The Classic Cattleyas

THE CLASSIC
Cattleyas

A. A. Chadwick
and
Arthur E. Chadwick

TIMBER PRESS

To Anne, with love

Frontispiece: *Cattleya jenmanii*

Published in 2006 by
Timber Press, Inc.
The Haseltine Building
133 S.W. Second Avenue, Suite 450
Portland, Oregon 97204-3527, U.S.A.
www.timberpress.com
For contact information regarding editorial, marketing, sales, and distribution
in the United Kingdom, see www.timberpress.co.uk.

Printed through Colorcraft Ltd., Hong Kong

Library of Congress Cataloging-in-Publication Data

Chadwick, A. A.
    The classic cattleyas / A. A. Chadwick and Arthur E. Chadwick.
      p. cm.
    Includes bibliographical references and index.
    ISBN-13: 978-0-88192-764-1
    ISBN-10: 0-88192-764-3
  1. Cattleyas. I. Chadwick, Arthur E. II. Title.
    SB409.8.C38C43 2006
    635.9'344—dc22
                                                                        2005027638
A catalog record for this book is also available from the British Library.

Contents

Preface and Acknowledgments

MANY THOUSANDS of orchids are known to botanical science, but only a few have become important horticultural plants. Still fewer have had an impact that extended beyond horticulture and into the social fabric of everyday life. Of the few stars that emerged since the discovery of tropical orchids over 200 years ago, only one has had an aura that transcends time.

This book is a tribute to that grande dame, that queen of the orchid world, that classic orchid whose bright lavender color became known as "orchid color" and whose image was the public's perception of what an orchid really looked like. What made this classic flower great was its large size, beautiful rose-lavender coloring, and thin, delicate substance with its look-but-do-not-touch air of femininity. The flowers had wonderful fragrances and were available every day of the year. Like people, no two flowers were exactly alike. They were similar, but very individual. They were the large-flowered classic cattleyas of orchid history.

It is not possible to write a comprehensive work like this without the help of many wonderful people and organizations. A special thanks goes to Enola Teeter, Evelyn Hansen, and Venice Bayrd of the Longwood Gardens library for their assistance with the many historical works needed to tell the story of the classic cattleyas. Equally appreciated was the assistance of James Watson, editor of the American Orchid Society publications, for his guidance and his help in obtaining copies of rare documents needed to authenticate the historical references in this work, and that of Gustavo Romero, curator of the Orchid Herbarium of Oakes Ames at Harvard University. In the area of art, we would like to thank the Royal Horticultural Society, particularly Charlotte Brooks, for help with the RHS award painting; Naturalia Publications for the *Lindenia* picture; and the Georgia O'Keeffe Foundation, Angela Mirro, and Anne Link for the use of their priceless paintings. Thanks also go to Anthony and Cheryl Alfieri and Joseph Grezaffi for access to the special varieties of *Cattleya* species and hybrids in their magnificent orchid collections.

ONE

Royal Flower of Imperial Europe

T HE 1800S are often referred to as the Golden Age of horticulture in Europe, but the century started out as a tragedy for orchids. As sailing vessels returned with their cargos of lumber, sugar, or spices from Asia or the Americas, they also brought an array of strange plants that were new to Europeans.

Among the plants was a scattering of tropical orchids that were so different from anything Europeans had seen before that no one really knew how to grow them. The orchids had been found growing on trees in their jungle habitats, so the horticultural and botanical authorities of the day assumed the plants were parasites like the familiar European mistletoe. Mistletoe grew on trees in Europe, and it was well established that it lived on their sap. To grow an orchid successfully, the experts felt you had to find a tree the orchids could parasitize, and the first decade of orchid culture was spent trying to find those trees.

Growers often notched through the bark of sapling trees in their hothouses, inserted the orchid plants into the sticky sap underneath, and tied them fast with twine. When the orchids died, their deaths were blamed on their incompatibility with the sap of the tree, not the ignorance of the grower who put them there. This practice went on for years, and by 1815, the cultivation of "tropical parasites," as orchids were called, was considered by most authorities to be "hopeless."

Botanists would eventually realize that orchids were epiphytes and that they grew on trees not to feed on the tree's sap as a parasite, but merely for support. The orchid roots clung tightly to the bark to prevent the plant from being blown or washed away, not to draw nourishment from the tree. The idea that orchids were parasites, however, echoed through horticultural circles during much of the early 1800s and led to the death of most of the tropical orchid plants that were imported at the time.

If orchids were not parasites and the kind of tree on which they were growing was not important, then what was important? Orchid plants sometimes arrived in Europe accompanied by a few comments from the collector on the conditions in the jungle where he found them growing. Most of this information said the plants grew in hot, dense jungles that dripped with moisture, so the standard recommendation from botanical experts for the next two decades told growers to keep the plants hot, heavily shaded, and very moist. Orchids were put in the "stove," a glass structure with a brick fluelike source of heat that developed high temperatures and a stagnant atmosphere—

9

sometimes charged with burned gasses. No one suggested the plants might need some fresh air or a cooler temperature and, as the orchid plants arrived in Europe by the hundreds, they soon died by the hundreds, and Europe became known as "the grave of tropical orchids." If an orchid plant bloomed once before it died, it was considered successful culture.

The large-flowered *Cattleya* species were, for the most part, spared the terrible fate of most orchids in the early 1800s. Cattleyas were difficult to find because they resided in the cloud forests and mountain valleys of the giant Andes Mountains of South America—areas that were largely inaccessible to early plant hunters. When a large-flowered *Cattleya* species was finally found in Brazil in 1817, the discoverer never told anyone where he found it, and speculation from horticultural and botanical experts placed its habitat more than 1000 miles from where it actually grew. It was not found again for another 70 years, and by then people knew how to grow cattleyas.

Only a few plants of the first large-flowered *Cattleya* arrived in Europe in 1818, and they went to the Glasgow Botanic Garden in Scotland. At the request of William Swainson, the man who discovered the plants, the Glasgow Botanic Garden sent some divisions of these new tropical parasites to a well-known plant collector named William Cattley, who lived in Barnet, near London. Cattley put the plants in his stove house where one of them managed to flower that autumn. A painting of the plant shows the pseudobulbs were badly shriveled and the flowers were forced out prematurely, presumably from the excessive heat to which they were exposed. The flowers, however, were spectacular compared with those of other orchids that were known at the time. They were large and richly colored, and Cattley was ecstatic.

The Glasgow Botanic Garden plants began flowering the next year, and the horticultural world slowly became aware of this magnificent new orchid. William Cattley hired a young botanist named John Lindley to draw and describe the new plants in his collection, and in 1821 Lindley wrote a book entitled *Collectanea Botanica* in which, along with other plants, he pictured and described the new orchid in plate 33. Lindley named the new orchid in honor of his patron, William Cattley, calling it *Cattleya labiata*. He used the term "labiata" to call attention to the remarkably large and distinctive labellum, or lip, of the flower. Lindley's *Collectanea Botanica* spread the word about the new *C. labiata* throughout the botanical and horticultural world of Great Britain and continental Europe. Plant lovers everywhere wanted to see this *C. labiata*, but the only plants available were owned by Cattley and the Glasgow Botanic Garden. If you did not know Cattley, or someone who could introduce you, or if you could not travel to Glasgow, you did not have much hope of seeing the flower. Nonetheless, people talked about *C. labiata* and began thinking of ways to acquire a plant.

Although his stove house was full of new tropical plants of every description, William Cattley considered his *Cattleya labiata* the most beautiful plant he owned. By 1825 he still had two live plants to show his horticultural friends and visitors, and his love affair with *C. labiata* lasted until his death on 24 May 1842.

William Cattley was not the only one, however, who was smitten by his encounter with *Cattleya labiata*. John Lindley felt *C. labiata* was the finest of all orchids, and despite the discovery of more than 150 new orchid species over the next 15 years from a wide range of genera, Lindley could not resist describing *C. labiata* again in Edwards's *Botanical Register* of 1836 in plate 1859. This time, Lindley threw away all restraint and said,

> There is certainly no plant of which I have any knowledge that can be said to stand forth with an equal radiance of splendour and beauty. For it is not merely the large size of the flowers and the deep rich crimson of one petal (the lip) contrasted with the delicate lilac of the others that constitute the loveliness of this plant, it owes its beauty in almost equal degree to the transparency of its texture, and to the exquisite clearness of its colours, and the graceful manner in which its broad flaglike petals wave and intermingle when they are stirred by the air.

No one has ever described a large-flowered cattleya with more eloquence than Lindley did with *C. labiata* in the *Botanical Register*.

Although John Lindley opened the door for *Cattleya labiata* to enter the horticultural world of Europe and extolled its beauty, he led many poor plants down a fatal path with his recommendations on how to grow them. Lindley's formula for success was based on the high-heat, heavy-shade, and lots-of-moisture system of culture. Few species of orchids grow well under these conditions. The majority produce weak growths, decline, and die. The recommendation is probably the worst possible one for growing cattleyas.

A second large-flowered *Cattleya* species was discovered in 1836. This time the cattleya came from Venezuela and was sent to George Green of Liverpool, who gave it to a local amateur orchid grower, Mrs. Moss. When the plant flowered, Mrs. Moss sent the flowers to botanist William Hooker at Glasgow, who was as captivated by them as John

Cattleya labiata

Lindley had been with *C. labiata*. Hooker immediately described the plant as a new species, naming it *Cattleya mossiae*, and suddenly there were two large-flowered cattleyas known to European horticulture. This time, however, plant hunters knew where to find the new species, and it was not long before plants of *C. mossiae* were being imported into Europe in large numbers.

By the time *Cattleya mossiae* came along, the greenhouse had begun to develop into a more satisfactory horticultural structure in which to grow plants. The old method of forming glass by blowing it into a circle, which produced crown glass, had given way to the production of flat sheets of glass. Glass was now blown into the shape of a cylinder which was cut in half lengthwise, reheated, and ironed flat. The flattening was even done by mechanical pressing at some factories, and glass was now available in good quality for anyone with the money to buy it. The old brick stove heaters were being replaced with hot water boilers and cast-iron pipe that carried heated water around the greenhouse. The pipe was packed at the joints instead of being threaded, so water leaks were common, but the climate in the greenhouse improved measurably. Plants were now being warmed rather than cooked by the heating system, and ventilators were beginning to introduce fresh air.

Greenhouses were also being separated by temperature, and three distinct temperature ranges were starting to be used—a cool house, an intermediate house, and a warm house. The cool house had a night temperature of 45° to 50°F. The intermediate house had a night temperature of 60°F, and the warm house had a night temperature of 70° to 75°F. Day temperatures were 10° to 15°F higher. When the same orchid plant was grown in each of these three greenhouses, it responded differently. It flourished at one temper-

Cattleya mossiae

ature, while it grew poorly at the others, and temperature became recognized as an important variable in growing orchids. Before this time, orchids were grown only at high temperatures in the stove house.

For a while a tug-of-war existed between the use of the terms "glasshouse" and "greenhouse" for these new horticultural structures. Since they were built of glass, with glass not only on the sides and ends but overhead as well, they were referred to by some people as glasshouses. The function of the glasshouses, however, was to grow green plants, and calling them greenhouses distinguished them from the many other glass structures that were starting to appear. People would eventually live in a glasshouse, but only plants would live in a greenhouse.

Human nature is such that there are always a few individuals who ignore the advice of experts and do things their own way. Disregarding the theoretical pronouncements of the academics, they decide how best to grow a plant by watching the way the plant responds to different cultural conditions. They experiment with the improved greenhouses and varied temperatures until the plants grow and flower better.

One of the pioneers in growing orchids by using commonsense observation was an Englishman named Joseph Paxton. Paxton was the head gardener to the sixth Duke of Devonshire at Chatsworth. The duke had one of the largest and most impressive collections of orchids in Britain during the 1830s, and even John Lindley had to admit after visiting the duke that

> the success with which epiphytes are cultivated by Mr. Paxton is wonderful, and the climate in which this is effected, instead of being so hot and damp that the plants can only be seen with as much peril as if one had to visit them in an Indian jungle, is as mild and delightful as that of Madeira.

Paxton did several things against the advice of Lindley and the other academic experts. He grew his orchids in greenhouses with different temperatures, and his cattleyas went out of the stove house and into the intermediate temperature greenhouse. He provided much more sun and fresh air into his greenhouses, particularly when the plants were actively growing in the summer, and he eliminated the dense wet atmosphere. He provided moisture to the air by watering the paths and stages of the greenhouse in the morning and afternoon, not saturating the air with a wet fog. He also improved the method of potting to give better drainage and greater attention to root development. The system Paxton devised to grow his cattleyas is essentially the one we use today for these orchids.

In 1837 an 18-year-old girl named Victoria ascended the throne of Great Britain, and with Queen Victoria came a new era of political stability throughout the world. The Napoleonic Wars had ended and, after the War of 1812, Britain reluctantly accepted the permanent independence of its North American colonies, now called the United States of America, and stopped harassing its ships at sea. The rest of the British Empire, however, stretched around the world so that it was commonly observed that "the sun never set on Her Majesty's empire." Under Victoria, Britain became the dominant military power in the world. With political stability, commerce and wealth increased, and thus merchants and nobles had time and money to indulge themselves in leisure activities. Horticulture became both an intellectual pursuit and a mark of wealth, and orchids became the pièce de résistance.

By 1841, the interest in orchids had grown to such an extent that botanist James Bateman observed that

> the number of collectors would seem to have increased as rapidly as the number of species in cultivation. In 1830 there were not more than five or six collections of the slightest note, and in these barely 100 species. The collections now cannot be counted, nor the species in their possession, but the latter must be estimated at 1000 at least.

As the age developed, an interesting phenomenon began to occur in the world of orchids. Just because orchids flourished in the Duke of Devonshire's greenhouses did not mean they could be grown well in anyone's greenhouse. The average homeowner could plant roses or four-o-clocks in a cottage garden and expect to find lots of reliable advice on how to grow them. With orchids, however, there was no reliable advice. The only published recommendations essentially told people how to kill them. Raising orchids was considered an art that only a few unusually talented growers had mastered. If you had only a greenhouse or two and one gardener, you were advised to stick to carnations, dahlias, or some other common greenhouse crop. To be successful with orchids, you had to have at least three greenhouses dedicated just to orchids and at least one full-time orchid grower, otherwise you were wasting your time and inviting disappointment.

Growing orchids soon became the province of only the most wealthy nobles and merchants who had large estates, numerous greenhouses, and a staff of gardeners. The lack of good information on how to grow orchids began to wrap these strange new tropical plants in a mystique that was unique to horticulture. Tropical orchids were now not only rare and special horticultural objects, but they were also becoming identified as the plants of aristocrats.

Saturday, 2 January 1841 saw the introduction of the most famous horticultural periodical of the 1800s, *The Gardeners' Chronicle*. The *Chronicle* was a 9-by-13-inch newspaper that you received through the mail once a week. In its first issue, the *Chronicle* described its mission as

> one of making a weekly record of everything that bears upon Horticulture and Garden Botany and to introduce such Natural History as has a relation to Gardening, together with Notices and Criticisms of every work of importance on the subject which may appear.

The *Chronicle* symbolized the growing interest in everything horticultural that was taking hold throughout the country, and it executed its stated mission with outstanding success over the rest of the century.

The list of contributors who had agreed to write articles and give advice in *The Gardeners' Chronicle* was virtually a Who's Who of the British horticultural world. It included the head gardeners of the dukes of Devonshire, Norfolk, Bedford, Newcastle, Buccleugh, Portland, and Sutherland; the gardeners for the earls of Derby, Surrey, Fitzwilliam, and Hopetoun; and head gardeners to the Archbishop of York, the Marquess of

Westminster, and the Countess of Grenville. It also included professors Daubeny of Oxford, Graham of Edinburgh, Henslow of Cambridge, Hoyle of Kings College, Hooker of Glasgow; George Bentham, secretary of the Horticultural Society of London; and John Lindley. It was an all-star cast, and with the depth of knowledge of its contributors, the *Chronicle* became a major source of guidance for growing new tropical plants, including orchids.

Fourteen *Cattleya* species were first described botanically in *The Gardeners' Chronicle*, including seven of the large-flowered ones—*C. dowiana, C. gaskelliana, C. lawrenceana, C. percivaliana, C. quadricolor, C. rex,* and *C. schroederae*. Because of the immense input from practical gardeners into the *Chronicle*, the debate over whether the large-flowered cattleyas should be species or just varieties of *C. labiata* was essentially won in the *Chronicle* in favor of making them individual species.

The Gardeners' Chronicle, however, was not a cure-all for the problem of educating people on how to grow orchids. The *Chronicle* did not go to everyone, and even subscribers wanted more information on the ever-increasing number of genera and species that were being discovered. They wanted a reference work, like a book, that would cover all aspects of raising orchids, from the type of greenhouse to build, to how to pot, repot, fertilize, and divide these plants.

The vehicle for this began to develop in the late 1840s when Bellenden Ker, who lived near Hoddesdon, England, decided to grow some orchids. The problem was that Mr. Ker's gardener did not have the faintest idea how to grow them, and Ker had to prevail upon his neighbor, Charles Warner, to let his gardener show Ker's gardener how to do it. Warner's gardener was an unusually successful orchid grower named Benjamin Samuel Williams, a man with 23 gold and 12 silver medals to his credit for orchids he had exhibited at Chiswick and Regent's Park. Under Williams's guidance, Ker's gardener became quite proficient at growing orchids, and an appreciative Ker encouraged Williams to make notes of the recommendations he gave his grower, and consider publishing them to help others. Williams managed to do this despite his many daily gardening duties, and a series of articles was written for *The Gardeners' Chronicle* in 1851 under the title, "Orchids for the Million," by B. S. Williams.

The articles were such a hit that they were put into book form and published as *The Orchid-Grower's Manual* the following April. The manual described 260 orchids then in cultivation and told prospective growers how to grow each of them. It gave advice on building greenhouses for orchids, including the best size, best heating system, glazing, and ventilation techniques. It even told growers how to handle newly imported plants and produce specimen plants for orchid shows and horticultural exhibitions. *The Orchid-Grower's Manual* soon became the bible on orchid culture for professional gardeners, and it grew into the most successful book on orchid culture ever written, dominating the field for over 50 years with seven editions.

By the 1850s, a newly imported tropical orchid could expect to live to a ripe old age in Europe, in a modern greenhouse, heated with soothing, circulating hot water, and ventilated with fresh outside air. It could expect to be carefully watered with room-temperature rainwater and tended by a knowledgeable grower who would grimace if you called it a "parasite." The stage was now set for the play to begin, and begin it did.

In 1851 Joseph Paxton re-entered the horticultural scene with a gigantic splash. He had developed a very special relationship with his boss, the Duke of Devonshire, who admired Paxton's boundless energy and imagination so much that the duke became his mentor. Paxton traveled with the duke throughout Europe, and the duke introduced Paxton to people who could help him develop his many talents. In 1834 Paxton began publication of *Magazine of Botany*, which continued until 1849 when he started another magazine, *Paxton's Flower Garden*. In 1840 Paxton published the first pocket-size botanical dictionary so growers could look up the names of plants as they walked through their greenhouses. He was first to use the ridge-and-furrow design for greenhouses and designed a display conservatory, "The Great Stove," at Chatsworth for the Duke of Devonshire that was architecturally as modern as if it had come out of the 21st century.

Joseph Paxton's greatest achievement, however, was his design of the Crystal Palace for the World Exposition of 1851 in London. The Crystal Palace was a huge glass building, some 18 football fields long and 8 football fields wide. Constructed of iron and glass, it had a remarkably large circular glass roof for the transept. The building housed full-sized trees and was a perfect display area for plants of all descriptions and an endless number of commercial stalls. It was so advanced for its time and so impressive that Queen Victoria in her excitement knighted Paxton for his achievement.

Sir Joseph Paxton's architectural endeavors soon prompted other architects to design an array of new glass conservatories that would adorn the estates and public areas of Europe. Horticulture was now on a collision course with destiny, and the Golden Age began to glow.

In 1855 *Cattleya trianaei* was beginning to be imported in large numbers into Europe by Horticulture Internationale, a large Belgian orchid firm owned by Jean Jules Linden. *Cattleya mossiae* was now common in European greenhouses, and together the two species gave a big boost to the interest in the large-flowered cattleyas. *Cattleya trianaei* flowered during the cold winter months when its beautiful pastel colors, delicate substance, and fine shape brightened the winter reveries. Its endless varieties were something to see and talk about and sometimes even an excuse for giving a party.

When *Cattleya trianaei* finished blooming, *C. mossiae* began to flower, and just in time for the spring flower shows that announced the end of winter. *Cattleya mossiae*'s bright lavender color, large size, and wonderful fragrance made it one of the most sought-after spring flowers for these shows, and competition among orchid growers moved into high gear. Plant entries in the horticultural shows were so numerous that gold and silver medals came in all sizes. At a typical exhibition in Regent's Park, there were Extra Gold Medals, Large Gold Medals, Medium Gold Medals, and just Gold Medals. There were Large Silver Gilt Medals, Large Silver Medals, Silver Gilt Medals, Silver Medals, Small Silver Medals, and, of course, Bronze Medals and an endless number of First Class Certificates and Certificates of Merit.

Large-flowered cattleyas became a particular favorite with exhibitors, not only because their flowers were so large and beautifully colored, but also because a single plant would make a grand display by itself. Most important, however, was that the large-flowered cattleyas were the best collectable plants to be found. Unlike most orchid species that had flowers so similar in color that they all looked alike, the plants of *Cattleya mossiae* and *C. trianaei* were distinctly individual. Like people, no two were exactly the same. Some had unusually beautiful color combinations in the lips and petals, or were a rare concolor, white, or white with a purple lip. Others had larger-than-normal flowers, with more frilly petals or a fuller shape. The variations that appeared in the flowers seemed endless. *Cattleya trianaei* had varieties with purple flares and featherlike markings in the petals, while the splash pattern on the lip of *C. mossiae* would sometimes coalesce into a solid purple.

Each new and rare variety commanded a higher price than the last one, and the prices paid by a duke or an earl for a single plant could exceed his grower's yearly wages. Soon hundreds of named varieties of *Cattleya mossiae* and *C. trianaei* were being exhibited, and the literature began to drip with royal varietal names.

The year 1865 was bittersweet for growers of the large-flowered cattleyas. On the bitter side, the three giants of the early 1800s who had ushered these cattleyas into the mainstream of European horticulture died within a few months of one another. Sir Joseph Paxton, who showed people how to grow cattleyas, died in June; Sir William Hooker, who described *Cattleya mossiae*, died in August; and Dr. John Lindley, who described *C. labiata* and established the genus *Cattleya*, died in October. The whole year seemed to be one of continuous mourning in *The Gardeners' Chronicle*.

On the sweet side, James Veitch and Sons received the first shipment of *Cattleya dowiana* plants that were alive and healthy. Veitch flowered the plants in the late summer of 1865, and to everyone's amazement, the beautiful yellow-petaled cattleya did exist after all. The plant collector, Josef Warscewicz, said it did in 1850. He said he found it in

Exhibition plant of *Cattleya trianaei* with more than 80 flowers

Costa Rica, but the plants he sent back to Hugh Low and Company died shortly after arrival and the herbarium specimens sent to the botanist Heinrich Gustav Reichenbach never arrived. For 15 years, no one really believed such a magnificent cattleya existed, and now, suddenly, they found it was real, and they could even buy a plant.

Cattleya dowiana not only had a completely different flower color from *C. mossiae* or *C. trianaei*, but it also extended the flowering season of the large-flowered cattleyas, because it bloomed in the summer in Europe. Its appearance increased the excitement over the large-flowered *Cattleya* species and accelerated efforts by commercial firms to find more of these species in the jungle.

The British firm Loddiges had dominated the importation and sale of tropical orchids in Europe for the first half of the 1800s, but Loddiges was never really a factor in the sale of large-flowered cattleyas. *Cattleya mossiae* was the only act in town from its discovery in 1836 until Loddiges was broken up in 1852, and Loddiges was not the first company to have *C. mossiae* for sale. That distinction went to Hornsey Nurseries. Loddiges also actively promoted the high-heat, heavy-shade, wet-atmosphere method of culture for orchids, and no large-flowered cattleya could survive for long with that treatment.

As the Victorian Era moved into the 1860s and 1870s, all this changed, and a new group of companies began to take the reins of the orchid business. Some, like Hugh Low and James Veitch, were old-line nurserymen who had sold a wide range of horticultural trees, shrubs, and tropical plants for almost 40 years. Others, like Frederick Sander, a general agricultural seedsman, were relatively new to the horticultural business. As the fruits of two decades of efforts by plant hunters began to pay off, however,

Cattleya dowiana

these companies began concentrating their efforts on the importation and sale of orchids. No sooner had the Costa Rican *Cattleya dowiana* flowered in Veitch's commercial greenhouses in Chelsea in 1865 then the clear-yellow petaled *C. dowiana aurea* was found in Colombia by collectors for Linden's Belgian company, Horticulture Internationale. The British firm Backhouse was close behind with *aurea* in 1872. Linden's collectors found *C. eldorado* in 1866, and it was a market staple by the mid-1870s.

Cattleya warscewiczii had been described as a new species back in 1854 by botanist Heinrich Gustav Reichenbach, but no one in Europe had ever seen a live plant. Even Reichenbach had only seen the dried specimens when he described it. The description of the large size of the flowers and the formidable bloom-spike, however, had a lot of companies looking for it, and in 1870 the plant hunter Benedict Roezl, working for Linden, found it in Colombia. *Cattleya warscewiczii* was soon imported in large numbers to the excitement of cattleya collectors. The same year (1870) also saw the discovery of *C. mendelii*, that large, delicately colored cattleya that was considered by many Victorian growers to be the finest of the large-flowered species.

If you were the first to have a new large-flowered *Cattleya* species for sale, you could sell it for ten times the price you could get for a plant of a species that had been around a few years, and the theme of the orchid business everywhere became "find a new large-flowered *Cattleya* species." A plant hunter who found a new species and was working for himself instead of a commercial company could retire on the income from a single shipment. The collector Eric Bungeroth actually did this when he managed to get a shipment of *C. rex* from the wilderness of Peru into England.

Big rewards also came from the sale of unusually beautiful or rare varieties of the large-flowered *Cattleya* species. Jean Jules Linden, commenting on *C. mendelii* in *Lindenia* (plate 55) said,

> *Cattleya mendelii* is an elite orchid and we can quite understand that certain varieties are priced as high as they are. We have seen some specimens of it sold at public auctions in England, which reached as much as ten pounds per bulb.

In the mid-1800s, one British pound was often more than a week's wage for many people, and the cost of a four-bulb plant of a special *C. mendelii* could equal the better part of a year's income, unless, of course, you were a wealthy baron or duke. By 1880 the large-flowered cattleyas were the playthings of the richest people in Europe, and prices of cattleyas were being increasingly quoted in gold guineas instead of silver pounds.

One of the more charming peculiarities of the Victorian Era was its system of money. While the United States of America had a simple system of currency in which the dollar was divided into 100 cents and everything was priced in dollars and cents, the British had a system based on history rather than financial logic.

The basic unit of British currency was the pound, which was backed by silver and was often called the "pound sterling." Twenty silver shillings made one pound, but the shilling itself was divided into 12 copper pennies, which gave an odd 240 pennies to the pound, not 100. Half a shilling was called a "six pence," immortalized in English literature in works like *The Moon and Six Pence*. Half a six pence was a three pence called a "thruppence" or "thrippnney bit." The copper penny was even divided into a half penny, called a "hay'penny," and a quarter penny, called a "farthing"—which inspired the old English expression, "not worth a farthing." Other silver coins included the crown, worth 5 shillings; the half crown, worth $2\frac{1}{2}$ shillings; and the 2 shilling florin. A typical price was quoted in pounds (£), shillings (s), and pence (d).

There was something for everyone, and the something for orchid buyers was the guinea. The guinea was a gold coin valued at 21 shillings or one shilling more than a silver pound, and it was commonly referred to as "a rich man's pound." Luxury goods were usually quoted in guineas because common people would never pay 21 shillings for something worth only 20 shillings. Only a duke or an earl with money to burn, an appetite for luxury goods, and a deep concern for his place in society would do something like that.

By the 1880s the large-flowered cattleyas were beginning to reach a new level of desirability within the orchid world. When Frederick Sander introduced the first plants of the December-flowering *Cattleya percivaliana* and the late spring-flowering *C. gaskelliana* in 1882 and 1883, he announced in *The Gardeners' Chronicle* that "with these two species, cattleyas are now in flower every month of the year." No other orchid was in flower every month of the year—only the large-flowered cattleyas. If you grew cattleyas, you could have them all the time. There was no cattleya season, and the excitement over these plants blossomed into a mild hysteria.

In 1889 the large-flowered cattleyas came full circle as *Cattleya labiata* was finally rediscovered in the Brazilian state of Pernambuco after 70 years of hunting for it. Its appearance was heralded as the horticultural event of the year, and the first *Cattleya* to be imported and described was now available in large quantities for everyone to grow. By 1892 *The Gardeners' Chronicle* reported that 25,000 plants of *C. labiata* were being imported annually into Great Britain alone.

During the 1880s commercial companies were making so much money from orchids that they could afford to indulge themselves in creating glamorous and expensive publications to help sell their newest imported species, or raise the level of recognition of the company's name and reputation. Spurred on by his success with *The Orchid-Grower's Manual* and the profits from his new Victoria and Paradise Nurseries, Benjamin S. Williams in cooperation with Robert Warner began publishing *The Orchid Album* on 1 June 1882.

The Orchid Album was a collection of paintings of some of the best varieties of the most popular orchids in cultivation at the time. Thomas Moore, curator of the Chelsea Botanic Gardens, wrote the botanical descriptions of the orchids, Williams wrote his advice on culture, and John Nugent Fitch did the original watercolor paintings. *The Orchid Album* was issued monthly but numbered as annual volumes. It was an impressive and beautiful work in royal quarto size of $9\frac{1}{2}$ by 12 inches—large enough to be distinctive, but small enough for easy handling. It was the first cocktail-table type of book that concentrated on eye-catching pictures of showy orchids, and the large-flowered *Cattleya* species were well represented.

Jean Jules Linden had dabbled in the production of orchid books between 1854 and 1860 when he published his book *Pescatoria*, but in 1885 Linden embarked on an orchid project on a grand scale with his *Lindenia*. *Lindenia* was an 11-by-14-inch monthly publication of four beautifully colored lithographs of orchids, accompanied by botanical descriptions of the plants in Latin and Linden's comments on historical perspective and culture in French. Several fine botanical artists painted the portraits of the orchids, with P. de Pannemaeker being the lead artist. The publication continued for more than 20 years and is one of the most beautiful works on orchids ever produced. It pictured 359 cattleyas, most of them varieties of the large-flowered species that Linden was so effective in introducing to European orchid growers.

Although most orchid companies catered to the wealthy nobles and merchants of Europe, Frederick Sander seems to have been the premier supplier of orchids to the top nobility. He knew most of them personally and was rewarded with rich orders for orchids and even royal honors. Following closely in the footsteps of Linden, Sander introduced in 1888 the first volume of the most impressive orchid book ever published, the *Reichenbachia*. Sander named the book in honor of his friend, the leading orchid botanist of the day, Heinrich Gustav Reichenbach. Sander captioned the book "Orchids Illustrated and Described."

The regular edition was a mammoth 21½ inches tall by 16 inches wide, and the imperial edition an even larger 29½ by 23½ inches. The imperial edition, which was limited to 100 copies, was printed with a little more clarity and brilliance than the regular edition, with the paintings matted to show them off. It was 3 inches thick and, at 44 pounds, was too heavy for a dainty Victorian lady to even lift. *Reichenbachia* was published in three languages—English, French, and German—and most of the paintings were done by Henry G. Moon who later married Sander's daughter. Many of the pictures were actually hand-touched by the artist himself to highlight the colors.

Sander dedicated the first volume of *Reichenbachia* "By Special Permission to Her Most Gracious Majesty The Queen"—in other words, to Queen Victoria. Two years later, in 1890, Sander published the second volume of *Reichenbachia*, this time dedicated "By Special Permission to Her Majesty Augusta Victoria, Empress of Germany and Queen of Prussia." In 1892 the first volume of a second series of *Reichenbachia* was published which Sander dedicated to "Her Majesty Maria Feodorova, Empress of Russia," and in 1894 the final volume was published and dedicated to "Her Majesty Marie Henriette, Queen of the Belgians." What was interesting about Sander's dedications was that all four ladies, Victoria, Augusta Victoria, Maria Feodorova, and Marie Henriette, were very good customers for Sander's orchids. It was clear that if horse racing was the sport of kings, orchid growing was the hobby of queens and Sander was their orchid supplier.

Sander pictured 34 cattleyas in *Reichenbachia*, including all the major large-flowered species. *Cattleya mendelii* received particular attention with paintings of the varieties 'Duke of Marlborough', 'Quorndon House', and 'Measuresiana'. The illustration of *C. mendelii* 'Measuresiana' is one of the most beautiful and inspiring paintings of a large-flowered *Cattleya* species ever made. *Reichenbachia* took orchids to the pinnacle of acclaim in Victorian Europe and almost bankrupted Sander's orchid company in the process. Unlike *Lindenia*, *Reichenbachia* was not designed so much to sell particular varieties of orchids, but rather to honor Sander's best orchid customers and establish Sander as supplier of orchids to European nobility—the people who could afford to pay the highest prices for special plants.

By the time *Reichenbachia* was published, Frederick Sander was the undisputed commercial leader in orchids. Queen Victoria appointed him Royal Orchid Grower; he was awarded the Victoria Medal of Honor; the Romanoffs made him a baron of the Holy Russian Empire; and the British magazine *Punch* dubbed him "The Orchid King." Sander became so famous that a letter from South America addressed merely to "Sander, Orchid King, England" had no trouble finding its way to Sander's company in St. Albans.

Painting of *Cattleya mendelii* 'Measuresiana' from *Reichenbachia*

Other companies with a different, less glamorous approach to using orchids to promote themselves also entered the field of publications in the late 1800s. In 1887 James
Veitch and Sons published the first volume of *A Manual of Orchidaceous Plants*. Volume
I was entitled *Epidendreae*, and the first genus discussed, of course, was the most important of the day, *Cattleya*. One of Veitch's purposes in writing the manual was to bring
everyday horticultural nomenclature in line with current accepted botanical thinking,
but Veitch sometimes found himself complaining about the very botanical classifications he was trying to promote. In the case of the large-flowered *Cattleya* species, the
manual contributed little more than confusion to the future course of botanical classification of these species and left the closely related laelias on a slippery course that would
eventually fall apart. Veitch's *Manual* however, was a comprehensive work with considerable historical and scientific background not covered in works like Williams' *Orchid-
Grower's Manual*. It ended up with 10 slender volumes with the last one published in
1894, and it gave Veitch significant recognition in the orchid community.

In 1878 Count Francois du Buysson in Paris had published a 536-page book on the
culture of orchids entitled *L'Orchidophile*. During the 1880s he expanded this into a
monthly French-language periodical, *L'Orchidophile*, that billed itself as the journal for
amateur orchid growers and provided useful information on new orchid introductions,
culture, and history. The need was felt for a similar journal in English, and in 1893
botanist Robert Allen Rolfe launched *The Orchid Review*, a chatty little monthly magazine that was in many ways a reflection of Rolfe's personality and his dedication to
orchids. In it Rolfe visited the great orchid collections of England, recorded the history
of orchid hybrids, gave cultural advice, and generally acted as a forum for everything

Brassocattleya Empress of Russia

pertaining to the realm of orchids. *The Orchid Review* was fun to read, and its readers never spared Rolfe the sting of any objections they had to what he wrote. The two orchid journals, *L'Orchidophile* and *The Orchid Review*, were not sponsored by commercial companies, but were the labor of love of their editors. They provided information on orchids the way *The Gardeners' Chronicle* had done for horticulture in general, and they were another symbol of the important place held by orchids during the Golden Age.

As the 19th century faded into a new millennium, the parade of the large-flowered cattleyas was almost complete. Only *Cattleya jenmanii* remained undiscovered in the jungle. These cattleyas had become the most popular collectors' orchids in cultivation with endless varieties named for orchid dignitaries, royal monarchs, and their regal entourage. The large-flowered cattleya itself had become the queen of the orchid world, and it would remain the queen for all of the next century.

When the Empress of Russia decided to send her sister a birthday gift, she did not need to decide what the gift should be. She would send a plant of the newest *Cattleya* hybrid, *Brassocattleya* Empress of Russia. The hybrid was beautiful beyond description, and it would be a striking addition to her sister's collection. Yet, as beautiful as it was, *Bc.* Empress of Russia was only the barest glimmer of the great things to come for the classic cattleyas.

TWO

Five-Star American Lady

As THE 20TH century opened, the Victorian Era quietly came to a close in Europe. On 22 January 1901, Queen Victoria died, and the long years of political stability that characterized the age of Victoria slowly turned into a nightmare of regional warfare that culminated in a world war in 1914. The world war wreaked havoc with European orchid companies and almost ruined the orchid leader, Frederick Sander.

Sander operated two giant orchid nurseries, one in England at St. Albans and one in Belgium at Bruges, and a small company in the United States in Summit, New Jersey. The long German occupation of Belgium largely destroyed the Bruges nursery, and literally thousands of large-flowered cattleya plants perished in the process. Sander's company in Summit had to be sold to provide cash to operate St. Albans which suffered from fuel shortages and low sales because of the war. The Bolshevik Revolution eliminated all of Sander's wealthy customers in Russia. As other European companies shared in the suffering, the eyes of the orchid world turned toward the United States which was insulated by a great ocean from the land wars of Europe.

In the United States the 20th century opened with the excitement of a young child entering a candy store. Inventors like Thomas Edison, Alexander Graham Bell, and Henry Ford were shaping a new world of incandescent light, electricity, telephones, and automobiles. The Industrial Revolution had created more multimillionaires in the United States than existed among the nobility of Europe, and the driving force for orchids spilled out of Europe and into America. The estates of wealthy Americans soon mirrored the pattern of the great estates of Europe during the 1800s: American estate owners hired gardeners, built greenhouses, developed beautiful landscaping, and started large orchid collections.

One of the largest and most famous of these orchid collections was owned by industrialist Albert C. Burrage, who had made a fortune in copper with his Amalgamated Copper and Chile Copper Companies. His Orchidvale estate in Massachusetts had 18 greenhouses 75 feet long by 20 feet wide and contained over 30,000 orchids, including 2000 *Cattleya trianaei*, 1400 *C. labiata*, 1000 *C. mossiae*, 1000 *C. warscewiczii*, and 4000 *Cattleya* hybrids.

Not quite as well known but equally fine was the Ronaele Manor Collection, belonging to Fitz Eugene Dixon of Elkins Park, Pennsylvania. "Ronaele" was the name of

Dixon's daughter Eleanor spelled backwards, but other than this light-hearted gesture, Dixon took his orchids very seriously. Dixon had over 20,000 orchids, including one of the largest collections of named varieties of the *Cattleya* species anywhere in the world. Because the whole area around Elkins Park was estate country, the region boasted the most concentrated group of private orchid collections in the United States. Elkins Park itself had the orchid collections of Fitz Dixon, George Widener, Joseph Widener, William L. Elkins, and Wharton Sinkler. Sinkler's collection was well known for having the finest white forms of the *Cattleya* species.

In nearby Kennett Square, Mary E. House had 20,000 orchid plants with mostly cattleyas of exceptional quality because she had bought each one in flower. The duPont fortunes from explosives and chemicals were represented in Kennett Square by Pierre S. duPont's magnificent collection at Longwood and, in neighboring Wilmington, by the Harry G. Haskell and Mrs. W. K. duPont collections. Having an orchid grower and a range of greenhouses full of orchids was as much a part of the estate culture of the early 20th century in the United States as riding stables and beautiful mansions.

Many of the fine cattleyas for these collections had been purchased from the leading European orchid companies before the world war, but as the demand for orchids by wealthy estate owners increased, the orchid industry in the United States also blossomed. Sander's company in Summit, New Jersey, was bought by two adventurous young American orchid growers named John E. Lager and Henry Hurrell. While European plant hunters had dominated the discovery of new orchids during the 1800s, U.S. collectors now became important contributors to finding new jungle plants, and John Lager was the premier U.S. orchid hunter.

Lager was particularly fond of the large-flowered *Cattleya* species, and he discovered a host of fine varieties that became famous, including the magnificent white clones *C. warscewiczii* 'Firmin Lambeau' and *C. schroederae* 'Hercules'. He thought so much of *C. schroederae* 'Hercules' that he put its picture on Lager and Hurrell's letterhead. *Cattleya warscewiczii* 'Firmin Lambeau' became one of the most famous and expensive large-flowered *Cattleya* species of all time when a division sold in 1910 for $5,000 ($50,000 in 2004 dollars). Lager personally hand-carried the division to Europe to be sure it arrived at its destination safely. He also discovered the finest semialba, *C. schroederae* 'The Baron', and the remarkably large and well-shaped *C. percivaliana* 'Summit'. Lager's colorful tales of his travels through Colombian cattleya areas are some of the best documentations in the literature of orchid collecting in the early 1900s.

Other plant hunters, like Lee Arthur Fennell, who developed the famous "Orchid Jungle" in South Florida, also introduced important *Cattleya* varieties like the fine dark *C. trianaei* 'Mary Fennell' and *C. lueddemanniana* 'Jungle Treasure' and the fine medium lavender *C. trianaei* 'Jungle Queen'. Lager and Hurrell and Fennell were only two of a dozen young American orchid companies that began supplying orchid plants to estate owners and other hobbyists in the United States in the early 1900s, but unlike the others, these two combined growing and selling orchids with actually collecting them in the jungle.

The year 1922 was a banner year for orchids in the United States. Although the first *Cattleya* hybrid had been made by James Veitch and Sons' grower John Dominy back in

One of the most expensive *Cattleya* species was the alba variety of *C. warscewiczii* 'Firmin Lambeau' FCC/RHS, which sold in 1910 for $5,000 ($50,000 in 2004 dollars) to a Belgium financier for whom it is named.

Cattleya trianaei 'Mary Fennell' HCC/AOS is one of the finest dark varieties of this species ever found. It was collected in the jungles of Colombia by the American plant hunter Lee Arthur Fennell in the early 1900s.

1852, raising orchid seedlings had always been a haphazard affair. Back in the 1800s and early 1900s, cattleyas were grown from seed by shaking the seed onto pots filled with peat and topped with wet burlap or a ground-up medium like milled peat, with glass or a Bell jar over them to keep them warm and moist. The seedling mortality from this system was horrendous, and only a few plants survived to maturity.

All this began to change, however, in 1922, when a young Cornell University researcher named Lewis Knudson published the results of his experiments with sterilized cultures for growing orchid seed. Knudson sowed his cattleya seed in sterilized flasks on laboratory agar, much as botanists culture strains of bacteria or fungi. His initial objective was to find out if newly germinating cattleya seedlings had to be infected with a natural fungus to enable them to grow—a commonly held belief by botanists in the 1920s. Knudson's fungus-free cattleya seed, planted on a sterilized medium in sterilized flasks not only germinated well but also grew magnificently. Knudson carried his experiments to their logical conclusion and, after seven years of growth in a completely sterilized environment, a *Laeliocattleya* hybrid actually flowered in a sterilized 12-liter flask. It was a breakthrough with far reaching consequences for commercial orchid growers, and it would revolutionize the industry. Using Knudson's sterilized planting technique, growers could now raise literally thousands of seedlings from a single *Cattleya* seed pod with little seedling mortality.

In the same year that Knudson published his experiments on growing cattleyas in a sterilized medium, a group of leading orchid people in the United States met in the Treasurer's Room of the Massachusetts Horticultural Society to form a society that could "advance the culture of orchids in America." They called the organization the American Orchid Society (AOS), and the Society embarked on a program that touched every facet of orchids in the United States from importation, hybridization, and cultivation to exhibitions, lectures, and plant judging. It became a driving force for orchids all over the country and, unlike the Royal Horticultural Society in Britain which was involved with a wide variety of plants, the AOS specialized in just one group of plants, orchids. Its concentrated efforts gave it unparalleled success in moving orchids to the forefront of horticulture in the United States. In June 1932 the AOS began publishing a quarterly journal, the *American Orchid Society Bulletin*, which grew into a monthly journal in 1940, and eventually into a glamorous full-color monthly magazine called "*Orchids*." The familiar figures of the early years of orchids, Albert Burrage, Fitz Eugene Dixon, and Wharton Sinkler, became the first, second, and third presidents of the AOS, and the Society soon provided the same important educational information and forum for American orchid growers that *The Gardeners' Chronicle* and *The Orchid Review* together had given growers in Britain.

As the 20th century moved past its second decade, the large-flowered cattleya emerged as not only an important plant for the estate trade and hobbyist in the United States, but also as an important cut flower for florists. Most people think of cattleyas as corsage flowers, but cattleyas were a widely used flower in vase arrangements long before they became the standard for corsages. Cattleyas were important vase flowers as early as the mid-1800s in Europe, as soon as there were enough *Cattleya* species in cultivation to provide a supply of blooms. Large-flowered cattleyas had many attractive qualities that made them a useful addition to common vase flowers like roses and carnations. Cut cattleyas lasted longer than cut roses, and their large size, unusual shape, and rich colors gave a striking accent to a vase arrangement.

Cattleya flowers were available year-round in Europe by the late 1800s, and *The Gardeners' Chronicle* even began quoting average weekly prices for them in their "Markets" column by 1889. On 9 September 1889, cut cattleya flowers sold for 10 to 15 shillings a dozen, while roses by comparison sold for only 3 to 5 shillings a dozen, and carnations sold as low as 1 shilling 6 pence a dozen. By the late 1800s, cattleyas had already become an elite cut flower in Europe, and if they appeared in a vase arrangement, you knew the arrangement was expensive. Elaborate, large arrangements for royal dignitaries were usually filled with cut *Cattleya* flowers.

During the 1920s the large-flowered *Cattleya* species were being imported in such large numbers at such a low cost that growers could sell the flowers at fairly reasonable prices. This in turn stimulated florists to use them more often in arrangements. Eight of these species, *C. labiata, C. percivaliana, C. trianaei, C. schroederae, C. mossiae, C. gaskelliana, C. warscewiczii,* and *C. dowiana,* were not only the most abundant of the species, but they also flowered at different times of the year and together they provided a continuous supply of cut flowers year-round. *Cattleya mossiae* was the most abundant of the species, and it flowered for Easter, Mother's Day, and all the spring parties when demand for cattleya flowers for table arrangements was the greatest. It cost so little to import these particular species that cut-flower growers could import a thousand plants, flower them for a year or two and, as the plants began to lose their jungle vigor and produced fewer flowers, throw them away and buy a thousand new plants and still make a

Classic wedding bouquet using white cattleya flowers

profit on the sale of the cut flowers. The practice had a ruinous effect on the species in their native countries and led to the depletion of whole areas in the jungle where the plants had once grown luxuriantly.

As the demand for cut cattleya flowers increased and prices began to go up, even companies that just sold orchid plants began to cut their cattleya flowers and sell them to floral distributors. Cut cattleyas became so popular for vase arrangements, wedding bouquets, and even casket covers during the late 1920s that there is an instance of one florist who had sold vase arrangements containing over 300 cattleya flowers for a fashionable ball, who had to retrieve the flowers at 1 A.M., float them overnight in water, and use them in a large casket cover the next day for a deceased dignitary. The Roaring Twenties fed on luxury goods like cattleya flowers, and cattleyas were used to cater to every wild whim, including flavoring the bathtub gin—a uniquely American experience.

As Herbert Hoover took office as president of the United States in early 1929 at the height of the financial boom and prohibition, Joseph A. Manda of West Orange, New Jersey, named a new *Cattleya* hybrid for Hoover's wife, Lou. The flower, *Brassolaeliocattleya* Mrs. Herbert Hoover, was the first cattleya named for a sitting first lady, but following the stock market crash a few months later in October, it would be the last cattleya named for a first lady until Dwight Eisenhower became president 24 years later.

The 1930s were a quiet time for orchids as far as the public was concerned, as luxury products faded from public view in the shadow of the Great Depression. Orchids, particularly large-flowered cattleyas, were still very popular with the wealthy estates that had survived the financial collapse, but the public only saw orchids at flower shows. Flower arrangements full of cattleyas were still made, but were the special enjoyment of the very rich.

Coffin cover made of white cattleya flowers

The 1930s saw the disappearance of some of the famous early private orchid collections as the owners either died or retired from orchid growing. The Mary House collection in Kennett Square was sold to a relatively new orchid company, L. Sherman Adams in Massachusetts. Thomas Young's collection, which had started as a hobby in 1905, had grown out of control by 1929 and was sold to a New York investment banker, Charles D. Barney, for the unbelievable sum of $3\frac{3}{4}$ million dollars. Thomas Young became Thomas Young Nurseries, then Thomas Young Orchids, and concentrated its efforts on the growing demand for cut cattleya flowers. By the end of the 1930s, Thomas Young Orchids had become the largest grower in the United States of cattleya cut-flowers and had almost 10 acres under glass in Bound Brook, New Jersey. It also had 29 huge greenhouses, the largest of which was 48 feet wide by 500 feet long and ran the length of a city block. With its dominating presence in the big eastern U.S. flower markets, Thomas Young Orchids eventually became the leading spokesman for the whole cattleya cut-flower industry.

As the United States slowly recovered from the Great Depression and the world moved inexorably toward the Second World War in the 20th century, a new fashion began to develop that would make the large-flowered cattleya the national symbol of the exotic orchid. Women have always enjoyed wearing flowers for special occasions and, in the United States, the fashion seems to have had much of its roots in the culture of the southern states where ladies picked flowers from their own camellia bushes to wear to dances. The cut camellias came in delicious feminine shades of pink and white and lasted all evening in a corsage. Camellias were, for a while, important corsage flowers even in the northern states, but the chaste, white, sweet-smelling gardenia soon replaced them in florist shops and, in time, the large-flowered cattleya replaced the gardenia.

When the cattleya came along, however, it seemed to add a new element of high fashion to corsages that had been missing with the other flowers. As the fashion took hold, the demand for cut cattleya flowers for corsages exceeded the supply and, by the 1940s, virtually the entire orchid industry in the United States was involved in one way or another in supplying cut cattleyas to the corsage trade. At a time when a pound of butter cost 35 cents, soldiers and sailors leaving for the battlefields of Europe would pay $20 for a cattleya corsage to give to the wives or girlfriends they would leave behind. Cattleya corsages became the fifth star of a lady's attire to accompany a beautiful gown, a fancy hair-do, high-spiked heeled shoes, and a pearl necklace at a formal reception or ball.

Cattleya mania became so pervasive that cattleya corsages were worn to luncheons, plays, operas, in fact to any event where a woman wanted to be elegantly dressed and look her very best. No boy would dare go to a high school prom in the late 1940s without giving his date a cattleya corsage. Florists' corsage business boomed and often overwhelmed their other floral activities, and the biggest problem was usually finding enough cattleya flowers to fill their customers' orders. The biggest cut-flower producer, Thomas Young Orchids, actually began advertising in the *American Orchid Society Bulletin* in 1945 asking private orchid growers to sell it their cattleya flowers so it could meet commitments with distributors. The advertisements ran for the rest of the 1940s. Even the Dixon estate in Elkins Park began selling its cattleya flowers to ease the burden of the wartime taxes.

As the leader in cut-flower production, Thomas Young Orchids had a large advertising campaign to promote cattleya flowers for corsages which appeared in both newspapers and magazines throughout the country during the 1940s. In designing the campaign, Young felt the word "cattleya" was not familiar enough to the public and was too
difficult for the public to pronounce. Many people called cattleyas cat-a-LEE-nas, like
the flying boats of the Second World War. Others called them cat-ta-LAAY-ah which
sounded like a maiden from a south sea island, so Young put a picture of a cattleya
flower in its ads, but used the word "orchid" to describe it. The word "orchid" soon
became synonymous with cattleya in the public's mind, and the bright lavender color of
a typical *Cattleya* species became known as "orchid color."

Cattleya flowers suddenly moved into a strange realm of their own. One of the largest
wholesale flower distributors in the eastern United States, S. S. Pennock, felt cattleya
flowers were more than a necessity in their business, but also said "their rank in the cut-
flower world is the same as diamonds and other precious stones in the jewelry business."
Other distributors compared the cattleya's place with the great masterpieces of art or
literature in their fields. A cattleya was the "most elegant flower for evening wear," or the
"corsage deluxe for real flower lovers," or "the only flower when the demand is for something choice." It seemed the whole industry could barely find enough superlatives to
describe the greatness of cattleyas at the peak of their success as cut flowers for corsages.

For the eight years Dwight Eisenhower served as president of the United States, his

At the height of their popularity, cattleya corsages were
worn by women not only to formal receptions and din-
ner-dances, but also to the theatre, opera, luncheons,
and any other event where they wanted to look their
very best.

the Orchid...
flower of fashion

If the occasion is special, wear orchids. If it is not, wear
orchids and make it so.

Thomas Young Orchids include the world's largest collection
of magnificent, American-grown hybrid orchids. These rare
and distinctive flowers acknowledge no equal in color, variety,
size and long-lived freshness.

Obtainable through florists in every city.

THOMAS YOUNG ORCHIDS INC.
America's Foremost Growers
BOUND BROOK, NEW JERSEY
New York 1, N.Y., 804 Avenue of the Americas
Boston 16, Mass., 537 Tremont Street.

During the 1940s Thomas Young Orchids, the leading
wholesaler of cattleya flowers, pictured a cattleya in its
advertisements and called it "an orchid." The word *orchid*
soon came to mean "cattleya" to the general public.

wife, Mamie, was the greatest advertisement for cattleya corsages that ever graced the White House. Mamie never seemed to go anywhere without wearing a corsage of two beautiful cattleya flowers. Whether it was to a political rally, a government function, or just a pleasure trip, the cattleya corsage was always present. In 1953 the Rod McLellan Company in San Francisco honored Mamie by naming a new *Cattleya* hybrid for her. The flower was a beautiful, large, floriferous white with a purple lip, and the company called it *Laeliocattleya* Mamie Eisenhower.

Unlike 1929, this time the idea of naming a cattleya for the first lady caught on, and it soon became a tradition. In 1961 the large New Jersey cut-flower producer H. Patterson and Sons named another lovely white with purple lip flower—*Cattleya* Jacqueline Kennedy—for the next first lady. Lines Orchids even named a beautiful white with purple lip cattleya in 1961 for former first lady Bess Truman. In 1969 Chicago cut-flower grower Orchids By Hausermann named yet another white with purple lip flower, *Laeliocattleya* Patricia Nixon, for the next first lady. It was all very grand, and if the orchid grower worked it right, he could even present the flowers to the first lady in person at the White House.

The cattleya cut-flower corsage mania of the 1940s and 1950s was like a supernova star that blazed unbelievably brightly for over 20 years before slowly beginning to die away as fashions changed and less glamorous things took center stage. Cattleya corsages had always been sold through florists' shops where the style and design of the corsage

President Eisenhower's wife, Mamie, was seldom seen in public without a corsage of cattleya flowers, and in 1953 the Rod McLellan Company named a *Laeliocattleya* in her honor.

Laeliocattleya Hillary Rodham Clinton 'First Lady'

were as important as the flower itself. After it was made, the corsage was placed on a fluffy bed of shredded wax paper in a large white box that had a luxurious big bow and a tasteful card. It gave the impression of elegance no matter how you looked at it.

By the late 1950s, however, the cattleya corsage had an important competitor as another orchid, the *Cymbidium*, flooded the market with flowers. Cymbidiums were longer-lasting flowers than cattleyas, and they were smaller and more compact, but still large enough that a corsage could be made out of one flower. Cymbidium flowers had heavier substance than cattleyas, so they resisted damage better when shipped long distances from growers to the market. Cymbidiums were also cool-growing orchids, which made them appealing to growers because they required less heat to grow than cattleyas, and cymbidiums produced so many flowers that one plant could fill two or three shipping boxes with blooms.

Before long, so many cymbidiums were available that they became a glut on the market during important spring holidays, like Easter, when demand for corsages was the greatest. In desperation, suppliers began marketing them through grocery stores and other mass merchandisers, and the surplus of cymbidiums and their cheap marketing had a profound effect on the corsage market. Cymbidium corsages were sold like cellophane-packaged Easter eggs and chocolate Easter bunnies that piled up at the checkout counter. They conveyed no message other than cheapness, and they soon destroyed the elegant image cattleyas had established for corsages so triumphantly over the previous decades. Florists could not sell their $12 cattleya corsages when their customers could buy a cymbidium corsage for $1.98 at the supermarket. When the glamour was gone, women soon lost interest in wearing orchid corsages altogether.

The tremendous growth in the production and sale of cut cattleya flowers during the 1940s, however, had not diminished the excitement that had developed in the plant side of the business. The Second World War had been hard on the orchid industry because greenhouses were consumers of precious wartime resources like coal and oil. In Britain, many plants were left to die in unheated facilities when fuel supplies were short. Orchid firms like Stuart Low, H. G. Alexander, and Black and Flory had made tremendous strides in breeding fine large-flowered cattleya hybrids during the 1930s, and now with the war, they were threatened with losing everything they had accomplished. The British industry was scattered throughout the countryside so it missed most of the destructive bombing that concentrated on the big cities, but the losses were still sizable. Continental Europe, however, was in shambles and the Second World War would be a turning point in the commercial growing of orchid plants. The United States would emerge as the undisputed leader in their production for the next 30 years.

The 1930s had seen numerous researchers and commercial companies in the United States experiment with Knudson's sterilized technique for growing cattleyas, varying the nutrients, the pH, and/or the disinfecting solutions, and new *Cattleya* hybrids were flowing into American greenhouses at a phenomenal rate by the 1940s. Many hybrids were bred at first to fill the gaps in cattleya cut-flower production. The cross between *Cattleya mossiae* and *Laelia purpurata*, called *Laeliocattleya* Canhamiana, was produced in large quantities to meet the huge demand for white cattleyas with purple lips that had developed for June weddings. The standard, medium lavender *Cattleya* species were replaced with rich, dark purple hybrids that had become more popular with the public. There had never been enough large white cattleyas at any time of the year to meet the demand for these flowers, so hybridizers plunged into the breeding of white *Cattleya* hybrids with a passion.

Despite all the production, however, cattleya plants were in such demand right after the war that two of the leading suppliers of orchid plants for hobbyists, Armacost and Royston, and L. Sherman Adams, literally ran out of hybrid seedlings to sell and had to withdraw their recently published price lists through notices in the *American Orchid Society Bulletin*. As time went on and supplies improved, hybridizers began producing not only lavender and white *Cattleya* hybrids, but a variety of unusual colors, and beautiful shades of yellow, orange, red, and green cattleyas began to appear. The public identified the colors lavender, purple, and white with cattleyas for corsages, but hobbyists, who just grew plants, recognized the uniqueness of the new yellow, red, or peach flowers and were excited about buying them. By the late 1940s and 1950s, a whole new world of color existed in cattleyas, and many companies were actively hybridizing for these "art shades" for sale to hobbyists.

In addition to the expansion in colors in cattleyas, the 1950s also saw the emergence of orchid companies that specialized in selling fine, named varieties of large-flowered *Cattleya* species and hybrids. The most famous of these orchid companies was Jones and Scully in Miami, Florida, which offered what it called its "Imperial Collection" of large-flowered cattleyas "for the connoisseur." In its 25th anniversary catalog for 1970–1971, Jones and Scully offered over 400 named varieties of the finest cattleyas to be found in the world. So many varieties were available that Scully had to group them by color to make them understandable. There were groups of lavenders, blues, whites, semi-albas, pastels, flares or darts or feathers, and yellows. The company offered more than 100 red shades, and some were priced as high as $150 per bulb. It was an impressive collection that appealed to hobbyists who wanted the finest cattleyas available regardless of cost. If you were a grower or hobbyist who had just received an American Orchid Society award on a cattleya, you could expect a telephone call from Bob Scully asking if you would sell him the awarded plant so he could add it to his Imperial Collection.

Researchers had known for a long time that some of the cattleya stud plants used in breeding had twice the normal number of chromosomes and that these tetraploid plants produced more vigorous hybrids with better quality flowers. As commercial orchid companies became aware of this phenomenon, they began testing their best stud plants to see if they were tetraploids and then selectively breeding with these tetraploid plants. H. Patterson and Sons, a major cut-flower producer in Bergenfield, New Jersey, even hired a full-time scientist to determine tetraploidy in its plants and began offering hobbyists dozens of cattleya crosses made with tetraploid studs along with lots of advertising hype on the superiority of these crosses over their competitors' crosses. During the 1950s Patterson produced literally thousands of unusually fine traditional lavender or white large-flowered *Cattleya* hybrids using this advanced system of hybridizing.

Lewis Knudson had given orchid growers their first major breakthrough in the production of orchid plants in 1922, with his sterilized method for planting orchid seed. Knudson's simple technique, which could use anyone's kitchen as a laboratory, made it possible to produce the hundreds of thousands of cattleya plants needed for the enor-

Brassolaeliocattleya Sayette 'Olive' reflects the trend toward new cattleya colors that emerged in the late 1940s and 1950s.

mous expansion of the cattleya cut-flower market and for the orchid plant sales of the 1930s to the 1950s. Growing plants from seed, however, produced new plants that varied, to some degree, in size, shape, or color even though they came from the same seed pod. The crosses never produced plants that were exactly like the parent plants. The offspring of two large, round, dark purple cattleya stud plants might have flowers with petals that ranged from narrow to wide with varying shades of lavender to purple.

Then, in June 1964, the French orchid company Vacherot and Lecoufle in Paris announced a breakthrough in orchid growing that would revolutionize the production of the parent plants themselves. Vacherot and Lecoufle claimed it could reproduce the parent plants of a wide range of orchid genera, including cattleyas, by cutting out the tiny tip, or meristem, of a new growth when the growth was only 2 or 3 inches tall, and planting the tiny tip in a sterilized nutrient solution on a slowly rotating wheel. The technique was much more sophisticated than Knudson's had been and could not be done in a typical home kitchen. If handled correctly, however, in a properly equipped laboratory, a single meristem tip could develop into 300 or more plants that were genetically identical to the original plant.

Before the advent of this tissue culture, or meristem, method of reproducing plants, the high-priced, extra fine varieties of cattleyas were always scarce because there was no economical way to reproduce them. They could only be reproduced by cutting the plant in half. This usually gave a three- or four-bulb front division and a backpiece of several old bulbs that took another two or three years to grow into a commercially salable plant. No one could grow enough plants by this method to supply the potential demand, and

Laeliocattleya Dorset Gold 'Orchidhurst' AM/RHS (1952) sold for $50 per bulb in Jones and Scully's Imperial Collection in 1970. It was eventually meristemmed by Vacherot and Lecoufle and sold for $13.50 for a whole plant.

prices for these fine varieties were always high. Vacherot's ability to produce "clones" of the original plant by using tissue-culture suddenly made it possible to reproduce these fine plants at a modest cost per plant. Instead of an extra fine cattleya variety selling for $500, the same plant, as a meristem, could sell for $10.

At first, everyone was skeptical of Vacherot's claim about its "mericlones," as Vacherot called them, but people bought a few plants, and as the plants flowered and were found to be just like the original plant, the concept took hold everywhere. Tissue-cultured cattleya plants were soon available from many orchid growers, and even Jones and Scully saw the writing on the wall and began selling meristems of some of its Imperial Collection. Vacherot had opened a new era in orchid production, and now anyone could own some of the finest varieties of cattleyas in existence at a reasonable cost.

Eventually so many meristemmed plants of fine cattleyas were for sale from so many orchid companies that Jones and Scully's Imperial Collection of fine cattleyas became a thing of the past. By the end of the 1970s, most orchid companies were offering meristems of a few fine cattleya varieties in their catalogs for less than $15 a plant, and hobbyists were buying them regularly. Vacherot and Lecoufle had become the leading supplier of meristem orchids soon after it announced their availability, but the company's success was short lived because it had no valid patent on the meristem process that could be enforced in a court of law. It was not long before many major orchid companies had set up laboratories to produce meristems, and Vacherot's monopoly disappeared.

As the world moved into the late 1970s and early 1980s, a new market for orchids began to emerge that would, once again, change the public's perception of these plants.

Laeliocattleya Culminant 'La Tuilerie', one of Vacherot and Lecoufle's popular mericlones, was its own hybrid. It received a gold medal and U.S. Patent 2658.

For the first 150 years after their introduction, tropical orchid plants had been sold primarily to hobbyists who usually knew something about the plants and how to care for them. Although you could occasionally find a large-flowered cattleya plant like a *Cattleya percivaliana* for sale in flower in a florist shop at Christmas, or a *C. mossiae* at Easter, orchid plants were not really sold to the general public like African violets and geraniums.

By the 1980s, however, the modern world was catching up with the orchid, and advanced technology, with its meristem tissue culture, fast long-distance transportation, and emphasis on business efficiency, was changing everything. The Second World War had seen great strides in the design of aircraft for the military and, with the peace, the leading aircraft manufacturer, Boeing, introduced its large transport and cargo jets, the 707 and 747, to the commercial market. It was now possible to ship high-value crops like orchid flowers and orchid plants by air from low cost tropical growing areas like Hawaii to the big markets on mainland America and avoid the high cost of growing the plants locally.

Not all orchids were suitable for sale to the general public, however. If they were going to survive on a typical home windowsill, they had to grow well at household temperatures around 70°F day and night. Since not all windowsills were in a sunny location, the orchids also had to grow fairly well under low light conditions in a shaded window. It would be nice if the orchids had flowers that lasted a long time, because homeowners were used to having long-lasting African violets and *Streptocarpus* inhabiting their windowsills. Most important of all, however, was that the orchids had to be tolerant of the abuse they would receive from homeowners who knew no more about growing an orchid plant than they knew about growing a mango tree.

One good candidate for this new homeowner's market was the *Phalaenopsis* orchid. Considerable progress had been made in breeding phalaenopsis over the previous 20 years, and phalaenopsis were now available with cascading sprays of 7 to 12 large, round flowers, and they came in an assortment of colors. Phalaenopsis would last in bloom for three months under normal conditions, and they loved warm household temperatures. Phalaenopsis were also very popular with commercial growers because they could be grown from seed to flowering-size plants in less than three years compared with cattleyas that took seven years and cymbidiums that took even longer.

Phalaenopsis soon began appearing in roadside nurseries along with pansies and evergreens, and they were for sale in grocery stores and mass-market outlets bunched up and shivering with the forced tulips and hyacinths. During the 1990s literally millions of phalaenopsis were produced in tropical and subtropical growing areas, then shipped to major cities to be "finished" or just sold "as is." By the late 1990s, phalaenopsis had become the second largest pot plant sold in the United States. Only the traditional Christmas poinsettia sold more plants annually.

Large-flowered cattleyas, despite their appealing beauty and fragrances, were not well suited to growing year-round on windowsills. They needed more sunshine, moving air, humidity, and space than a home windowsill could provide when they were actively growing, and a lot more knowledge to grow than the typical homeowner was interested in learning. A 70°F night temperature was simply too hot for most large-flowered *Cattleya* species or hybrids and, without lots of sunshine, there was not much hope of getting any flowers. A typical large-flowered cattleya plant in a 5- or 6-inch pot would not even fit on most modern-day windowsills.

The industry responded to these limitations by breeding miniature cattleyas that were more tolerant to heat and were small enough to populate a windowsill. The miniature cattleyas took up no more space than a typical African violet in a 3- or 4-inch pot. Despite their bright colors, small size, ease of culture, and the name "cattleya," however, these miniatures did not have the appeal of the large-flowered cattleya that was still the "real orchid" in the eyes of most people.

The large-flowered cattleya remained out of reach of the homeowner market. Its magnificent large lavender, white, or art-shade flowers were beyond the horticultural capability of the average homeowner or even most of the merchants who sold them. When a grower sent plants of a large-flowered cattleya to a mass merchandiser, they were often handled so poorly on arrival that the flower buds did not open well, and the life of the flowers was shortened to only a few days. Despite all the modern technology, production improvements, and growing efficiency of the 1980s and 1990s, the classic, large-flowered cattleyas remained the special plants of the orchid-growing hobbyist who had a greenhouse and a real interest in growing them.

As women's interest in wearing corsages had faded in the 1970s and the cut-flower industry declined, thousands and thousands of beautiful large-flowered cattleya plants, both species and hybrids, had perished. So many fine cattleyas were lost as the giant cut-flower growers went out of business that even the meristemming of cattleyas suffered

The most enduring of the large-flowered *Cattleya* species, *C. mossiae* was the first cattleya to fill the greenhouses of European nobles in the early 1800s and the last *Cattleya* species to leave the cut-flower greenhouses in the United States in the late 1900s.

because the remaining producers of cattleya plants often could no longer locate particular fine old varieties to meristem. Some of these fine varieties still existed in private collections, but it was often difficult to find the owners and, once in a private collection, many of these varieties were no longer for sale to anyone at any price.

With the many people who actively grew orchids as a hobby, however, cattleyas still remained the premier collectors' plants they had always been, and this is where we find them today. Their appeal has not diminished, nor their beauty and diversity. Many of the rare and beautiful varieties still command unusually high prices, and when in bloom, they are still a justification to have a party to show them off to your orchid friends. They are not the kind of plant you can buy in a supermarket or mass-merchandising outlet. You need a greenhouse to grow cattleyas well year-round in a temperate climate and enough plants so a new plant will begin blooming every three weeks or so if you want a constant supply of flowers. Although the world has changed dramatically over the past 100 years, the classic large-flowered cattleya has not. It is still the elegant queen of the orchid world and the flower of the orchid connoisseur.

Looking back on the history of the large-flowered cattleyas, *Cattleya mossiae* stands out as perhaps the most enduring of these classic orchids. It was the first large-flowered cattleya to fill the private greenhouses of European nobility during the early 1800s, and it was the last *Cattleya* species to leave the commercial cut-flower greenhouses in the United States in the late 1900s. It was the first cattleya to appear on the cover of the *American Orchid Society Bulletin* and the first orchid to grow on the nutrient agar in Lewis Knudson's sterilized flasks, and it is still one of the finest orchids in existence anywhere. Its large flowers, classic bright lavender colors, floriferousness, wonderful fragrance, and endless varieties epitomize the legacy of the large-flowered cattleya. *Cattleya mossiae* is as beautiful as any flower, orchid or non-orchid, that ever stepped onto the horticultural stage, and it is an orchid that you can still buy, grow, and enjoy in the 21st century.

THREE

A Touch of Botany

T HE CLASSIC cattleyas are a group of species within the genus *Cattleya* that made the genus famous and that largely established tropical orchids themselves as being rare, exotic, and expensive plants. Like the other *Cattleya* species, they are found growing wild in South America, although one species, *C. dowiana,* is also found in Central America, primarily in Costa Rica. These species only grow in South and Central America.

We have also included as classic cattleyas, the six large-flowered Brazilian species that are called "cattleyode laelias" (chapter five, "The Orphanage"). These species show no meaningful differences from the traditional large-flowered *Cattleya* species and, although they have eight pollinia instead of the usual four, we feel this is a trivial difference botanically compared with their overwhelming similarities. We feel their difference in number of pollinia should never have been used to exclude them from the genus *Cattleya.*

The classic cattleyas can be separated from the other *Cattleya* species by the large size of their flowers, their unbroken or entire lip structure, and the single leaf at the top of the pseudobulb. The term "entire" means that the outer edge of the lip is continuous and there are no cuts separating the front and side lobes. These species are sometimes referred to as "unifoliate cattleyas" because of their single leaf, but this is not a good descriptive term because other *Cattleya* species like *C. luteola, C. iricolor,* and *C. walkeriana* also have a single leaf at the top of the pseudobulb, but do not belong in this group. *Cattleya luteola* and *C. iricolor* have small flowers and *C. walkeriana* does not have an entire lip.

A better general term to describe these classic cattleyas is "large-flowered cattleyas" because it is the flower size, including the large and full lip, that primarily distinguishes them from the other *Cattleya* species. There are 17 traditional large-flowered *Cattleya* species and they have sometimes been referred to historically as the "Labiata Group," although not all writers have included all 17 species when they use the term. James Veitch in his book *A Manual of Orchidaceous Plants,* published in 1887, described the Labiata Group as the "collective name for a group of cattleyas remarkable for the size and extraordinary beauty of their flowers," and this is the way most people think of them. With the addition of the six large-flowered Brazilian species referred to earlier, this gives a total of 23 large-flowered *Cattleya* species in the classic group.

The Cattleya Plant

Botany, like all sciences, has its own vocabulary, and in the following text, we will define those terms useful in understanding cattleyas.

Cattleyas are epiphytes, which means they grow *on* another plant without parasitizing that plant. Cattleyas are not parasites and, when they are found growing on trees, they only use the tree for support and do not in any way feed on the tree's sap. When cattleyas grow on rocks, they are called lithophytes.

Botanically, the *Cattleya* plant is a horizontal creeping stem called a rhizome with an enlarged storage stem called a pseudobulb (literally "false bulb") that grows vertically from the rhizome. A single fleshy leaf arises from the top of the pseudobulb in the large-flowered cattleyas, and roots emerge from the base of the rhizome. The primary function of the pseudobulb is to store moisture so the cattleya can survive dry periods in the jungle. The pseudobulb also stores nutrients for future vegetative growth and flower production. The thick fleshy leaf at the top of the pseudobulb also acts as a reservoir for moisture.

When the cattleya begins to grow, an axillary bud, or eye, at the base of the newest or youngest pseudobulb swells and breaks through its covering scales and becomes a new lead (pronounced "leed"). The lead grows forward horizontally for an inch or so and then turns upward to become a new pseudobulb. The initial inch of horizontal growth becomes a new rhizome.

While the pseudobulb is actively growing, it is protected from damage from insects and weather by thin, overlapping sheathing leaves. As the pseudobulb matures and its tissues harden, this sheathing turns brown, becomes dry and loose, and eventually falls away from the pseudobulb.

The *Cattleya* has a sympodial manner of growth, which means it grows forward, producing one pseudobulb after another as it goes. This is different from orchids like vandas and phalaenopsis which only grow upward from a single point—a growth pattern called monopodial.

To be able to live in the air on another plant, *Cattleya* roots must have a covering that protects them from drying out. Roots that grow in the soil do not need this protective covering because the moist soil protects them from desiccation. The protective covering on a *Cattleya* root is called the velamen and, in addition to protecting the root from drying out, the velamen has the ability to cling tightly to any porous surface like tree bark, rocks, or clay flower pots. The velamen also acts as a sponge and rapidly absorbs any water that falls on it. When the outside of the velamen is dry, it is white in color even though the inside may still be moist and green where it surrounds the root.

The growing tip of the root where the velamen is forming is a light green color and extends about $\frac{1}{2}$ inch beyond the end of the root. The root has the ability to send out new growing tips not only at the end of the root, but also anywhere along the length of the root. These secondary root tips usually form when the primary root tip is broken off or eaten by an insect.

In the large-flowered *Cattleya*, the flower stalk that supports a group of flowers is called a raceme, and the raceme emerges from the top of the pseudobulb where the leaf

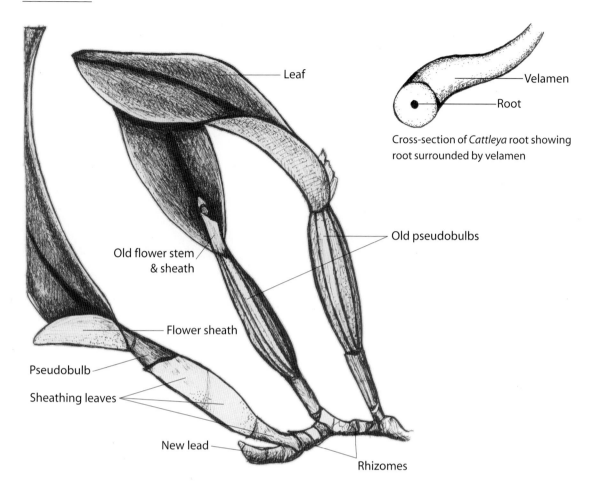

Cross-section of *Cattleya* root showing
root surrounded by velamen

Typical *Cattleya* plant showing rhizomes, pseudobulbs, leaves, flower
sheath, sheathing leaves, and new lead

and pseudobulb meet. The raceme and flower buds are enclosed initially in a protective
envelope called a sheath which is about 1 inch wide and 1 to 3 inches long depending on
the species. When the raceme and buds emerge from the top of the sheath, they grow
upward into a head of flowers called an inflorescence. The inflorescence contains from
2 to 10 flowers depending on the species. Two of the large-flowered *Cattleya* species, *C.
labiata* and *C. warneri*, normally have a double sheath with one sheath inside the other
as an extra protection against damage to the raceme and buds.

Botanists use the term "whorl" to describe the various layers of a flower's structure.
The outer whorl of a large-flowered *Cattleya* flower is made up of three sepals which are
essentially the same size and color. The sepal that stands straight up in the back is called
the dorsal sepal and the other two are called lateral sepals. All three sepals together are
referred to as the calyx of the flower. The next whorl is made up of three petals which are
larger and broader than the sepals. All the petals together are called the corolla, and all
the sepals and petals combined are termed the perianth. The *Cattleya* actually has only
two normal petals since the third petal has been modified into the structure we call the
lip or labellum.

The *Cattleya* flower has a bilateral symmetry, which means the flower can be cut in only one vertical plane to obtain halves that are the mirror image of each other. A daisy, by comparison, has a radial symmetry where the flower can be cut vertically in any plane through the center to produce halves that are mirror images.

The lip of the *Cattleya* flower is made up of three lobes, two side or lateral lobes, and one front or midlobe. The midlobe of the lip protrudes and sometimes hangs down

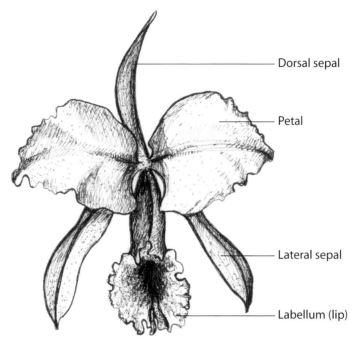

Flower of large-flowered *Cattleya* showing sepals, petals, and lip

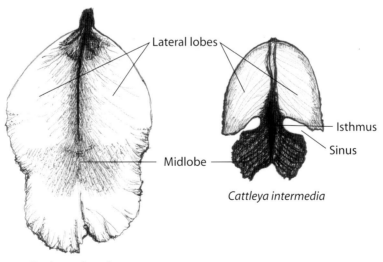

Cattleya schroederae

Cattleya intermedia

Unrolled and flattened lips of *Cattleya schroederae* (left) and *C. intermedia* (right) showing the three lobes of the lip

and has the most varied color pattern. No deep indentations or cuts, called sinuses, separate the three lobes of the lip in the large-flowered *Cattleya* species and this is an important distinguishing feature. The bifoliate *Cattleya* species, by comparison, do have sinuses separating the lateral lobes and the midlobe, and they have an area between the sinuses called the isthmus. Some botanists describe the lip of the large-flowered cattleyas as "obscurely three-lobed" because the lip often looks like it does not really have separate lobes when compared with the distinct lobes of a bifoliate *Cattleya.*

Another distinct feature of the large-flowered *Cattleya* species is that the labellum completely surrounds and hides the column. The column is a structure unique to orchids that contains both the male pollen sacs, the pollinia, and the sticky female surface, the stigma. The stigma is the place where pollen is caught and held during pollination. This is quite different from most common flowers like lilies or tulips where the pollen is held on separate male structures called anthers and the stigma is on a separate female structure called the pistil.

The pollen in cattleyas is not free to blow around in the air as it does in most garden flowers and trees. It is molded into solid waxy sacs, called pollinia, which are yellow in color and located in the anther cap. Because it is in a solid mass, the pollen can only be transferred mechanically by insects or man. The anther cap is located at the front end of the column and is held in place by a tiny flexible structure at the tip of the column that resembles a bird's beak. The structure is sometimes referred to as a hinge.

Cattleyas have four pollinia in the anther cap which are held together as two pairs and the Brazilian Laelia/Cattleyas have eight pollinia as four pairs. A tiny flap called a rostellum separates the male pollen sacs from the female stigmatic surface of the column in cattleyas and prevents self-pollination of the flower. As an insect enters the flower, the anther cap depresses slightly where it touches the rostellum so the insect can move past the rostellum without disturbing the pollinia. When the insect leaves the flower, however, the anther cap does not depress but opens slightly to expose the tails or caudicles of the pollinia. The rostellum exudes a sticky fluid onto the back or head of the insect that catches and glues the caudicles with their pollinia to the insect as it moves out of the flower. The pollinia are then carried on the insect to another flower where the pollinia are pulled off by an even-more sticky stigmatic fluid.

Once the pollinia are on the stigma, the pollen begins to grow like tiny threads down the inside of the column toward the ovary which contains the female eggs, the ovules. It takes the pollen several weeks to grow down the column to the ovules, so fertilization does not occur for a month or two after pollination. The ovules themselves are also not fully mature and able to be fertilized while the flower is still in bloom.

Once pollinated, a *Cattleya* flower will usually begin to fold or wilt after two days even though its flowers normally last three or four weeks. The *Cattleya* flower has an inferior ovary which means the ovary is below the flower not above it. Because it is below the flower and attached directly to the flower stalk, it is sometimes mistaken for a flower stem. The ovary in cattleyas also twists as the bud enlarges so that the lip is on the lower side of the flower when the flower opens. This twisting process is referred to botanically as resupination.

Bees are the primary pollinators of cattleyas in the wild, and nature seems to have designed the cattleya flower so the sepals and petals are large and colorful and attract these pollinators to the flower. The brightly colored lip then guides the bees to the nectar at the base of the column and, on their way, they pollinate the flower. When the cattleya flower is pollinated and the ovules fertilized, they develop into seeds and the ovary grows into a large seed pod which botanists call a capsule.

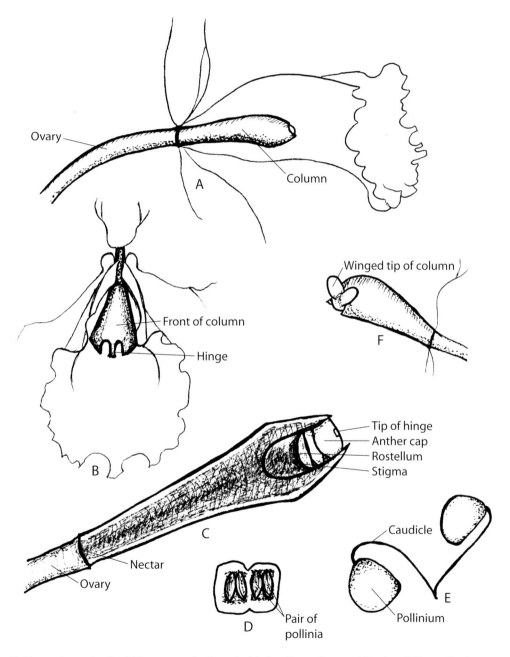

Cattleya column details. A: Placement of column inside lip of large-flowered *Cattleya*. B: Front of column showing hinge which holds anther cap in place. C: Underside of column showing anther cap, rostellum, stigma, nectar, and ovary. D: Inside of anther cap showing four pollinia arranged in two pairs. E: Pair of pollinia with caudicles still attached to each other. F: Wing-tipped column of *Cattleya lueddemanniana*

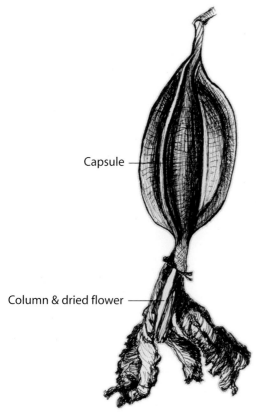

Capsule —

Column & dried flower —

Capsule (seed pod) of *Cattleya mossiae* six months after pollination

Cattleya capsules have three lobes with six prominent ribs and vary somewhat in size and shape from plant to plant, but there is no constant difference in the shape of the capsule from species to species. In other words, you cannot identify a *Cattleya* species by the size and shape of its capsule. There is often more variation between the size and shape of the capsule within a species like *C. mossiae*, for example, than there is between the capsules of *C. mossiae* and *C. warscewiczii* or *C. trianaei*.

Cattleya capsules normally ripen in about 9 months but can take as long as 14 months or more if the plant is weak or virused. When the capsule ripens, it splits or dehisces along the three lobes of the capsule, and seeds fall out and drift through the air to a suitable site on a tree's rough bark where they germinate. The seed has virtually no endosperm or stored food to sustain it the way most other seeds do, so it must find a place to grow as soon as possible if it is to survive. A *Cattleya* capsule contains hundreds of thousands of dust-size seeds because only a very few seeds will land in an environment where they can grow.

In nature, *Cattleya* seeds are usually infected by a fungus that provides them with the nutrients they need to germinate and begin to grow. The relationship between the fungus and the orchid seed is beneficial to both of them and is said to be symbiotic. A fungus is not needed to germinate and grow cattleya seedlings in a laboratory because the required nutrients are provided in the agar medium.

Classification of Large-flowered Cattleyas

The genus *Cattleya* was established by a 22-year-old British botanist named John Lindley when he published a description of the large-flowered species, *C. labiata* in his book *Collectanea Botanica*. The book shows a publication date of 1821, but the book was not completely published in that year which is why some authors show dates up to 1824 for establishing the genus. Lindley himself considered the publication date to be 1821 and referred to it that way in his 1831 book *Genera and Species of Orchidaceous Plants*. Lindley's botanical descriptions were in Latin and his general comments in English in *Collectanea Botanica*.

Lindley described *Cattleya labiata* as an American parasitic plant in keeping with the botanical thinking of the 1820s when botanists still considered orchids to be parasites. He later re-described it as an epiphyte as botanists realized that orchids only used trees for support and did not feed on the tree's sap as a parasite would. Lindley had no trouble adding new species to the genus *Cattleya* right after he established it because the new plants were obviously different from *C. labiata*. He added *C. loddigesii*, a small, lavender bifoliate that had a cut lip, at the same time he described *C. labiata* in plate 33, and *C. forbesii*, another small yellow-green bifoliate without a cut lip in plate 37 of *Collectanea Botanica*.

Lindley added a second large-flowered species, *Cattleya maxima*, in 1831 when he published his *Genera and Species of Orchidaceous Plants* (p. 116) based only on dried specimens that had been collected over 50 years earlier by two Spanish botanists, Hipólito Ruíz and José Antonio Pavón. In his description of *C. maxima*, Lindley had to say the flowers were "probably lavender" because he could not really tell. The thing that impressed Lindley so much about *C. maxima*, however, was the 7-inch spread of the flowers which made them the largest *Cattleya* flowers he had ever seen and the reason he called the species "maxima."

In 1836, however, when botanist William Jackson Hooker described *Cattleya mossiae* as a new species in Curtis's *Botanical Magazine* (65, plate 3669), everything came to a halt. As Lindley saw it, *C. mossiae* had flowers that were the same size and shape as *C. labiata* with similar lavender coloring. Even *C. mossiae*'s distinctive splashed lip pattern sometimes resembled the purple lip of *C. labiata*. The pseudobulbs of the two plants were slightly different, but not always, and all their vegetative characteristics seemed at times to overlap. *Cattleya mossiae* bothered Lindley so much that he wrote a refutation of Hooker's original description of the species in the *Botanical Register* of 1840 (plate 58) in which he re-described *C. mossiae* as "*C. labiata* var. *mossiae*." In his 1840 comments, Lindley took exception to each point Hooker had used to establish *C. mossiae* as a new species.

Lindley's re-description of *Cattleya mossiae* set off a botanical debate over whether the large-flowered cattleyas were really separate species or just varieties of *C. labiata*, and the debate lasted for over 60 years. Each new large-flowered *Cattleya* species that was discovered was subjected to a botanical inquisition with some botanists classifying the plant as a species, others classifying it as a variety of *C. labiata*. One of the foremost botanists of the day, H. G. Reichenbach, even vacillated between the species and variety concept, describing *C. warscewiczii* as a species in one article (*Bonplandia* 2 [1854]: 112), and as *C. labiata* var. *warscewiczii* in another (*The Gardeners' Chronicle* 19 [1883]: 243). One of the main problems was that Lindley was a highly respected pioneer in classifying orchids and most people were reluctant to challenge his pronouncements even when they appeared to be wrong.

When Lindley died in 1865, the situation moderated somewhat, but when James Veitch in his book, A *Manual of Orchidaceous Plants*, in 1887 described the large-flowered *Cattleya* species as varieties of *C. labiata*, the confusion was as bad as ever. Following Veitch's lead, Frederick Sander described the large-flowered cattleyas as varieties of *C. labiata* in the first three volumes of his book *Reichenbachia*. The weight of the horticultural evidence, however, finally overwhelmed the critics and in Sander's fourth and final volume of *Reichenbachia*, he dropped the variety concept and called all the large-flowered cattleyas pictured "species."

One of the most influential people in the argument to make species of all the large-flowered cattleyas was James O'Brien, one of the most knowledgeable horticulturists of the late 1800s and early 1900s. O'Brien's influence as a writer and advisor for *The Gardeners' Chronicle* and his position as secretary to the Royal Horticultural Society's Orchid Committee for 34 years is largely responsible for correcting the situation and firmly establishing the large-flowered cattleyas as species in their own right, and not varieties of *Cattleya labiata*.

John Lindley's problem with the classification of the large-flowered *Cattleya* species lay in his classification system, not the similarity of the species themselves. Like most botanists of his time, Lindley classified orchids based primarily on their floral structures with some consideration given to vegetative similarities or differences. This gave a static-two dimensional view of the plants that worked for most orchids but not for the large-flowered cattleyas. The large-flowered cattleyas were too similar to each other to be separated into species based exclusively on their floral and vegetative structures and colors. It took a third dimension, a dynamic one that looked at the plants' growing and flowering habits, to do this. Hooker knew *C. mossiae* was very different from *C. labiata* when he called *C. mossiae* a new species in 1836, but he could not describe the difference in the botanical framework of the day.

Only one large-flowered *Cattleya* species, *C. lueddemanniana*, has a structure that is different from all the other *Cattleya* species. *Cattleya lueddemanniana* has a column with a winged tip. No other *Cattleya* species has this winged structure on the tip of the column, and it makes *C. lueddemanniana* an easy species to identify.

When it comes to color, only two *Cattleya* species have unique color patterns. *Cattleya maxima* is the only species with a yellow stripe running down the center of the lip of all its varieties, including the white (alba) and white with purple lip (semialba) forms. *Cattleya dowiana* is the only species with sepals and petals that are yellow or yellow suffused with purple, and it is the only species that does not have an alba or semialba form. The rest of the large-flowered *Cattleya* species are basically lavender-colored flowers with alba and semialba forms that have no structural differences. Their color patterns occasionally overlap so that one species can, at times, look just like another species based on color patterns alone. For these lavender large-flowered *Cattleya* species, it is essential to know their growing and flowering habits if you want to separate them into individual species.

Cattleya Growth and Flowering Habits

Although Reichenbach could not tell it from the dried specimens he received from plant hunter Josef Warscewicz, a major difference between *Cattleya warscewiczii* and *C. labiata* or *C. mossiae* was its flowering habit. Both *C. labiata* and *C. mossiae* complete their growths, then rest a month or more before buds appear in the sheath. *Cattleya warscewiczii*, however, flowers before its new growth is completed, and the flower buds emerge from the sheath while the pseudobulb is still actively growing. *Cattleya warscewiczii* also flowers at a different time of the year than either *C. labiata* or *C. mossiae* under greenhouse conditions in the United States.

These growth and flowering patterns of the large-flowered *Cattleya* species have significant botanical value in describing these species for they are as much a part of these plants as their entire lips or single leaves. The 17 species can be divided into two groups based on whether or not they have a resting period after completing their new growth. They can be divided further based on how long they rest. If they begin to flower without a rest, they can be separated based on whether their buds emerge from the sheath before the new growth is mature or whether they appear as tiny buds at the bottom of the sheath at maturity of the pseudobulb.

Rogerson (2004) has shown that the *Cattleya* species can also be divided into two groups based on whether they send out roots before or after they flower. Based on Rogerson's data, it appears that the *Cattleya* species that root before they flower are the same species that rest before they flower. The species that root after they flower are those that flower without a rest period.

Table 1. Large-flowered *Cattleya* species that flower after a rest period.

SPECIES	APPROXIMATE LENGTH OF REST PERIOD (IN MONTHS)	APPROXIMATE FLOWERING SEASON IN THE UNITED STATES
C. labiata	1	September–October
C. jenmanii	2–3	October–November
C. maxima	2–3	November
C. percivaliana	2–3	December
C. quadricolor	4	December–January
C. trianaei	4	December–February
C. schroederae	4	February
C. lawrenceana	4	March
C. mossiae	5–6	February–May
C. mendelii	6	April–May

Table 2. Large-flowered *Cattleya* species that initiate buds and flowers with no rest period.

SPECIES	FLOWER BUDS APPEAR IN SHEATH AS SOON AS THE PSEUDOBULB IS MATURE	FLOWER BUDS APPEAR WHILE PSEUDOBULB IS STILL ACTIVELY GROWING	APPROXIMATE FLOWERING SEASON IN THE UNITED STATES
C. lueddemanniana		X	March–April
C. gaskelliana	X		May–June
C. warneri	X		May–June
C. warscewiczii		X	June–July
C. eldorado		X	July
C. rex		X	July
C. dowiana		X	August

Although the flowering times of the large-flowered *Cattleya* species are very reliable, it is important to recognize that the months shown in Tables 1 and 2 apply only to greenhouse conditions in the United States. In northern Europe where there is less sunlight and shorter winter days, these species usually flower a month or two later than the times shown in the tables. Under natural conditions in the jungle, the flowering times are also influenced by the hemisphere in which these species grow. *Cattleya labiata*, for example, flowers in the fall, in September–October in the United States and January–February in Brazil. These species are also subjected to a variety of microclimates in their native countries which can affect their flowering time. The only reliable way to see the differences in flowering times is to grow the species side by side in a common environment.

You will notice as you go through the chapters on the individual *Cattleya* species that each species has a distinctive appearance and a typical lip color pattern. *Cattleya lueddemanniana* flowers, for example, usually have an oval shape, while *C. trianaei* flowers tend to be more circular in form. *Cattleya mossiae* has a "splash" pattern in the lip, while *C. warscewiczii* has a yellow eye on either side of the lip. Although each species has a typical lip color pattern, there is enough variation in these color patterns that the flowers of one species can occasionally look so similar to another species that you cannot tell them apart based on color pattern alone. Color patterns are only a general guide to the species and not definitive characteristics like the plant's growing and flowering habits.

We have not yet found a way to describe fragrances in simple words, so it is not possible to discuss the differences in fragrances between the *Cattleya* species. This is unfortunate because each species has its own distinct fragrance which anyone who grows them can come to recognize. These differences in fragrance clearly label these plants as different species because they suggest different pollinating insects.

FOUR

The Large-flowered *Cattleya* Species

THE FOLLOWING descriptions of the individual large-flowered *Cattleya* species give a summary of their history, characteristics, and culture. The species are presented in the order in which they were first described botanically to show their relationship with each other and with the events that fashioned their acceptance into the horticultural and botanical world of the 19th century. The publication in which the species was first described botanically follows the species name.

Table 3. Large-flowered *Cattleya* species by year in which they were described.

SPECIES	YEAR	PUBLICATION WHERE FIRST DESCRIBED
C. labiata	1821	Lindley, *Collectanea Botanica*, plate 33
C. maxima	1831	Lindley, *Genera and Species of Orchidaceous Plants*, p. 116
C. mossiae	1836	Hooker, Curtis's *Botanical Magazine*, plate 3669
C. warscewiczii	1854	Reichenbach fil., *Bonplandia* 2:112
C. lueddemanniana	1854	Reichenbach fil., *Xenia Orchidacea* 1:29
C. trianaei	1860	Linden & Reichenbach fil., *Botanische Zeitung* 18:74
C. warneri	1862	Moore, *Select Orchidaceous Plants* 1:plate 8
C. quadricolor	1864	Bateman, *Gardeners' Chronicle* 24:269
C. dowiana	1866	Bateman, *Gardeners' Chronicle* 26:922
C. eldorado	1869	Linden, *Flore des Serres et des Jardins* 18:plate 1826
C. mendelii	1872	Dombrain, *Floral Magazine*, plate 32
C. percivaliana	1883	O'Brien, *Gardeners' Chronicle*, n.s., 20:404
C. gaskelliana	1883	Reichenbach fil., *Gardeners' Chronicle*, n.s., 19:243
C. lawrenceana	1885	Reichenbach fil., *Gardeners' Chronicle*, n.s., 23:338
C. rex	1890	O'Brien, *Gardeners' Chronicle*, 3d series, 8:684
C. schroederae	1895	Rolfe, *Orchid Review* 3:268
C. jenmanii	1906	Rolfe, *Kew Bulletin* 20:85

Cattleya labiata Lindley

Collectanea Botanica, plate 33. 1821

Cattleya labiata was discovered by the naturalist William Swainson in the province of Pernambuco in northern Brazil in early 1817. Swainson was collecting plants at the time for the Glasgow Botanic Garden in Scotland, and he shipped the *C. labiata* along with his other plants from Pernambuco to Glasgow in June 1817. Swainson then traveled south to Rio de Janeiro where he made another shipment of plants in August 1818 which did not include *C. labiata*. Swainson wrote a letter to a Professor Jamieson giving the details of his trip through Brazil which was published in the *Edinburgh Philosophical Journal* of 1819 (1: 369–373) under the title "Sketch of a Journey through Brazil in 1817 and 1818." Swainson then left on a collecting trip to New Zealand and disappeared from the horticultural scene.

At Swainson's request, the Glasgow Botanic Garden sent divisions of the *Cattleya labiata* plants they received to a tropical plant collector in Barnet, England, named William Cattley. Cattley flowered the first *C. labiata* in November 1818, and the Glasgow Botanic Garden flowered theirs the following fall. Cattley hired a young botanist, John Lindley, to describe the plants in his collection, and in 1821 Lindley published a book, *Collectanea Botanica*, in which, along with other tropical plants, he described *C. labiata* as a new species and established the genus *Cattleya*, naming it in honor of his patron, William Cattley.

Cattleya labiata created such a sensation right after its discovery with its large lavender flowers and rich, dark purple lip that commercial companies wanted to import

Cattleya labiata 'Amensiana', a light lavender form of the species

more plants, but no one knew where to find them. William Swainson was now foraging through New Zealand and out of touch with everyone in England, and his account of his trip through Brazil lay buried and unread in library archives. With few facts to work with, the botanical and horticultural authorities of the 1820s began speculating about Swainson's trip and decided he must have collected *C. labiata* near Rio de Janeiro because they knew he made a shipment of plants from Rio. They did not seem to know about his shipment from Pernambuco.

This speculation turned to "fact" when another naturalist, George Gardner, made a trip to Brazil in 1836 and found the beautiful large-flowered, lavender-colored *Laelia lobata* blooming on Top Sail and in the Organ Mountains just north of Rio and mistakenly took it for *Cattleya labiata*. Gardner even sent dried specimens of *Laelia lobata* back to the Royal Botanic Gardens Kew where they were put in the herbarium under the name "*C. labiata*."

The herbarium specimens were not examined, however, until 1907 when Robert Allen Rolfe soaked them out to evaluate the remarks of a French plant hunter, Louis Forget. Forget had written an article in the 1897 *Le Jardin* entitled "Erreurs geographiques concernant les Orchidées"(pp. 246–248) in which he stated emphatically that Pernambuco was the home of *Cattleya labiata* and that the species never existed in the Organ Mountains or anywhere else in the state of Rio de Janeiro. When Rolfe discovered that Gardner's specimens were *Laelia lobata* and not *C. labiata*, he realized Forget was correct. *Cattleya labiata* had never existed in the Organ Mountains and virtually all 19th-century writers, including Rolfe himself, had misstated its origin.

Since everyone was looking in the wrong place for *Cattleya labiata*, it became known for over 70 years as "the lost orchid." When it was finally re-discovered in 1889, it was found by someone who was not even looking for orchids—a collector for a Mr. Moreau of Paris. Moreau was a distinguished entomologist who had dispatched a collector to central and northern Brazil with a view to adding specimens of new insects to his museum. Since Moreau grew some orchids as a hobby, his collector sent him 50 plants of a large lavender orchid from Pernambuco. By an unbelievable coincidence, Frederick Sander stopped to visit Moreau when the plants were just starting to flower and realized they were the long-lost *C. labiata*. Having no commercial incentive to keep its location secret, Moreau happily explained to Sander where his collector had found *C. labiata* and by 1892, over 25,000 *C. labiata* plants were being imported annually into Great Britain alone.

Because it was the first large-flowered *Cattleya* to arrive in Europe, *C. labiata* has been the victim of an endless number of fanciful tales about its discovery. One of the most frequently heard stories tells us that Swainson's *C. labiata* plants were mistaken for the packing material surrounding his ferns and mosses. No one thought they had any value, and William Cattley threw them under his greenhouse bench where, after a few months and to everyone's amazement, the packing material flowered. This myth grew out of an article written in 1893 by Frederick Boyle entitled "The Lost Orchid" in which Boyle was speculating on where Swainson may have discovered *C. labiata*. In 1893, no one knew where he found it, and with typical British humor, Boyle said Swainson probably did not know himself where it grew and, "The orchids fell in his way—possibly collected in distant parts by some poor fellow who died at Rio. Swainson picked them up and used them to pack his lichens." Boyles's bit of fun and nonsense, however, was taken seriously by later writers who created a grand myth out of it that has been retold by an endless number of "orchid experts" ever since.

Unfortunately for the myth-tellers, the facts show that Swainson shipped all his *Cattleya labiata* plants to the Glasgow Botanic Garden with instructions to send some of them to William Cattley. Glasgow, of course, had to know what the plants looked like to do this. Swainson himself knew how beautiful *C. labiata* was because he arrived in Pernambuco on the eve of its flowering season and stayed six months. Having seen the flowers, Swainson knew Cattley would love them, and Cattley took such good care of the plants that they flowered a year ahead of the plants Glasgow kept for themselves.

Among the large-flowered *Cattleya* species, *C. labiata* is one of the most interesting, not only because of its fascinating history, but also because it captures the middle ground of the large-flowered *Cattleya* species. In this sense it was probably a good selection for a type species for these plants, which are often referred to as the Labiata Group of cattleyas.

Cattleya labiata is not the best-shaped *Cattleya* species, but it is far from the worst shaped. It does not produce the most flowers on a flower spike, but it is a reliable producer of four or five flowers per spike. It is a relatively tall growing member of the large-flowered cattleyas, taller than *C. mossiae* and *C. trianaei*, but not as tall as the Sanderiana forms of *C. warscewiczii*. It is a robust grower with a proud carriage and produces good-sized 6- to 7-inch flowers that separate well on the spike. Flowers are normally produced from a double sheath unlike the Colombian and Venezuelan *Cattleya* species that flower from a single sheath. *Cattleya labiata* is the only large-flowered *Cattleya* species that blooms in the early autumn in the United States and is easily separated from its close Brazilian relative, *C. warneri*, by its flowering season since *C. warneri* blooms in the spring. *Cattleya labiata* is also light controllable and, as you shorten the length of daylight, you can actually make it flower at any time of the year. It flowers naturally when nature shortens the day length in the autumn.

Sun shining through the sheath of this *Cattleya labiata* showing its distinctive double sheath

More than any other *Cattleya* species, *C. labiata* passes on good carriage to its hybrids. The flowers stand high on the plant and do not crowd each other. Good carriage is a quality sorely needed in many modern *Cattleya* hybrids, since round-shaped flowers are not worth much on a plant that does not display them well.

Cattleya labiata has a lot more color forms than *C. warscewiczii*, but not as many as *C. trianaei*. Its most common lip pattern is a solid dark purple with a pale lavender edge. There have been a number of fine white varieties of *C. labiata* found over the years. Two of the most famous are E. Ashworth's old clone 'Harefield Hall' and John Lager's 'Alba Plena'. The earliest whites to be awarded were 'Alba' FCC/RHS (1892), and 'Alba Purity' FCC/RHS (1907), which, like 'Alba Plena', had only a trace of yellow in the throat.

The most famous semialba varieties of *Cattleya labiata* are 'Cooksoniae' FCC/RHS (1895) and 'Mrs. E. Ashworth' FCC/RHS (1896). Both of these plants produce striking flowers and have survived the last 100 years quite well and are still grown by hobbyists today.

Good lavender varieties of *Cattleya labiata* vary from pale lavender to some impressive dark clones like 'Monarch'. Some breeding has been done between these fine old lavender clones to produce better-shaped flowers like *C. labiata* 'Aruba' AM/AOS (1982) and 'Bahia', but many of these hybrid labiatas have lost much of their beautiful natural species appearance, and the old original jungle plants are more attractive.

Although *Cattleya labiata* announces the beginning of the autumn season, its dominance of this time of year in orchid shows and for cut-flower sales was relatively short-lived as many more brilliant and floriferous autumn-blooming *Cattleya* hybrids rapidly replaced it. By the late 1940s primary hybrids like the intensely dark purple *C.* Fabia (*C. labiata* × *C. dowiana*) and the brilliant *C.* Peetersii (*C. labiata* × *C.* Hardyana) were the standard September cut-flower, not *C. labiata*. Many complex hybrids filled the October and November need for cattleya flowers, and *C. labiata* all but disappeared from commercial production. This rapid replacement of *C. labiata* by autumn-bloom-

Cattleya labiata 'Cooksoniae' FCC/RHS (1895)

ing hybrids led to the disappearance of most of the fine old awarded lavender varieties of the species and, sadly, only a few remain in cultivation today.

Culture

Cattleya labiata is one of the most vigorous *Cattleya* species and undoubtedly one of the easiest to grow. It normally begins growing in February in the United States and will complete its new growth by June. If the growth is completed early enough, it will make a second growth that will mature in late July or early August and both growths will

Cattleya labiata 'Monarch'

flower at the same time in the fall. Depending on the variety, *C. labiata* will flower from September into November. After flowering, it should be allowed to rest and should be given water sparingly. Too much water during its rest period will rot the roots and retard growth in the spring.

Like most other large-flowered *Cattleya* species, *C. labiata* benefits from lots of sun and moving air. The leaves should be a light green color if you want its five-flowered bloom spikes. Repotting should be done in the spring as soon as the front pseudobulb begins to send out a flush of new roots.

Cattleya maxima Lindley
Genera and Species of Orchidaceous Plants, p. 116. 1831

Although *Cattleya labiata* was the first large-flowered *Cattleya* species described botanically, *C. maxima* was actually the first species discovered by Europeans in the jungles of South America. It was found 44 years before *C. labiata* by Spanish botanists Hipólito Ruíz and José Antonio Pavón in 1777 while they were working for the Spanish government investigating the quinine forests of what is now Peru and Ecuador. Ruíz and Pavón sent dried herbarium specimens of the plants back to Spain, but nothing was done with them for over 50 years.

Ruíz and Pavón's herbarium specimens were eventually sold to Aylmer Bourke Lambert, an author of several horticultural and botanical books. Lambert recognized the unique character of the lavender orchid in the collection and took the dried specimens to John Lindley who, in 1831, decided they were a new species of *Cattleya* and gave them the name *C. maxima*. He included a description of *C. maxima* on page 116 of his book *Genera and Species of Orchidaceous Plants* published in 1831.

The dried herbarium specimens were the only evidence European horticulturists had of *Cattleya maxima* until 1842 when Karl Theodor Hartweg, a collector for the Horticultural Society of London, discovered some plants in the immense forests that border the Rio Grande near Malacotes, Ecuador. Hartweg sent the plants back to England where they flowered in 1844, and Lindley wrote another description of *C. maxima* in the *Botanical Register* of that year. Then for some strange reason, Hartweg's plants quietly disappeared from cultivation, and it was another 10 years before *C. maxima* appeared again in Europe.

The plants collected by Hartweg were the first live *Cattleya maxima* to reach Europe, and they had plump, short pseudobulbs with relatively short upright leaves and three to five dark lavender flowers on a flower stem. This type of *C. maxima* is found on the western slopes of the Andes from southern Colombia into northern Peru and Ecuador at elevations of 3000 to almost 6000 feet above sea level. It is referred to as the "upland" *C. maxima* and was the only *C. maxima* known to horticulturists until 1864.

In 1864 Gustav Wallis, a collector for Jean Linden's company, Horticulture Internationale in Belgium, sent Linden some truly giant *Cattleya maxima* plants, up to 2 feet tall with 12 to 21 flowers on a spike, which he collected at sea level in Ecuador. These tall plants had pale to medium lavender flowers with none of the intense dark purple of the short-pseudobulb type. Despite their beauty, however, Wallis's tall-pseudobulb, "lowland" *C. maxima*, again disappeared from cultivation in less than 10 years. It wasn't until 30 years later in 1894 that a large number of the tall-pseudobulb *C. maxima* arrived in Europe, and the two forms of *C. maxima* finally established themselves in European horticulture.

Cattleya maxima had a variable popularity over the years, which has undoubtedly accounted for its disappearance now and then from cultivation. Sander did not include a picture of *C. maxima* in his famous book *Reichenbachia*, although he featured most of the other important *Cattleya* species. Helen Adams also gave a cursory treatment to *C. maxima* in her series on the *Cattleya* species in the *American Orchid Society Bulletin* during the 1940s. The problem seems to be that *C. maxima* is thought of as a large-flowered, labiata-type *Cattleya* species, but it lacks the size and full shape of most of these species. There is no round-shaped *C. maxima* or anything even close. The flowers are all starry, and the petals often come forward. *Cattleya maxima* was not grown for cut flowers during the 1940s and 1950s because of its narrow petals despite the long-lasting qualities of the flowers and their attractive flowering season which went from Thanksgiving through early December.

The only one who really glamorized *Cattleya maxima* was Linden in his famous book *Lindenia*, where he included pictures of two striking short-pseudobulb plants, 'Virginalis' and an unnamed dark clone, and two magnificent tall-pseudobulb varieties, one of which, 'Florbunda', received a two-page spread. Linden felt the tall-pseudobulb, lowland *C. maxima* was the best type because of the large head of flowers that made such an impressive display. Linden, of course, was the first one to have large numbers of the lowland type for sale, so this may have colored his opinion.

The upland type of *Cattleya maxima* can have four or five very dark purple flowers on a relatively short-growing spike.

Like a small child playing peekaboo in the hallway, *Cattleya maxima* has poked its face into the horticultural world, only to quickly pull it back, then reappear to surprise the viewer. The beauty of the tall lowland form, with its exquisite pastel pink flowers, goes in and out of fashion as the growing space in the greenhouse shrinks and expands, while the upland *C. maxima* is popular when small plants with dark flowers are in vogue—as they are today.

Cattleya maxima flowers in late autumn in the United States, from mid-November into early December. It blooms after *C. labiata* has finished flowering and before *C. per-*

The tall-growing form of *Cattleya maxima* comes from the warm lowland areas of Ecuador and can stand over 3 feet high with 15 flowers on a spike. Lowland forms also are paler in color than the upland type.

civaliana begins. The flowers of *C. maxima* have a lovely fragrance and are very long lasting, sometimes staying in bloom until Christmas. The species has all the color forms of the typical large-flowered *Cattleya* species from albas and semialbas to dark purple and lovely pale pinkish-lavender. There are also some attractive coerulea varieties.

This species is one of the few large-flowered cattleyas that is easy to identify by its color pattern. *Cattleya maxima* has a characteristic yellow stripe running down the center of the lip in all color forms, including the albas, and it is the only *Cattleya* species with this yellow stripe.

Much has been written about the name "maxima" that John Lindley gave the species because it does not seem to fit the plant. Veitch, in his *Manual of Orchidaceous Plants* in 1887, described the name as "scarcely appropriate, as most of the labiata varieties have still larger flowers." Many people today, including some writers, assume that Lindley gave *Cattleya maxima* its name to reflect the tall pseudobulbs and many-flowered bloom spikes of the lowland form, because these are some of the largest heads of flowers of any of the *Cattleya* species. The facts, however, point to a different conclusion. There was no way to tell from Ruíz and Pavón's herbarium specimens how tall the pseudobulb was since it had been cut off 1 inch below the leaves. The flower spike was also not complete. It was only 8 inches long with the top broken off, and it showed evidence of only five flowers. No one would name a plant "maxima" based on this evidence.

On the other hand, the single dried flower that was preserved was 7 inches across, which was not only large for *Cattleya maxima*, but made it the largest *Cattleya* flower Lindley had seen up to that time. The year 1831 was early in the discovery of the *Catt-*

The yellow stripe down the center of the lip in *Cattleya maxima* is so characteristic of the species that it even appears in the alba varieties.

leya species. Only five species—four bifoliates (*C. forbesii, C. intermedia, C. guttata,* and *C. loddigesii*) and one large-flowered species (*C. labiata*)—had been described botanically. The bifoliate cattleyas had flowers less than 4 inches across, and the painting of *C. labiata* that accompanied Lindley's description of the species in 1821 shows a flower that is only two-thirds its normal size because the plant was so poorly grown. In 1831 then, a *C. maxima* with a 7-inch flower was the largest *Cattleya* species around.

Even as late as 1844, Lindley said in the *Botanical Register* that *Cattleya maxima* rivaled *C. labiata* and "its flowers are as large," and Hooker in Curtis's *Botanical Magazine* for 1856 (plate 4902) subtitled his description of *C. maxima* "Largest Cattleya." Thus *C. maxima* was named "maxima" because of the size of its flowers. The name had nothing to do with the size of the plant or its flower spike. There are lots of *Cattleya* species, of course, that have flowers that are larger than 7 inches across, but that is now, not in 1831.

The color of the flowers in the short-pseudobulb plants seems to give this type of *Cattleya maxima* most of its appeal, while the large size of the plant and flowerhead in the tall-pseudobulb type is both an asset and a liability, depending on the amount of space a grower has available to give the plant. Both types of *C. maxima* have charming flowers, however, and are well worth the time spent to grow them.

Culture

Although *Cattleya maxima* is an easy plant to grow, the short- and tall-pseudobulb types have slightly different cultural requirements. They both begin to grow in the

The typical *Cattleya maxima* has light lavender sepals and petals and a dark purple lip with a yellow stripe running down the center of the lip. It normally flowers in late autumn in the United States.

spring in the United States, and both flower in late November to early December. Their night temperature requirements, however, are not the same. As a mountain plant, the short-pseudobulb, upland *C. maxima* requires the normal cattleya night temperature of 58°F and can take temperatures down to the low 50s if it is kept dry. The tall-pseudobulb *C. maxima*, however, grows near sea level where night temperatures are in the high 60s to low 70s. To grow the tall-pseudobulb *C. maxima* well, the night temperature should be around 65°F, so the plant should be put in the warmest part of the intermediate greenhouse.

Day temperatures for both types of *Cattleya maxima* should be about 85°F. The upland *C. maxima* likes more sun than the lowland, but both grow and flower well if their leaves are a light green color. Both forms also benefit from lots of moving air. The upland type often has some purple pigment in the foliage, while the lowland is normally just green. To enjoy the full size of the tall pseudobulbs of the lowland type, the plant must develop a good root system, and it will help to keep the plant slightly underpotted so it can be watered more frequently.

Cattleya maxima grows well for us in clay pots. We do not recommend growing it on cork slabs because the plants require watering too frequently to produce good growths. *Cattleya maxima* should be repotted as soon as it makes new roots from the lead pseudobulb and should be fertilized only when actively growing in the spring and summer.

Cattleya mossiae Hooker
Curtis's *Botanical Magazine*, plate 3669. 1836

One of the wonderful things about the *Cattleya* species is that there is always one in bloom every day of the year and you come to associate each with a particular season. So when the days begin to lengthen and the spring sun grows stronger, you know the greenhouse or sun porch will soon be filled with one of the brightest, largest, and loveliest rose-lavender cattleyas in nature's storehouse, *C. mossiae*. Springtime is mossiae time.

Since *Cattleya mossiae* blooms in abundance during March, April, and May, it is in bloom for Easter, Mother's Day, all the spring dances and graduations, and most of the spring flower shows. It is often called "The Easter Orchid," and it is no wonder that it was the darling of the commercial cut-flower industry in the 1940s and 1950s. It was still grown for cut flowers long after the other *Cattleya* species had given way to fancier hybrids.

Cattleya mossiae was not discovered until 1836, which was over 15 years after John Lindley established the genus *Cattleya* and described *C. labiata* as a new species. The first *C. mossiae* plant to reach Europe was sent to George Green of Liverpool, England, by a friend in Venezuela. Green gave the plant to a friend of his, a Mrs. Moss who owned a stove, or warm greenhouse, full of tropical plants in Otterpool. When the plant bloomed, Mrs. Moss was so thrilled with it that she sent the flowers and her own pencil sketch of the plant to William Jackson Hooker, a professor of botany at the University of Glasgow, Scotland. The flowers were a mammoth 8½ inches across and had a beautiful rose-lavender color and a lovely fragrance that Hooker described as "powerful." Hooker was so impressed he decided to describe it as a new species, *Cattleya mossiae*, naming it after Mrs. Moss. He published the description in Curtis's *Botanical Magazine* of 1836 (pl. 3669). The colored lithograph that accompanied Hooker's description was done by Walter Fitch, one of the most outstanding botanical artists of the period.

Unlike *Cattleya labiata*, which was so scarce it was virtually unavailable in 1836, *C. mossiae* was plentiful and was soon imported in large numbers by Hornsey, Loddiges, and other British nurseries. Within a few years most orchid collections in Europe grew *C. mossiae*, and it became a favorite for exhibitions because of its great abundance of large flowers. *Cattleya mossiae* not only produced large individual flowers but also bore four or five flowers on a bloom spike and numerous growths with several spikes. A plant in a 10-inch pot could have more than 20 flowers and produce a magnificent display. Between 1865 and 1913, the Royal Horticultural Society gave 37 Awards of Merit and 16 First Class Certificates to various clones of *C. mossiae*. The number of named varieties of *C. mossiae* was almost endless, and more than 150 were recorded in the literature before the end of the 19th century.

Europe was not the only place that loved *Cattleya mossiae*, of course. It was so admired in its native Venezuela, where it was called the "Flor de Mayo," that it was eventually named that country's national flower. Since Venezuela is home to eight major *Cattleya* species, including the impressive large-flowered *C. lueddemanniana*, *C. gaskelliana*, and *C. percivaliana*, it speaks volumes for the peoples' love for *C. mossiae*.

For the hobbyist, *Cattleya mossiae* has all the qualities to make it a true treasure. It is one of the easiest *Cattleya* species to grow and the easiest to flower, and it adapts bet-

Cattleya mossiae 'Ed Patterson' AM/AOS is a fine example of a classic rose-lavender wild plant of this species.

ter to more adverse growing conditions than any other species in the genus. For this reason, it is often recommended as a beginner's orchid. Yet, its enduring qualities keep it high on the list of favorites of longtime orchid growers. When a friend of ours gave up his large cattleya collection because he could no longer take care of his greenhouses, the only plants he kept to grow in his home solarium were his four plants of *C. mossiae*, because, as he put it, "They are as much a part of spring as the daffodils and you can always count on them."

Cattleya mossiae was one of the most abundant of the large-flowered *Cattleya* species in its natural habitat in the 1800s, and literally hundreds of thousands of plants were imported into Europe and the United States during the last two centuries. It is still one of the most common species found in the wild today. Enough alba varieties of *C. mossiae* were found that the British orchid company Sander could tell its collectors to include a case or two of alba plants with every shipment, which is remarkable when you realize that only one or two alba plants were found with most other large-flowered *Cattleya* species over 100 years of collecting.

The first alba form of *Cattleya mossiae* to reach Europe was actually described as a new species, *C. wagneri*, by botanist Heinrich Gustav Reichenbach (*Xenia Orchidacea* 1: 28, pl. 13). When *C. wagneri* was finally recognized as a variety of *C. mossiae*, Sander continued the name "wagneri" by using it as a clonal name on an alba that received a First Class Certificate from the Royal Horticultural Society in 1885. The clonal name ('Wagneri') soon became so associated with the alba form that it was virtually a generic

Cattleya mossiae reineckiana 'Young's Variety' has been the standard of quality in semialba forms of *C. mossiae* for over 70 years, and the plant has a long history of producing outstanding hybrids. The original plant was collected in the Venezuelan jungle.

description for it. As a result, we see alba varieties of *C. mossiae* today with labels that read only "*C. mossiae* Wagneri." Sometimes Wagneri is followed by a clonal name but not always. The word "alba" does not appear anywhere in the name.

A similar thing happened to the semialba variety of *Cattleya mossiae*. The Royal Horticultural Society gave a First Class Certificate to a plant in 1871 that had white sepals and petals and a lip with rosy crimson veins that was exhibited by Torrdesborough. *The Gardeners' Chronicle* published two articles about the plant in 1883 and 1884 when its reporter visited the estate of Sir N. de Rothschild who also grew the plant. Sander even put a painting of it in its book *Reichenbachia* (plate 52). Once again, the variety became so well known that the term "reineckiana" was soon synonymous with a semialba *C. mossiae*. One of the most famous breeding semialba forms of *C. mossiae* of all time, *C. mossiae reineckiana* 'Young's Variety', still carries this descriptive name.

Most famous, old cultivars of *Cattleya mossiae* have the classic mossiae shape where the broad petals tend to fall forward. This unique shape distinguishes *C. mossiae* from most of the other large-flowered *Cattleya* species. Since many *C. mossiae* have petals that are very wide, this fall-forward shape is still very attractive. The only First Class Certificate awarded to *C. mossiae* by the American Orchid Society for over 50 years went to 'Mrs. J. T. Butterworth', which had this fall-forward petal shape. *Cattleya mossiae* is apparently so proud of its shape that it passes it on to its hybrids, and the shape is really rather nice, even though it does not fit the arbitrary international standards for *Cattleya* judging.

Cattleya mossiae 'Mrs. J. T. Butterworth' FCC/AOS (1941) sold for $10,000 during the heyday of the cut-flower era in the United States. It had petals that measured $9^1/_2$ inches across and was the only *C. mossiae* plant to receive a First Class Certificate from the American Orchid Society until the end of the 20th century.

The lavender forms of *Cattleya mossiae* present a wide range of color in the petals from pale rose to dark purple. Most of them have the typical lip pattern where the purple has a splashed appearance, but a few varieties lack this pattern. One of the most famous lavender-breeding cultivars is 'R. E. Patterson' (not to be confused with 'Ed Patterson', which is a different variety). *Cattleya mossiae* 'R. E. Patterson' has normal-size flowers with petals that are upright instead of falling forward. Its shape is the main reason it was so widely used in breeding, but it also had a unique lip pattern where the dense lavender splashing went all the way to the edge of the lip. There have also been several lavender *C. mossiae* that were tetraploids like Patterson's famous 'Orchidhaven' and John Mossman's 'Julie'.

Without *Cattleya mossiae*, spring hybrids would be few and far between. Virtually all of our good spring *Cattleya* hybrids today have this species in their background. The most famous of these hybrids is the semialba form of *Laeliocattleya* Canhamiana, which is a primary hybrid with semialba *Laelia purpurata* (syn. *Cattleya purpurata*). This hybrid so dominated the June cut-flower market at one time that it was known as the "Bridal Orchid." Thomas Young Orchids in Boundbrook, New Jersey, grew more than 10,000 semialba *Lc.* Canhamiana plants in 8-inch and 10-inch pots (150,000 flowers) for this June market but could not begin to meet the demand for the flowers. It is difficult to praise *C. mossiae* too much because it is a truly wonderful plant. The word "magnificent" has been used by many authors to describe it, and in this respect William Hooker in his original description of the species said it best when he wrote that *C. mossiae* is simply "the most magnificent of all orchidaceous plants."

Cattleya mossiae 'R. E. Patterson' has been widely used in breeding because of the unusual upright shape of its petals. The variety is unique because the dark lip color extends to the edge of the lip.

Culture

Because it flowers in the spring, *Cattleya mossiae* does not begin growing until early summer, after species such as *C. labiata* have completed their growths. *Cattleya mossiae* usually completes its growth in the United States by late September and then rests for about six months before it flowers. It will typically send out a flush of roots from the new growth as soon as the growth is mature. If repotted at this time, it will still produce a strong flower spike in the spring. Like other cattleyas, *C. mossiae* should only be repotted when it begins sending out these new roots.

Cattleya mossiae likes lots of water while actively growing in the summer, and then should be watered sparingly during the cold winter months when it is dormant. It grows best if you allow it to dry out thoroughly before watering it again. When you do water, give it a thorough watering that wets all the roots in the container. *Cattleya mossiae* requires plenty of sun and air and will give more flowers the more sun it receives. It is receiving too much sun, however, if the leaves feel warm to the touch or become yellow-green. *Cattleya mossiae* requires a normal *Cattleya* temperature of 58° to 60°F at night and up to 85°F during the day.

Fertilizer is not needed to produce good growths or flowers but can benefit plants grown in bark mixes. We recommend ¼ teaspoonful of a soluble 20–20–20 fertilizer per gallon of water be given weekly during active growth in July and August. Use a cup of this solution per plant per watering. Never use slow-release fertilizers since these can release nitrogen when the plant is dormant, and this could cause injury to the plant.

Cattleya mossiae 'Anthony Alfieri' AM/AOS is probably the best-shaped lavender *C. mossiae* ever exhibited. It was a selection from a selfing of John Mossman's famous stud plant, *C. mossiae* 'Julie.'

Cattleya warscewiczii Reichenbach fil.
Bonplandia 2: 112. 1854.

Cattleya warscewiczii is not only the largest-flowered species in the genus, with flowers that can reach 12 inches across from petal tip to petal tip, but it also produces the largest flower spikes with as many as 10 huge flowers per spike. When well grown, the flower spike stands almost vertical, unlike most of the other *Cattleya* species, which produce flowers in a horizontal plane. This vertical placement of the flowers adds to the overwhelming grandeur of the bloom spike and makes *C. warscewiczii* truly the king of the *Cattleya* species.

Some 50 years or so ago, when this species was common in commercial greenhouses in the United States, no one ever called it *Cattleya warscewiczii*. In fact, few people would know what you were talking about if you called it that. The old growers called it *C. gigas* (pronounced "GI-gus"). The name *gigas*, which means "giant," was given to it by Jean Jules Linden in 1873, when he believed he was first to describe it botanically. He wasn't the first, because H. G. Reichenbach had done that 19 years earlier in 1854 in the German botanical publication *Bonplandia* (2: 112), where he named it in honor of his "dear friend" Josef Warscewicz. But, although Reichenbach named it officially, Linden was the one who actively promoted it under the name *C. gigas*, which soon became the common name for *C. warscewiczii*—and still is today.

While we are all indebted to Josef Warscewicz for his contributions to the discovery of many orchid species, one has to be something of a linguist to handle the name *warscewiczii*, where the *w* is pronounced like a *v* and the sounds and spelling are not famil-

A fine example of the Imperialis type of *Cattleya warscewiczii*

iar to the English language. Most people still find it easier to use Linden's name, "gigas," for this reason. They use it as a common horticultural name much as we do when we call *Pyrus communis* "a pear" or *Prunus armeniaca* "an apricot."

There are two major types of *Cattleya warscewiczii*. One of these blooms from late June into early July in greenhouses in the United States and has pseudobulbs about 8 inches tall. *Cattleya warscewiczii* 'Firmin Lambeau', 'F.M.B.', and the lavender Imperialis forms belong to this group. The other major type blooms from mid to late July and has taller pseudobulbs with larger flowers and larger, darker lips. The Sanderiana forms of *C. warscewiczii* are in this second group.

A third type of *Cattleya warscewiczii*, not seen in cultivation since the late 1940s, has tall pseudobulbs with up to 12 flowers per spike. The flowers are fairly dark but only half the size of the other two types. Because of its relatively small flowers, this third type was never held in high regard by commercial growers or hobbyists, which is why we no longer see it.

Cattleya warscewiczii is often described as having "two large yellow eyes" in the lip, but although a few clones do have large eyes, most have relatively small yellow eyes like the variety 'Powhatan'. An occasional plant has been found with a solid dark purple lip and no eyes, and two such plants were awarded by the Royal Horticultural Society many years ago: 'Rothschild's' AM/RHS (1895) and 'Saturata' FCC/RHS (1906).

Among large-flowered cattleyas, *Cattleya warscewiczii* is one of the easiest to recognize, not only because of its flowering season and growth habit, but also because it has relatively few color forms and most lavender varieties of the species look somewhat similar. This is quite different from many of the other large-flowered *Cattleya* species, which have so many diverse color forms that it is sometimes difficult to tell one species from another.

There has been considerable confusion in recent years over the term "Sanderiana" when it refers to *Cattleya warscewiczii*. Sanderiana is a type of *C. warscewiczii* and not a specific clone, but some writers and growers still use 'Sanderiana' as though it were a clonal name. Unfortunately, Sander himself contributed to this present-day confusion by describing "var. imperialis" and "var. sanderiana" in the 1927 edition of *Sanders' Orchid Guide*. Sander did not mean "variety" in the sense of "clone" when he wrote this, but it is sometimes misinterpreted to mean that.

To confuse things even more, the Royal Horticultural Society in 1893 gave an Award of Merit to a plant named *Cattleya warscewiczii* 'Sanderae'. The RHS has never awarded a plant named *C. warscewiczii* 'Sanderiana', although some authors have described Sanderae as Sanderiana. So when you see a label on a plant that reads "*C. warscewiczii* Sanderiana," it means a large, late-flowering type of *C. warscewiczii* and not that great clone you have always wanted to own.

Unlike *Cattleya mossiae* and *C. trianaei*, which have hundreds of named varieties, *C. warscewiczii* has relatively few. The varieties that are named, however, are some of the most famous in the annals of orchid history. The most well known is *C. warscewiczii* 'Firmin Lambeau' FCC/RHS (1912), the first true alba form ever found. While Sander could tell his collectors in Venezuela to ship him a case or two of alba forms of *C. mossiae*, no one had ever seen an alba *C. warscewiczii* until 'Firmin Lambeau' came

Cattleya warscewiczii is famous for its rich, dark velvety purple lip with two small yellow eyes on large flowers that can reach 12 inches across. The flower spike gives a vertical presentation of the flowers unlike most other *Cattleya* species where the flowers are spread in a horizontal plane. The variety shown is 'Powhatan'.

along. 'Firmin Lambeau' sold in 1910 for a fabulous $5,000 (equal to about $50,000 today), and John Lager, co-owner of the venerable orchid firm of Lager and Hurrell that found the plant, personally took it across the Atlantic to be sure it made it to its new owner safely.

Much has been written about the genetics of 'Firmin Lambeau' because the early crosses made between it and the alba forms of *Cattleya mossiae*, *C. gaskelliana*, and *C. warneri* produced only lavender-flowered hybrids. It was not until 'Firmin Lambeau' was crossed with an alba form of *C. trianaei* that white flowers were produced and geneticists realized there were two distinct types of albinism in the *Cattleya* species.

'Firmin Lambeau' is still an exceptional white form of *Cattleya warscewiczii*, although its selfings, like Leo Holguin FCC/AOS (1985), have received more publicity lately. Because of its large size and good shape, 'Firmin Lambeau' would be considered a fine form of the species if it had lavender flowers.

Semialba forms of *Cattleya warscewiczii* are not as rare as the alba form, but they are still rare compared with most other *Cattleya* species. The most famous is undoubtedly 'Frau Melanie Beyrodt' (Mrs. Melanie Beyrodt) FCC/RHS (1904). This plant is commonly referred to by the abbreviation "F.M.B." and it is the best and most widely used form of the species used for breeding semialba *Cattleya* hybrids.

The combination of *Cattleya warscewiczii* 'Frau Melanie Beyrodt' and *C. mossiae reineckiana* 'Young's Variety' produced the exceptionally fine strain of semialba *C.* Enid sold by H. Patterson and Sons in the 1940s and 1950s. Because of Enid's excellent qualities, Patterson made this cross over and over again, year after year, for both plant sales

One of the most beautiful of all *Cattleya warscewiczii* and one of the best breeders is the semialba 'Frau Melanie Beyrodt' FCC/RHS (1904), commonly referred to as 'F.M.B.'.

and cut flowers. *Cattleya* Enid received many awards, including an FCC/AOS (1951) for the variety 'Orchidhaven'. A primary hybrid, *C.* Enid, has been an essential building block to many of our most floriferous *Cattleya* hybrids because one parent, *C. mossiae*, also contributes size and ease of flowering to the partnership. *Cattleya* Enid is particularly interesting because it can flower at any time of the year and is not restricted to the flowering season of its parents.

The famous, dark flowered *Cattleya warscewiczii* 'Low' FCC/RHS (1910) (see chapter seven, "Cattleyas in Art") is in the background of most of our darkest *Cattleya* hybrids, including *Brassolaeliocattleya* Norman's Bay, *Blc. Memoria* Crispin Rosales, and *Blc.* Oconee. Another well-known dark clone is *C. warscewiczii* 'Meteor' AM/RHS (1914), but many other fine dark clones are simply not named.

Cattleya warscewiczii produces some of the most vivid shades of purple in the genus, and it is no wonder that *C.* Hardyana, its natural hybrid with *C. dowiana aurea*, has such magnificent rich coloring. The lip patterns are remarkably brilliant, and while *C.* Hardyana was widely used in making early crosses, it and other fine, old, dark, wild-collected forms are no longer in existence.

Among the beautiful old blush clones of *Cattleya warscewiczii* is 'Rosslyn' AM/RHS (1904), which can produce a breathtaking flower spike. And, of course, the most famous of the blue clones is *C. warscewiczii* 'Helena de Ospina'.

Because it produces the greatest number of flowers on a spike of all the large-flowered *Cattleya* species, *C. warscewiczii* has been invaluable in hybridizing to increase flower count. Virtually all the primary hybrids of *C. warscewiczii* have been important historically for this reason.

Cattleya warscewiczii 'Rosslyn' AM/RHS (1904) is one of the most beautiful of the pastel-colored varieties.

It is difficult to say too many nice things about *Cattleya warscewiczii*. John Lager, the dean of orchid collectors in the United States and an expert on the *Cattleya* species, who tramped through the jungles of Colombia for many years, had an unusually high regard for this species. In his lecture to the Massachusetts Horticultural Society in 1907, after leading his listeners through the maze of spurs, ridges, valleys, canyons, and precipices of the Colombian mountains, Lager observed that

> on crossing the Magdalena River going northeast, we find *Cattleya gigas* San-
> deriana in the state of Cundinamaca. This cattleya is without doubt the grandest
> of all the South American cattleyas. The enormous size of the flowers and
> as many as 10 on a spike is a sight worth seeing.

It is no wonder that Jean Jules Linden felt he had found the pot of gold at the end of the rainbow when he found his *Cattleya gigas*. Linden, however, went straight to the point when he said, "*Cattleya gigas* is quite simply the most beautiful orchid in the world."

While its flower spikes are awe-inspiring, *Cattleya warscewiczii* is also known for its strength and determination to survive. It was Lager, again, who said,

> I have seen this cattleya climb up the mountain until actually stopped by the cold;
> the plants in such localities are, as a rule, stunted, struggling as they do for an
> existence, the front part of the plant somehow will push out new leads repeatedly,
> while the pseudobulbs behind will lose their leaves and die off.

This is not a soft, spineless orchid, but a giant among orchids in many different ways, and it is the undisputed king of the Colombian mountains.

Culture

Most hobbyists in the United States do not grow or flower *Cattleya warscewiczii* well. If you want to enjoy a really strong flower spike, you should start the plant growing as early as possible in late January or early February. You do this by giving it full sun and by teasing it with a light spray of water on sunny days. After the "eye" breaks and begins to grow, continue to give the plant light sprays of water and as much sun as it can take without burning. The leaves should be a yellow-green, and you will need lots of air movement around the plants to keep the leaves from getting warm. Once the leaves feel warm to the touch, you will have to add enough shade to prevent the plants from burning.

Cattleya warscewiczii should not receive much water until the new growth is about 4 inches tall. Too much water too early seems to retard rather than stimulate good flower production, and even early growers like Linden felt this was important enough to call to the attention of their customers.

As the growth gets taller, slowly begin to increase the amount of water, but even when you give the plant heavy waterings, always let it dry out thoroughly before water-ing again. The old pseudobulbs should be fully plump by the time the new leaf begins to emerge.

If you want a fine tall spike of flowers, be careful not to allow the plant to get too warm as the buds emerge from the sheath; otherwise, the spike will tend to curve over and spread the flowers horizontally rather than keep its normal beautiful vertical conformation. It can be difficult to keep *Cattleya warscewiczii* cool enough when the outside summer temperature is over 90°F. We often move our plants from the greenhouse onto a cool porch once the buds emerge until the whole spike is open.

The right time to repot *Cattleya warscewiczii* is immediately after it has flowered, since this is the time it will normally send out a flush of new roots from the newest pseudobulb. Never repot it just before it begins to grow in the spring because it will need all the roots it has to handle the new growth and flower spike.

Because it makes such a heroic effort to grow, root, and produce its huge flower spike in such a short time, *Cattleya warscewiczii* needs a long rest after flowering if you want another good flowering the following year. Avoid allowing it to make another growth after flowering, although we have found that a really strong-growing plant may not always cooperate with you on this.

Cattleya lueddemanniana Reichenbach fil.
Xenia Orchidacea 1:29. 1854

Spring is a particularly appealing time of year for those who grow the *Cattleya* species because several of the best species flower then. It is a time for *C. mossiae*, *C. mendelii*, and the charming *C. lawrenceana*. It is also a time for one of the most beautiful and elegant members of the spring entourage, *C. lueddemanniana*.

Cattleya lueddemanniana is native to Venezuela, where it has always stood a little in the shadow of the grand and glorious national flower, *C. mossiae*. Since it flowers at the same time as *C. mossiae*, it can be overwhelmed by *C. mossiae*'s huge presence. It is like a beautiful but shy young girl who is always upstaged by her ever-present older sister.

The orchid aficionados of Venezuela, of course, adore *Cattleya lueddemanniana* and hold it in high esteem because it has several virtues that *C. mossiae* lacks. The most important one is its fine shape: *C. lueddemanniana* has some of the best-shaped flowers in the genus. Unlike *C. mossiae*, the everyday plants of *C. lueddemanniana* can have good form. Fine shape is a dominant characteristic of the plant, and when *C. lueddemanniana* is crossed with other cattleyas, it helps to improve the form of all the resulting hybrids. *Cattleya lueddemanniana* also has some unusual flower colors that border on shades of peach-lavender, and some beautiful very dark purple varieties where the color has an almost iridescent glow which is unique to the large-flowered *Cattleya* species.

With its many virtues, you would think *Cattleya lueddemanniana* would have established itself in cultivation the day after *C. mossiae* arrived. There were, after all, dozens of plant hunters searching the jungles of Venezuela, collecting *C. mossiae* during the 1830s and 1840s, and *C. lueddemanniana* was, so to speak, just down the road or over the hill. When it finally did find its way to Europe, it was given a new species name each time a new plant appeared. *Cattleya lueddemanniana* has had more trouble with its name than virtually any other large-flowered *Cattleya* species. Its name was so little known after its discovery that the plant was actually described as three different species and the name "*C. lueddemanniana*" was the least known of all of them.

The official botanical name, *Cattleya lueddemanniana*, was given to it by H. G. Reichenbach in 1854 when he described the species in *Xenia Orchidacea* (1: 29). Reichenbach's description was based on a plant given to him by a Mr. Lüddemann, in whose honor Reichenbach named the species. Lüddemann was a friend of Reichenbach and the grower for the famous Pescatore orchid collection in Paris. It was already a bad omen, however, that the plant Lüddemann gave Reichenbach was mislabeled "*C. maxima*."

Eight years later, in 1862, Robert Warner saw a plant of *Cattleya lueddemanniana* in the collection of a Mr. Dawson of Meadow Bank, near Glasgow. Believing it to be a new species, Warner named it *C. dawsonii* in *Select Orchidaceous Plants* of 1862 (1: pl. 16).

Cattleya lueddemanniana was a rare plant in cultivation after Reichenbach first described it. There were essentially no plants for sale until 1868 when Hugh Low and Company in England imported a large number. Neither Reichenbach nor Warner had known where the plants they described grew naturally, so when Low's collectors found them in a previously unexplored area of Venezuela, Low treated them as a new species and another description was published in *The Gardeners' Chronicle* of 1868 (28: 404) under the name "*C. speciosissima*." Low's large commercial supply of plants spread the name *C. speciosissima* with them over all of Europe, and for the next 100 years, *C. speciosissima* was the name most widely used by commercial growers and amateurs alike for *C. lueddemanniana*. The commercial orchid grower's bible of the day, the 7th edition of *The Orchid-Grower's Manual*, does not even mention *C. lueddemanniana* except to refer the reader to *C. speciosissima*.

After reviewing the situation in 1880, Reichenbach paid *Cattleya lueddemanniana* the ultimate compliment when he said, "Well, this cattleya boasts three names and all of them deserved, since the species is worth three." *Cattleya lueddemanniana*'s troubles with its name continued, however, and the first *C. lueddemanniana* hybrid to flower was recorded as a *C. mossiae* cross by Mr. Dominy of Veitch, who raised it.

Because *Cattleya lueddemanniana* flowers at the same time as *C. mossiae*, but produces fewer flowers per stem than *C. mossiae*, it was not popular with commercial cut-flower growers in the United States during the 1930s and 1940s. Its flowers were also not quite as long lasting or as fragrant as those of *C. mossiae* and were sometimes crowded on the flower stem. Despite its abundance in Venezuela, it was never imported in the large numbers that occurred with *C. mossiae* and *C. trianaei*. *Cattleya lueddemanniana* was looked upon by commercial growers as a minor species not worth much attention except for hybridizing to improve flower shape in spring hybrids. Linden, in his magnificent orchid book, *Lindenia*, pictured only one *C. lueddemanniana* and even then he called it "*C. malouana*." Helen Adams, in her articles on the *Cattleya* species in the *American Orchid Society Bulletins* of the 1940s, never included an article on *C. lueddemanniana*, although she included articles on virtually all the other important large-flowered *Cattleya* species.

In its native homeland of Venezuela, *Cattleya lueddemanniana* grows along most of the north slope of the coastal mountains, the Cordillera de la Costa, from sea level to about 1500 feet. From there it extends inland into the state of Lara at a slightly higher elevation. Plants in the two areas differ somewhat in color and size, and some authors have considered them not only distinct types, but also even separate species. The coastal

C. lueddemanniana is generally larger, better-shaped, and lighter in color, while plants from Lara, the Larense type, are smaller and darker. Because of the intense dark color of a few plants of the Larense type, they have had a significant impact on hybridizing over the years. It is a dark Larense-type plant of *C. lueddemanniana* crossed with *Laeliocattleya* Callistoglossa (*Laelia purpurata* × *Cattleya warscewiczii*) that gave us *Lc.* Lustre, which in turn appears in the background of such outstanding dark hybrids as *Brassolaeliocattleya* Norman's Bay, *Blc.* Memoria Crispin Rosales, and *Blc.* Oconee.

White clones of *Cattleya lueddemanniana* have also garnered their share of recognition, largely because of their good shape compared with the poorer shape of *C. mossiae.* The Royal Horticultural Society has given them three First Class Certificates (FCC) and the American Orchid Society has given one. The first FCC was awarded by the RHS in 1892 to a 'Sanderiana' clone. The flower was even pictured in the book *Reichenbachia.* A second FCC was given in 1898 to a plant exhibited by a W. Duckworth, Esquire of Manchester, England. A third clone, 'The Queen' FCC/RHS, is considered one of the best-shaped albas in the genus *Cattleya.* The hybrid *Cattleya* Lady Veitch (*C. lueddemanniana* 'The Queen' × *C. warneri* alba) made by Sander in 1915 was truly outstanding and the variety 'Superbissima' was magnificent with wide, overlapping petals. It was as good as the finest *C.* Bow Bells.

There are several fine semialba clones of *Cattleya lueddemanniana,* among them 'Margaret' AM/AOS (1979), which has very good shape and large size. The most famous semialba is the old variety 'Stanleyi' FCC/RHS (1901), which has been pictured in many publications over the past 100 years. 'Stanleyi' is so well known and distinctive that some growers have used the name 'Stanleyi' on *C. lueddemanniana* plants that look

Cattleya lueddemanniana 'Stanleyi' FCC/RHS (1901) is the most famous of the semialba varieties of the species and is still in cultivation today.

THE LARGE-FLOWERED CATTLEYA SPECIES

similar but are not actually the same plant; this unfortunate situation leads to endless confusion.

Many fine lavender clones of *Cattleya lueddemanniana* exist, and one of the very best is named for A. A. Chadwick's father, 'Arthur Chadwick' AM/AOS. This remarkably large flower has an exceptional shape and a large classic *C. lueddemanniana* lip. It was a wild-collected plant imported in 1935.

The most famous dark purple clone is an old one named *Cattleya lueddemanniana* 'Ernestii' FCC/RHS (1896), which *The Orchid-Grower's Manual* described as "the finest variety of *C. speciosissima* we have ever seen." Two of the best dark clones available today are Lee A. Fennell's 'Jungle Treasure' and 'Stewart's', both of which have excellent dark color. 'Jungle Treasure' has a particularly beautiful lip. There are also some good coerulea clones like 'Siquisique' AM/AOS, 'Ana Beatrix', and 'Mariauxi', which have very good shape for a coerulea.

In the trivia category, *Cattleya lueddemanniana* is a candidate for the *Guinness Book of Records* with a plant that produced four lips on one flower (*The Orchid Review* 7 [1899]: 292).

In nature *Cattleya lueddemanniana* breeds with *C. mossiae* to produce a lovely natural hybrid, *C. Gravesiana*. Over the years hybridizers have produced some particularly fine white strains of *C. Gravesiana*, but most of these seem to have been lost to cultivation. Although *C. Gravesiana* is rare in cultivation in the United States today, it is still fairly common in Venezuela.

Among large-flowered cattleyas, *Cattleya lueddemanniana* is the only one with a distinct structure that the other *Cattleya* species do not have. The tip of the column is

Cattleya lueddemanniana 'Arthur Chadwick' AM/AOS is an unusually large and fine-shaped medium lavender variety with a classic *C. lueddemanniana* lip pattern. It was discovered in the Venezuelan jungle in 1935.

"winged," and this winged column is an excellent way to identify the species if you are in doubt about a particular plant. *Cattleya lueddemanniana* also has a lot of round purple spots on the leaves when they are young and actively growing. The spots normally fade and disappear after the leaves mature.

Cattleya lueddemanniana is a distinct and lovely large-flowered species that is only now beginning to enjoy the recognition it deserves. Its greatest success since its discovery has been as a parent to improve the shape of spring-blooming *Cattleya* hybrids, but it is a beautiful flower in its own right with an iridescent coloring and charm not found in the other *Cattleya* species.

Culture

Cattleya warscewiczii has the reputation as the *Cattleya* species that requires the most sun to make it bloom well, but the greatest sun-lover is actually *C. lueddemanniana*. Unlike most of the other large-flowered *Cattleya* species which grow at relatively high altitudes in the mountain valleys, *C. lueddemanniana* grows close to sea level in its native Venezuela. It grows where there is almost full sun, so it takes lots of sun for most clones to bloom well. British orchid growers often consider it a shy bloomer because of the reduced sunshine levels in Britain and northern Europe, but under the hot, sunny conditions we have in the United States, it flowers freely. To bloom well, the leaves of a *C. lueddemanniana* plant should be light green. With this much sun, you have to have plenty of moving air to keep the leaves from burning. Feel the leaves with your hand, and if they are warm, you must provide more air or more shade.

Because it grows at sea level, *Cattleya lueddemanniana* also likes a slightly warmer

One of the finest dark purple varieties of *Cattleya lueddemanniana* of all time is the clone 'Ernestii' FCC/RHS (1896).

Cattleya lueddemanniana is the only large-flowered *Cattleya* species with a wing-tipped column.

night temperature (63°F) than most of the other large-flowered species. Young transplanted seedlings will not tolerate cold night temperatures, and we recommend a night temperature of 70°F if you want to avoid rot. These seedlings also like more sun than other *Cattleya* species.

In the United States, *Cattleya lueddemanniana* begins growing during the winter, and as soon as the new growth is mature, it sends up buds and flowers in March and April with no rest period. After blooming, it will usually make another growth that will not flower, and the plant will then rest until next winter. Under low-light conditions, however, it can occasionally flower only on the second growth in September or October and not in the spring. This phenomenon occurs more often in Europe than the United States.

While it is actively growing, *Cattleya lueddemanniana* requires lots of water, but like other *Cattleya* species, it should be allowed to dry out thoroughly between waterings. If you are growing plants in a bark mix, *C. lueddemanniana* will benefit from light fertilizing while it is actively growing.

Cattleya trianaei Linden & Reichenbach fil.
Botanische Zeitung 18:74. 1860

Winter may be a dreary time of the year with its overcast days and long somber nights, but for those who grow *Cattleya trianaei*, it is a time to enjoy one of nature's most colorful and captivating flowers. Because it blooms in the winter, *C. trianaei* is one of the most beloved *Cattleya* species, for it appears when we need nature's beauty most. Yet, its appealing flowering season tells only a small part of the story of this wonderful orchid. Of all the *Cattleya* species, *C. trianaei* stands out as a model of perfection, for it possesses the best qualities of the genus.

Cattleya trianaei has the finest-shaped flowers of all the large-flowered cattleyas and the greatest range of color. It has many lovely pastel shades, varieties with flares and feathering in the petals, and the most delicate and glistening substance. Despite its delicate substance, *C. trianaei* lasts in flower longer than any other *Cattleya* species, and five or six weeks is not uncommon. Only *C. schroederae*, a close relative, and *C. eldorado* equal it in the longevity of the flowers.

A vigorous grower, *Cattleya trianaei* makes two growths a year, one right after the other, and it flowers on both of them. It is quite resistant to rot and handles overwatering better than most *Cattleya* hybrids. Had *C. trianaei* been discovered at the same time as *C. labiata*, it would undoubtedly be the type species today for the large-flowered cattleyas instead of *C. labiata*.

Cattleya trianaei was first described by botanist H. G. Reichenbach in the German publication *Botanische Zeitung* in January 1860, but it was actually discovered by Europeans 18 years earlier. The first to find it was the Belgian Jean Jules Linden, who came across it in 1842 as a young man while traveling near Fusagasuga, Colombia. Although he did not collect any plants, Linden did fall in love with the species and would eventually become the leading force in introducing it to European orchid growers.

In 1851 Colombian botanist José M. Triana, while working for Linden, found large numbers of *Cattleya trianaei* in the Eastern Cordillero and sent a shipment back to Linden in Belgium. By 1855 Linden was offering plants for sale in his orchid catalog for 150 francs each under the name "Cattleya Trianae." The species was dedicated, Linden said, "to that erudite and modest author of *Flora Columbiana*, José M. Triana."

Of the many new orchids Linden introduced to the horticultural world in Europe in the 1800s, *Cattleya trianaei* seems to have been his favorite. The plentiful supply and wide variety of color types made it a collector's dream, and Linden was happy and eager to promote it. He was the first to discover it and the first to have it commercially available. He pushed his friend Reichenbach to publish a description of it as a new species and pictured 41 different clones on 28 full-color plates in his famous book *Lindenia*, including a gorgeous double-page spread of eight. He featured it at flower shows and even produced a special exhibition for it in 1870 at the Brussels Zoological Gardens, where he displayed 240 different varieties with more than 900 flowers. Even Reichenbach acknowledged Linden's contribution to the plant by using Linden's name "*Cattleya trianaei*" in describing it and putting Linden's name next to his in the species description, "*Cattleya trianaei* Lind. Rchb. f.""

It seems only fitting that Linden named *Cattleya trianaei* in honor of a native Colombian, because Colombia and *C. trianaei* are inexorably tied together. *Cattleya trianaei* is the national flower of Colombia, and it grows abundantly in many parts of the country. It seems every Colombian has his or her own collection of favorite varieties of *C. trianaei* and despite what you read in the newspapers, Colombia is famous first as the home of *C. trianaei* and only second as the home of the cocaine cartel.

Cattleya trianaei in bloom during January 1948 at Thomas Young Orchids, Bound Brook, New Jersey. This was the smallest of six greenhouses full of flowering *C. trianaei* and, sadly, plants in all six greenhouses were thrown out on the dump to die right after this picture was taken.

The name "trianaei" is pronounced "tri-an-ee," which is strange because it ends in an *i*. Reichenbach in his original description spelled *trianaei* with an *i* at the end to reflect the male gender of José Triana. But almost everyone who followed Reichenbach for the next hundred years, including Linden, Sander, Veitch, and even the Royal Horticultural Society, left the *i* off the name, spelling it "trianae." The spelling matched the way the name was universally pronounced, so the word itself was only changed back to Reichenbach's original spelling in 1960 after much soul searching. But we still pronounce it "tri-an-ee."

Like *Cattleya mossiae* in Venezuela, the Colombian *C. trianaei* was found in such great numbers that literally hundreds of thousands of plants were imported into Europe and the United States after its discovery. *Cattleya trianaei* was so plentiful and inexpensive to import that it was rarely raised from seed, and the cut-flower growers of the 1930s and 1940s could actually import plants, grow and flower them for a year or two, throw them away, and still make a good profit on the cut flowers. It is a sad commentary to the history of cattleyas that such a practice was not unusual.

Cattleya trianaei ranks with *C. mossiae* in having the greatest number of named *Cattleya* clones. An inventory of the famous Dixon collection in Elkins Park, Pennsylvania, in 1930 listed 68 outstanding clones of *C. trianaei*, and there were hundreds more in other collections and in the literature. By 1916 the Royal Horticultural Society in England had awarded 22 First Class Certificates and 24 Awards of Merit to *C. trianaei*. The American Orchid Society has made *C. trianaei* one of its most-awarded large-flowered *Cattleya* species.

One of the finest of all *Cattleya trianaei* varieties is 'The President' FCC/AOS, which was featured on the cover of the June 1946 *American Orchid Society Bulletin*. The petals are almost 4 inches wide and the sepals are 1¼ inches wide.

Several fine white varieties of *Cattleya trianaei* have been found over the years. Linden pictured a particularly beautiful one in *Lindenia* (plate 29). In the 1930s and 1940s, *C. trianaei* 'Broomhill's' was the leading white variety, and it commanded a king's ransom because it bred true white color and had high fertility. It was used extensively in breeding winter-blooming white *Cattleya* hybrids during this period. More recently, *C. trianaei* 'Aranka Germaski' FCC/AOS has received much recognition because of its fine shape which resembles the alba in *Lindenia*. Like many of the finest-shaped forms of *C. trianaei*, however, it is not a good breeder.

Really fine semialba forms of *Cattleya trianaei* are rare, and *C. trianaei* 'Trenton' is the best we have seen. There are a few better-shaped semialbas, but they lack the rich lip coloring of 'Trenton'.

Fine lavender forms of *Cattleya trianaei* are plentiful and range from pale pastels like 'The Baron' FCC/RHS and the beautiful pinkish 'Mrs. F. E. Dixon', through medium lavenders like 'The President' FCC/AOS, 'A. C. Burrage' AM/AOS, 'Jungle Queen' AM/AOS, 'The Premier' FCC/RHS, and 'Clinkaberryana'. Really good dark forms like 'Mary Fennell' HCC/AOS are quite rare.

Cattleya trianaei has many lavender varieties with dark purple flaring along the tips of the petals. *Cattleya trianaei* 'Mooreana' FCC/RHS is perhaps the most famous. There are also some truly unique clones like Linden's *C. trianaei* 'Striata' and Fennell's 'Jungle Feather', which have a feathered pattern along the central vein of the petals. There are also some striking blue clones like 'Blue Bird' and Linden's 'Coerulescens'. But it is the many delicate pastel shades of color that set *C. trianaei* apart from the other *Cattleya*

Good dark-colored varieties of *Cattleya trianaei* are hard to find, and 'Mary Fennell' HCC/AOS (above) is one of the best. *Cattleya trianaei* 'Trenton' (below) is a rare semialba with an usually rich purple lip.

species. Even H. G. Reichenbach in his original description said of *C. trianaei* that "there may be no cattleya existing which has more beautiful coloring," and if you see a greenhouse full of them, you will know what he meant.

More than any other species, *Cattleya trianaei* gives fine round shape to *Cattleya* hybrids, and many primary hybrids of *C. trianaei* have better shape than some of our complex hybrids today. Some particularly fine primary hybrids of *C. trianaei* are *C.* Princess (*C. trianaei* × *C. lueddemanniana*), *C.* Ballantineana (*C. trianaei* × *C. warscewiczii*), and *C.* Maggie Raphael (*C. trianaei* × *C. dowiana*).

When the holiday spirits have drained away, and the winter winds begin to blow, and everything outside is cold and sad and colorless, don't be concerned, for that is when *Cattleya trianaei* will give you a carnival of happy color. Her sunny smile will warm your winter hibernation with grace and beauty, for she is truly a lovely lady of winter.

Culture

Cattleya trianaei is one of the easiest of the large-flowered *Cattleya* species to grow. Virtually all of the standard mediums used for cattleyas suit it well. If you start *C. trianaei* growing early in the spring in the United States, right after it finishes blooming, it will complete its first growth by early summer and rush into a second growth that will be completed in late summer. Be certain not to dry the plant off after the first growth is completed, however, or it may not start the second growth. Both growths should produce flowers in late December through February, after the autumn rest.

Cattleya trianaei 'Mrs. F. E. Dixon' is a lovely pastel-pink variety named for the wife of the second president of the American Orchid Society.

Cattleya trianaei 'Clinkaberryana' is an exceptionally large-flowered variety which shows the classic coloring that made *C. trianaei* so popular with collectors.

If you want to produce the best flowers, avoid repotting the plant as long as possible, and only repot when new roots emerge from the lead pseudobulb. Like other *Cattleya* species, *C. trianaei* should have lots of sun and air, and the leaves should be a light green color. Do not let the leaves get warm to the touch, however, because this is too much sun and may burn the leaves. Always keep *C. trianaei* slightly dry during its rest period to avoid rotting the roots, and start the plant growing right after flowering with frequent light sprays of water on sunny days.

Cattleya trianaei usually produces only two or three flowers per stem, unlike most other large-flowered *Cattleya* species, such as *C. mossiae*, *C. labiata*, and *C. dowiana*, which produce four or more flowers per stem. With two growths in succession, of course, *C. trianaei* will give you a splashy five- or six-flower display, so the net effect is about the same.

Cattleya warneri Moore
Select Orchidaceous Plants 1, plate 8. 1862

As the newness of spring begins to wane and the summer sun smiles down from its place high in the sky, we find ourselves with a greenhouse full of the lovely Brazilian *Cattleya warneri*. This delightful species provides a display of lavender and purple that rivals and is reminiscent of its autumn-flowering sister from Brazil, *C. labiata*. Were it not for their wide difference in blooming season, the flowers of one could easily be mistaken for the other.

The two major large-flowered Brazilian *Cattleya* species are no strangers to each other in botanical and horticultural lore. Few orchids have been haunted so much by a closely related species as *C. warneri* has by *C. labiata*. *Cattleya warneri*'s similarity to *C. labiata* has clouded its past and often unsettled its future, and the problems started even before *C. warneri* was officially discovered.

The first European to find *Cattleya warneri* was the naturalist Dr. George Gardner, who found it in the Brazilian province of Minas Gerais during a trip in the late 1830s. Unfortunately for *C. warneri*, Gardner was convinced he had rediscovered the lost *C. labiata*, so *C. warneri* started its trip into the wonderland of orchid nomenclature as "*Cattleya labiata*" and stayed there for the next 25 years.

In August 1862, all this changed when Robert Warner, a prominent orchidist of the time, published his magnificent *Selected Orchidaceous Plants*, in which he pictured four gorgeous lavender flowers under the name "*Cattleya warneri*" and included a botanical description of the new species by M. S. Moore. Warner pointed out in the text that *C. warneri* had to be a new species and not *C. labiata*, because it flowered at a completely different time of the year than *C. labiata*.

The 1880s, however, were not so kind to *Cattleya warneri*. During this period, the eminent horticulturalist James O'Brien championed the idea that all the large-flowered cattleyas should be species in their own right and not subspecies or varieties of *C. labiata*. O'Brien argued that these species were distinct and individual horticulturally and not at all like *C. labiata*. The only plant he left under *C. labiata* in the old mold was *C. warneri*, which remained *C. labiata* var. *warneri* for no apparent reason other than, like *C. labiata*, it came from Brazil. With time, however, *C. warneri* slowly rose to the same rank as the other large-flowered cattleyas, and today it is accepted as a distinct species.

Cattleya warneri has several characteristics that make it different from *C. labiata*: shorter and stouter pseudobulbs, a more compact habit, and broader leaves. Although both species have characteristic double sheaths, recent work by Érico de Freitas Machado in Brazil suggests that the double sheaths may not really be the same.

The most obvious difference between the species, of course, is the one Robert Warner alluded to in his original description in 1862—their different flowering season. *Cattleya warneri* flowers in the spring (late May and June in the United States), while *C. labiata* is an autumn bloomer (September through November). The two species also make new growths at different times of the year: *C. warneri* in the autumn and winter, and *C. labiata* in the spring and summer. Finally, they root at different times in their growth cycle: *C. warneri* after flowering and *C. labiata* before flowering (Rogerson 2004). These differences in growth, rooting, and flowering periods exist even when *C. labiata* and *C. warneri* are grown side by side on the same bench in the same greenhouse, so they are inherent in the plants and are not caused by environmental or regional factors, as some have suggested.

Cattleya warneri is certainly one of the nicest late spring-flowering *Cattleya* species. Its lavender color is unusually clear, and its large size and ease of culture make it a good plant for both the beginning hobbyist and the expert. It also has many color forms that make it attractive to collectors.

Like *Cattleya labiata*, *C. warneri* is not known for its well-shaped flowers. Clones have been found, however, with superior form, and several were awarded by the Royal Horticultural Society in London in the late 1800s.

The flowers of most alba forms of *Cattleya warneri* are more poorly shaped and smaller than the lavender forms, although one alba clone exhibited by A. A. Peeters of Brussels in 1903 received an FCC/RHS and was described as having "very fine large flowers." Certainly the alba *C. warneri* used by Sander in 1915 to make the original cross of *C.* Lady Veitch (*C. warneri* alba × *C. lueddemanniana* alba) must have been outstanding, because this cross produced magnificent round white flowers, and two clones received First Class Certificates from the Royal Horticultural Society. *Cattleya* Lady Veitch 'Superbissima' was a huge white with overlapping petals. Remakes of *C.* Lady Veitch, however, have all produced mediocre flowers because of the poorly shaped *C. warneri* parent. A commonly available alba form of *C. warneri* sold in the United States today is "McPeak's Variety," which is floriferous and easy to grow, but has narrow petals and sepals that can bend backward when fully open, an undesirable characteristic.

Semialba varieties of *Cattleya warneri* are very rare, and the most well known one is the clone 'Itabirana' which is pictured in L. C. Menezes's fine book entitled *Cattleya Warneri*. Menezes also includes in her book pictures of a wide variety of lavender varieties of *C. warneri*, which makes the book an excellent reference for color forms of this species.

Cattleya warneri has always had a number of dark clones like 'Ardenholm', and the species is noted for its dark varieties. Although some forms of *C. warneri* have petals that fall forward, most have petals that stand upright, giving the flower an attractive form even though the petals are not wide. Flowers of *C. warneri* range in size from 6 to 8 inches across, and one plant is recorded with four flowers, each measuring $9\frac{3}{4}$ inches across.

A fine typical lavender variety of *Cattleya warneri*

As a parent, *Cattleya warneri* passes on broad leaves to most of its hybrids, and if you look back into the parentage of a *Cattleya* hybrid that has broad leaves, you will invariably find *C. warneri* as a parent. The double sheath of *C. warneri* also sometimes appears in its hybrids.

Although *Cattleya warneri* seems to have been continuously available following its introduction in the 1860s, it was never in plentiful supply. Linden did not include a picture of the species in his famous book *Lindenia* because he did not have many plants to sell, and the species was never a significant factor in the cut-flower market of the 1930s to the 1950s in the United States. *Cattleya warneri*'s historical place has been as an exhibition and hybridizing plant, where its size and floriferousness produced a striking display, and its flowering season opened new doors to spring hybrids.

Because of its ability to produce late-spring-flowering hybrids, particularly June-flowering hybrids, *Cattleya warneri*'s place among the large-flowered *Cattleya* species will always be secure. Here the haunting specter of *C. labiata* fades into the shadows, because you cannot produce spring-flowering hybrids with *C. labiata*. The list of primary hybrids of *C. warneri* reads like a Who's Who of the late-spring cut-flower plants of the 1930s and 1940s. *Cattleya* Myra Peeters alba (*C. warneri* alba × *C. gaskelliana* alba) was one of the earliest fine white *Cattleya* hybrids to flower in the wedding month of June. *Cattleya* Dupreana (*C. warneri* × *C. warscewiczii*) was a standard of excellence in June lavenders and was the parent of most good June-flowering dark purple hybrids. *Cattleya* Comet (*C. warneri* × *C. dowiana*) can be an extremely dark June flower. *Cattleya warneri* crossed with *C.* R. Cadwalader is even called *C.* June Time.

When *Cattleya warneri* was first exhibited at a meeting of the Royal Horticultural

One of the most beautiful and well-shaped varieties of *Cattleya warneri* is this blush-colored clone, 'Santa Teresa.'

Most alba varieties of *Cattleya warneri* have petals that are narrower than those of the lavender forms. This unnamed white variety is typical.

Cattleya warneri has many dark lavender varieties like this famous 85-year-old 'Ardenholm.'

Society in 1860, it was awarded a Silver Medal with the remarkable citation that the award was given "as a mark of the esteem and admiration with which its appearance was hailed." No other *Cattleya* species has ever received such a compliment.

Happily, after 145 years, *Cattleya warneri* is still with us to add to the brightness and color of our long June days. Like a beautiful maiden from a long forgotten tale, *C. warneri* gently closes the gates of springtime and, with a radiant, bubbling smile, laughingly throws open the doors to summer, unaware that her haunting sister of the autumn wind, *C. labiata*, ever existed.

Culture

Although *Cattleya warneri* is not a difficult species to grow, it does have its unique requirements. It is actively growing, for example, during the winter months in the United States when most other cattleyas are dormant. Because of this, it is sometimes difficult to give it the best growing conditions.

Like most other cattleyas, *Cattleya warneri* needs a warm, moist atmosphere when growing, and this can be difficult to provide in the winter in a greenhouse when the sun is at a low angle and the outside temperature is well below freezing. This is compounded by the problem that most of the other *Cattleya* species like cooler, drier conditions in keeping with their dormancy in the winter. Since *C. warneri* will tolerate less than the best conditions and still produce a satisfactory growth, it can usually be grown with the other *Cattleya* species if you put it in the warmest and sunniest part of the greenhouse in the winter. This means you may sometimes have to hang it near the glass to give it the heat and sun it needs to grow well.

Most growers recommend that *Cattleya warneri* be grown with less sunlight than most other large-flowered *Cattleya* species, and we have also found this to be true. Your best guide for this, of course, is still the color of the leaves, which should be light green.

A well-flowered *Cattleya warneri* will produce four flowers on a spike, and five flowers is not unusual. If you have your *C. warneri* plants hanging near the glass during the winter, you should put them back on the bench as soon as buds appear in the sheath. High temperatures are not desirable after the buds form, and intense sunlight can actually cook the buds in the sheath and kill them. A strong growth will normally produce a double sheath. A weak or late growth will sometimes produce only a single sheath or no sheath at all.

Like all the *Cattleya* species, this one should be watered thoroughly and then allowed to dry out completely before the next watering. A continuously wet medium will rot the roots. Repot *C. warneri* only when it begins sending out a flush of new roots and preferably during the warm summer months.

Cattleya quadricolor Bateman
Gardeners' Chronicle 24: 269. 1864

Cattleya quadricolor first appeared in Europe in 1848 when an English orchid grower named Rucker received a single plant from a friend traveling in Colombia. When the plant flowered in 1849, Rucker sent the flowers to John Lindley, asking him what it was.

The only large-flowered *Cattleya* species known at the time were *C. labiata* and *C. mossiae*, and Lindley thought the flowers Rucker sent were different enough from these two species to mention the plant in an article he wrote for *Paxton's Flower Garden*. Because the new plant had four different colors in its flowers—purple, white, yellow, and lavender—Lindley gave Rucker's plant the simple name *C. quadricolor*. Lindley was reluctant to claim *C. quadricolor* as a new species, however, because too little was known about the *Cattleya* species in 1849. He merely said such a plant existed and let it go at that.

Nothing was heard of the new *Cattleya quadricolor* for the next 14 years, until Rucker again stepped into the picture and sent a plant to James Bateman, another English botanist. The plant flowered in 1864 in Bateman's greenhouses at Knypersley, and he described it as a new species on page 269 of *The Gardeners' Chronicle and Agricultural Gazette* of 19 March 1864, following up with a picture in Curtis's *Botanical Magazine* (plate 5504). Bateman called the new species "*C. quadricolor*," giving Lindley credit for the name, and, with a full Latin description, a full-sized picture of two flowers, a pseudobulb, and a leaf, the story should have ended there. For *C. quadricolor*, however, this was only the beginning of an interesting trip that would entangle it in a wonderland of botanical confusion.

Four years before Bateman described *Cattleya quadricolor*, botanist H. G. Reichenbach had described another new *Cattleya* species from Colombia that he called *C. trianaei*. This plant also had the same four colors in its flowers that Bateman had described in *C. quadricolor*. The botanical community looked at Bateman's *C. quadricolor* with skepticism and finally concluded that he had merely re-described *C. trianaei*. Bateman's *C. quadricolor*, instead of expanding the number of *Cattleya* species, suddenly passed into the mists of forgotten horticultural lore. No one seemed to notice Bateman's comment that the flowers of *C. quadricolor* did not open fully—a distinctive characteristic not shared with *C. trianaei* or any other *Cattleya* species.

Then *Cattleya quadricolor* received an almost fatal blow. In 1873 Linden and André, in the Belgian publication *L'Illustration Horticole* (part 1, 120, p. 43), described another new *Cattleya* species from Colombia that they called *C. chocoensis*, "The Cattleya of Choco." This species had the same half-open flowers as *C. quadricolor* and the same four colors in its flowers. On top of this, Linden's collector in Colombia had sent him a large number of plants of *C. chocoensis*, and Linden had to popularize it as strongly as possible or lose money on it. Linden decided to describe the flowers of *C. chocoensis* as "bell-shaped," rather than half-open, to make them more appealing, and he wrote glowingly about the lip, which he felt was shorter than normal and enhanced the flower's bell-shaped appearance. Linden also declared emphatically that *C. chocoensis* was not a *C. trianaei*—and who better to say this than the man who had introduced *C. trianaei* to European horticulture.

With Linden's promotional machinery in high gear, *Cattleya chocoensis* soon became a well-established species, and we find it mentioned in *The Orchid-Grower's Manual*, and W. Watson's *Orchids: Their Culture and Management*. Linden, of course, published a glamorous picture of it in his elegant book *Lindenia*. The famous American plant collector John Lager even wrote about collecting it in an article in *The Orchid Review* of 1894 entitled "*Cattleya chocoensis* at Home." The only negative comment came from orchid collector Benedict Roezl, who could not understand why the plant was named *"chocoensis"* when it did not grow in the Choco area of Colombia. Through all this, of course, *C. quadricolor* became a forgotten name.

It wasn't until 1898 that someone finally dusted off the image of *Cattleya quadricolor* and called it to the attention of the orchid world. In 1898 an American from Stockton, California, Dr. A. M. Hoisholt, wrote a letter to the British publication *The Orchid Review* complaining that *C. quadricolor* had been omitted from its listing of *Cattleya* species. He also sent live flowers and pictures of *C. quadricolor* to reinforce his complaint. Robert Allen Rolfe, editor of *The Orchid Review*, investigated the matter, and, in the process, discovered that *C. quadricolor* and *C. chocoensis* were the same species and, of course, *C. quadricolor* enjoyed the botanical priority and was the correct name. Rolfe also concluded that, although *C. quadricolor* "is not equal to *C. trianaei* in point of beauty, its distinctiveness seems now to be fully established."

Despite these clear statements on behalf of *Cattleya quadricolor* from one of Britain's foremost orchid authorities at the time, in one of the most widely circulated orchid magazines of the day, The International Registration Authority administered by the Royal Horticultural Society registered *C. quadricolor* hybrids only under the name *C. chocoensis* for all of the 20th century. When we became aware of this in mid-2001, we made a formal request to the Orchid Registrar to correct the name, and in December 2001 the Orchid Registration Advisory Committee agreed to do this. *Cattleya quadricolor* is now the official parent for these hybrids instead of *C. chocoensis.*

Cattleya quadricolor flowers have the same lovely pastel coloring as *C. trianaei,* but they do not open fully and they hang in a half-open position.

The half-open appearance of the flowers of *Cattleya quadricolor* is easily seen in this side view.

The similarity between *Cattleya trianaei* and *C. quadricolor* has always been a problem for botanists. The species have the same color patterns in their flowers. Both bloom at the same time of the year, and their growths mature at the same time. Both rest for several months before flowering, have the widest-petaled flowers of any of the large-flowered *Cattleya* species, and have exceptionally long lasting flowers. Because of these similarities, it is easy to say *C. quadricolor* is merely a variety of *C. trianaei*.

Cattleya quadricolor, however, grows in a different area of Colombia than *C. trianaei*, and all *C. quadricolor* have the same distinctive bell-shaped or half-open flowers, which is not characteristic of *C. trianaei*. *Cattleya quadricolor* has a fairly strong, pleasant fragrance, while *C. trianaei* has a more subtle, muted scent. *Cattleya quadricolor* also grows under somewhat different conditions from *C. trianaei*. In his 1894 article in *The Orchid Review* (2: 307), American plant hunter John Lager described the species as growing "on level land and to a great extent marshy and at time inundated, consequently the moisture the plants receive throughout the year is considerable." He went on to say that the conditions drench the plants in a heavy mist all year and that *C. quadricolor* requires more moisture than *C. trianaei* to grow well. *Cattleya quadricolor* is clearly a different plant from *C. trianaei* in many respects, although it took decades for this to be fully recognized.

As a *Cattleya* species, *C. quadricolor* has all the usual color forms of the large-flowered group. The plant originally described by James Bateman in 1864 was a lovely semi-alba. There are also true albas, albescens, and many lavender forms. Pale lavender flowers predominate, and there are very few really dark lavender clones. *Cattleya quadricolor* is noted for its wide-petaled flowers, and, in many clones, the petals actually touch or

Cattleya quadricolor is noted for having many well-shaped varieties like this beautiful off-white clone.

overlap. *Cattleya trianaei*, of course, is famous for having wide-petaled flowers, but wide-petaled *C. trianaei* are relatively few in number compared with *C. quadricolor*.

The big problem with *Cattleya quadricolor* is that its flowers are always opening, but never really open. Although its flowers have the wonderful four colors that make *C. trianaei* flowers so beautiful and popular, *C. quadricolor* remains a stepchild among the *Cattleya* species. When we look at it in the broadest sense, however, *C. quadricolor* may be the wisest of all the large-flowered *Cattleya* species. Its bell-shaped, half-open flowers are an important survival mechanism. They appeal to insect pollinators such as bees, but not to orchid predators like man. When you consider that *C. quadricolor* grows in a very limited area of Colombia, and the large-flowered *Cattleya* species were plundered mercilessly for almost a century, the fact that *C. quadricolor* is still available in these areas is testament to the effectiveness of its survival mechanism.

Hybridizers have done relatively little with *Cattleya quadricolor* compared with the other large-flowered *Cattleya* species. Most efforts have been aimed at trying to keep its wide petals while still enjoying fully open flowers in the hybrids. The color of its flowers are as beautiful as any you will find in the large-flowered group, so there is hybridizing potential in the species. A cross between *C. quadricolor* and *Brassolaeliocattleya* Helen Huntington was even good enough to be registered recently under the name *Blc.* Georgien Cataldo.

No *Cattleya* species collection would be complete without *C. quadricolor*. It usually flowers for us at Christmas, and on a festive Christmas Eve, we often look at it as Mother Nature's Christmas bells.

Culture

Cattleya quadricolor is one of the easiest of the large-flowered *Cattleya* species to grow. It is vigorous and has a greater-than-normal resistance to root rot. It will usually send out a new growth in late February or early March in the United States and complete the growth by early summer. It typically makes a second growth as soon as the first one is completed and will rest until late October before forming buds in the sheath. *Cattleya quadricolor* flowers about mid-December in the United States, just before the early *C. trianaei* come into bloom.

During its active growth period, it should receive lots of sun, moving air, and water. *Cattleya quadricolor* will tolerate a wet medium better than other large-flowered *Cattleya* species and can take extra water during its growing season. The medium, however, should never be allowed to become excessively wet or soggy because this can kill the plant's roots. *Cattleya quadricolor* should be repotted just after flowering, as soon as new roots appear on the front pseudobulb.

Cattleya dowiana Bateman
Gardeners' Chronicle 26: 922. 1866

Josef Warscewicz was one of the great plant hunters of the mid-1800s, and when he discovered a remarkable large yellow-flowered *Cattleya* species in Costa Rica in 1850, he collected as many plants as he could, packed them up, and sent them off to Low and

Company in Clapton, England. He also packed up some dried specimens of the plants with instructions to Low to send them to a young friend of his, botanist Heinrich Gustav Reichenbach, so the plants could be described as a new species. He even asked that the new species be named for Mrs. Lawrence of Ealing, one of the most liberal orchid patrons at the time.

In due course, the plants arrived in England, but to Low's dismay, they were in such terrible condition from the long journey from Central America that despite Low's best efforts, they all died before any of them could flower to display their beauty. The dried specimens for Reichenbach were dispatched as requested, but for some inexplicable reason they never arrived at their destination, and within a few weeks, the only thing that remained of the new *Cattleya* species was Warscewicz's letter with his glowing account of the color of the flowers. As the years went by, no more plants of the yellow *Cattleya* species were discovered, and European orchid growers began to wonder if the description of the plant was true or whether Warscewicz had simply created the story just to have some fun with them. Stricken twice with yellow fever, Warscewicz eventually returned to Europe a sick man, and the future of the yellow *Cattleya* was left to another generation of plant hunters.

In 1864 a local naturalist named Arce, who was collecting native insects, birds, and tropical plants in Costa Rica for George Ure Skinner, sent a shipment of his latest acquisitions to England. Veitch and Son purchased the plants and, in the autumn of 1865, to Veitch's amazement, one of the cattleya plants flowered with the beautiful yellow color Warscewicz had described. Botanist James Bateman wrote an account of the plants in *The Gardeners' Chronicle* of 29 September 1866 (p. 922), and a year later in 1867, he wrote a full botanical description in Curtis's *Botanical Magazine* (23, 3rd series, plate 5618). It was a great day for cattleya lovers, although something of a disappointment for Mrs. Lawrence, because Bateman named the orchid *Cattleya dowiana* and dedicated it to "a gallant officer in the American Packet Service, the well-known Captain J. M. Dow . . . for the many kindnesses shown and the frequent assistance rendered to English naturalists and men of science."

In 1868, three years after Veitch bloomed the plants from Costa Rica, another plant hunter, Gustav Wallis, working for Linden, discovered a similar yellow *Cattleya* species near Frontino, Colombia, and in 1872 Backhouse and Company's collector Butler found more of the Colombian plants. The new yellow species was over 600 miles from the one found in Costa Rica and, since it seemed to have a brighter yellow color, it created considerable speculation over whether it was really the same species or a different species.

After growing the Colombian plants side by side with his Costa Rican *Cattleya dowiana* for several seasons, Veitch concluded the plants were so similar they had to be the same species. For the clear yellow-petaled Colombian varieties, Veitch coined the name "*C. dowiana aurea*." The rest of the British orchid industry, after growing the plants together as Veitch had done, came to the same conclusion—there was no basic difference between the plants except their shades of color and their geographical separation. While this seemed to be the end of the story, it proved to be only the beginning.

Jean Jules Linden, owner of the Belgium orchid firm Horticulture Internationale, who had received the first plants Wallis collected in Colombia, decided there must be a difference between the Colombian and Costa Rican yellow cattleyas because, as a new species, he could sell the newly discovered plants for a lot more money than he would get if they were just another form of *Cattleya dowiana*. He talked about them everywhere as a new species and called them "*C. aurea*" to emphasize their brighter yellow color. Linden had done a similar thing with *C. trianaei* back in the 1850s and, because of his efforts then, the botanist Reichenbach had agreed to describe *C. trianaei* as a new species in 1860. This time, however, Reichenbach refused to go along with Linden, and Linden was left virtually alone with his *C. aurea*.

Since the leading botanist of the day would not describe the yellow Colombian *Cattleya* as a new species, Linden decided to do it himself. In 1883 he took the bold step of including a botanical description of the Colombian yellow *Cattleya* in his periodical *L'Illustration Horticole* (30: 125) under the name "*C. aurea*." The description was accompanied by a picture of a single flower that had clear-yellow sepals and petals and a dark purple lip with gold veining. Two years later he published a picture of three magnificent yellow Colombian cattleya flowers in his *Lindenia* under the title "*C. aurea*—Golden Cattleya," to re-enforce the name.

Linden was one of the great orchid promoters of the late 1800s and, despite the many objections he received to his new *Cattleya aurea*, his book *Lindenia* established it as a legitimate name for the clear yellow-petaled varieties from Colombia in the minds of some people. Linden, however, was not consistent in using the name *C. aurea* in *Lindenia* and, as the years went by, he used the name *C. dowiana* more and more for the yellow Colombian species. Although he called his eye-catching double-page spread of

The typical *Cattleya dowiana aurea* has clear yellow sepals and petals with a dark purple lip that is overlaid with gold veining. The bloom spike usually bears four or five of these flowers.

seven beautiful varieties *C. aurea*, he pictured the yellowest of all Colombian *Cattleya* varieties, one that had clear bright yellow sepals and petals and an almost all-yellow lip, *C. dowiana* 'Statteriana', without any reference to *aurea*. The last picture of the species he published in *Lindenia*, his Colombian variety 'Moortebeckiensis', which had some purple in the yellow petals, he also called *C. dowiana*.

It is not surprising that Linden reverted to the use of the name *Cattleya dowiana* for the yellow Colombian *Cattleya* species because he was basically a practical man and, when there was no commercial advantage to separating the Costa Rican and Colombian types into separate species, he called them both *C. dowiana* as everyone else. It was difficult to do otherwise when, after 50 years of growing thousands of them, commercial companies could see no clear difference between the Costa Rican and Colombian yellow cattleyas in the size of the plants, their growth habits, rooting habits, flowering season, flower shape, flower size, number of flowers on a flower stem, vigorousness, fragrance, and intensification of purple color in hybridizing. Certainly the majority of horticultural and botanical authorities today favor using the name *C. dowiana* for both the Colombian and Costa Rican plants, and the International Authority for the Registration of Orchid Hybrids feels the same way. The Authority does not recognize *C. aurea* as a species and will not register a hybrid using it as a parent. *Sander's List of Orchid Hybrids*, therefore, shows no crosses using *C. aurea* even though many yellow Colombian *Cattleya* species have been used in breeding over the years.

The flower color of plants from Costa Rica varies greatly from those that grow in

One of the darkest red-purple varieties of *Cattleya dowiana* is this clone from a selfing of the famous 'Rosita' FCC/RHS (1901).

Colombia, which is not surprising considering their wide separation. The brightest yellow varieties come from Colombia, including most of the clear yellow-flowered types and those with an abundance of yellow in the lips. By contrast, the plants from Costa Rica tend to have more lavender in their yellow sepals and petals. The famous 'Rosita' variety that received a First Class Certificate from the Royal Horticultural in 1901 had petals that were mostly purple, and selfings of it produced some red-purple varieties. While there are wide variations in the amount of yellow and purple in the flowers from each area, there are also flowers from both areas that look the same. They have yellow sepals and petals with some purple in them, and it is impossible to tell them apart.

The typical *Cattleya dowiana* has flowers with pale yellow sepals and petals with some purple or lavender in them and a lip that is intensely dark purple with fine gold veining. The flowers are fairly large, ranging from 5½ to almost 8 inches across. *Cattleya dowiana* was originally described in 1866 as having sepals and petals of a "mellow straw color," but there are flowers with petals that range from red-purple to tan, yellow suffused with lavender, pale greenish yellow, golden yellow, and even orange-yellow.

The lips of *Cattleya dowiana* vary from dark crimson-purple with and without gold veining to crimson with large yellow eyes, to lips that are virtually all yellow, sometimes beautifully edged in pale lavender. One of *C. dowiana*'s most unusual characteristics is the variability of the yellow color in the lip. One year the lip may have only a small amount of yellow or no yellow at all, and the next year it may be virtually all yellow. Many hobbyists have been fooled into believing they have a spectacular yellow-lipped

The yellow color in the lip of *Cattleya dowiana* is somewhat unstable and can vary considerably from one year to the next. These flowers of *C. dowiana aurea* 'Kathleen' AM/AOS show this color instability even between flowers on the same flower stem.

C. dowiana, only to find on the next flowering there is no yellow in the lip, just a few faint gold veins against an intense dark purple background. The amount of yellow can even vary from flower to flower on the same inflorescence.

The variability in yellow color even shows up in the old lithographs of the 1800s. One of the most famous yellow-lipped cultivars of *Cattleya dowiana aurea* is the clone 'Statteriana' which Linden featured in his *Lindenia* (plate 356). There, it had an almost completely bright yellow lip. *The Orchid Album* also published a picture of 'Statteriana' (plate 468) which showed a lip with only two enlarged yellow eyes with most of the lip being dark purple. There is also a record of a *C. dowiana* with petals that looked exactly like the typical dark purple lip, including all the gold veining. The plant appeared in the collection of E. G. Wrigley in Lancashire, England, and was described by R. A. Rolfe on page 493 of the 2 November 1889 issue of *The Gardeners' Chronicle*.

Cattleya dowiana is unique among the large-flowered *Cattleya* species because it is the only large-flowered species that does not have either an alba or semialba form. Some so-called semialba forms of *C. dowiana* that have been pictured in the literature over the years are really semialba varieties of the natural hybrid, *C.* Hardyana (*C. warscewiczii* × *C. dowiana*). The yellow color in the sepals and petals of *C. dowiana* is extremely recessive and disappears when it is crossed with other large-flowered *Cattleya* species. A semialba form of *C. warscewiczii* crossed with a clear-yellow-petaled *C. dowiana* produces only semialba varieties of *C.* Hardyana with no trace of yellow in the flowers. The yellow color can occasionally re-appear when a primary hybrid of *C. dowiana* is selfed, and there are a few rare yellow-petaled varieties of *C.* Hardyana, *C.* Fabia (*C. dowiana*

Cattleya dowiana has many color variations. This 8-inch Costa Rican variety has straw- or tan-colored sepals and petals.

× *C. labiata*), *C.* Empress Fredrick (*C. dowiana* × *C. mossiae*), and *C.* Maggie Raphael (*C. dowiana* × *C. trianaei*).

Because of its beautiful color and floriferousness, *Cattleya dowiana* has been used in breeding more than any other large-flowered *Cattleya* species. It has the unique quality of darkening and enriching the lavender color of other cattleyas when bred with them, and it is responsible for the intense dark color of many of our best lavender hybrids today. This darkening effect occurs when either the Costa Rican or Colombian type is used, although the degree of intensity varies with the clone.

Cattleya dowiana is one of the most beautiful cattleyas, and many writers have even called it "the" most beautiful. In addition to its magnificent colors, its flowers have a wonderful fragrance that fills every corner of your greenhouse or home. H. G. Reichenbach, who described some of the finest large-flowered *Cattleya* species, often complained in his later years that he should have been the botanist to describe *C. dowiana*, not James Bateman. He felt it was one of the great disappointments of his life, and Reichenbach's loss says a lot about the place of *C. dowiana* in the minds of the horticulturists and botanists of the 1800s. It tells us *C. dowiana* was the most prized species.

With its strange geographical separation and its ever-fluctuating yellow colors, *Cattleya dowiana* is like a mysterious woman whose face is hidden by a thin veil. As the veil moves now and then to expose a little more of her beauty and intrigue, it still keeps us from seeing her whole face. The veiled lady remains the great enigma of the large-flowered *Cattleya* species, constantly enticing new victims with the feeling they have solved her mysteries when, in fact, no one ever has.

Culture

Cattleya dowiana is a strong, vigorously growing plant that produces a tall four- or five-flowered bloom spike in midsummer in the United States. It will begin sending out a new growth in early spring and, as the growth matures in early July, the buds will already be in the sheath and will open a few weeks later. The flowers, unfortunately, are not long lived, and two weeks is about all you can expect from most varieties. The short life of the flowers undoubtedly accounts for their strong fragrance since they must attract pollinators as quickly as possible before the flowers die. *Cattleya dowiana* likes a warmer temperature than most other large-flowered *Cattleya* species with a minimum of 65°F at night. It should be kept as dry as possible when it is dormant from September to March to avoid developing root and pseudobulb rot which can kill the plant. Like *C. warscewiczii*, *C. dowiana* likes lots of sun and its leaves should always be light green in color. *Cattleya dowiana* also needs lots of moving air to keep it healthy.

Cattleya eldorado Linden

Flore des Serres et des Jardins de l'Europe 18, plate 1826. 1869–1870
L'Illustration Horticole, plate 7. 1870

Deep in the tangled jungles of tropical Brazil, among the many wandering tributaries of the Amazon Basin, lies the fabled land of El Dorado. The appetites of the Spanish conquistadors for the elusive riches of this Land of Gold were such that explorers believed it was worth risking a kingdom—or even their lives—to find this land. For the plant hunters of the mid-1800s, El Dorado was the realm of stinging insects, biting ants, bloodsucking bats, swarms of flies, clouds of mosquitoes, malaria, dysentery, and the promise of the golden treasure of a new *Cattleya* species.

Into this jungle in 1866 plunged the orchid collector Gustav Wallis as he explored the low-lying areas where the waters of the Negro River pour into the mighty Amazon River. It was here that Wallis encountered an unknown *Cattleya* species scattered among the branches of Macucu trees, its pale lavender-pink petals and orange lip reflecting sunlight between the gently moving leaves of the trees.

Wallis was collecting orchids for Jean Linden's company, Horticulture Internationale, in Brussels. It was exciting, often death-defying work to be a collector hunting tropical orchids. Plant hunters usually made a nominal wage for their efforts, while the company that employed them was highly rewarded when the plants they found were the first of a species to be introduced into European horticulture. Jean Linden was particularly fortunate when Wallis sent him a large shipment of the new *Cattleya* species. Not only was it different from any other known *Cattleya*, but Linden received enough plants to cover all his expenses and make a handsome profit as well. In 1867 Linden had more than 700 plants of the new species in bloom to select from for his display in Paris. Exhibited plants, of course, must have a name, so Linden casually christened the new species *C. eldorado* to orient his customers to its native home in the Land of Gold in the steaming Amazon jungle.

The typical *Cattleya eldorado* has flowers with pale lavender sepals and petals and a bright orange disc in the throat of the labellum. The disc is edged with white, and the lower edge of the lip is dark purple. This color pattern is distinctive to the species.

The Paris Show of 1867 was a huge success for Linden and his new *Cattleya eldorado*, and the horticultural world embraced the new species with such excitement that no one seemed concerned that *C. eldorado* had not been described botanically as a new species. The nearest thing to a botanical description appeared in 1869 when Louis van Houtte published a full-color picture of *C. eldorado* in his *Flore des Serres et des Jardins de l'Europe* (18: pl. 1826), along with a few flattering comments in French by Linden about the flowers. The picture was printed exactly to size for both the flowers and the plant itself and showed the identifying color pattern of the lip. It was not a botanical description in the normal sense, but, since a picture is often worth a thousand words, particularly botanical Latin words, it was sufficient to establish the uniqueness of the new plants. It was certainly clear that Van Houtte pictured *C. eldorado* as we know it today and the *Flore des Serres* reference is the one most often used as the first botanical description for the species.

In 1870, in the periodical *L'Illustration Horticole* (plate 7), Linden and André published another life-size picture, again in full color, of a *Cattleya eldorado* plant and flowers under the name *C. eldorado* 'Splendens'—'Splendens' being a clonal name for a particularly fine form. This picture was accompanied by a detailed description in French of the flowers, including color, size of segments, and crisping and a comparison of the plant with Van Houtte's 1869 *C. eldorado*. It also compared *C. eldorado* with some of the other large-flowered *Cattleya* species like *C. labiata* and, together with the earlier work by Van Houtte, gave a clear botanical description of *C. eldorado* as a new species.

Cattleya eldorado is one of the more distinct members of the large-flowered *Cattleya* species and is noteworthy for its lovely range of subtle colors. The most common color

Cattleya eldorado has a wide range of color forms, including good medium lavender varieties.

form has pale lavender-pink sepals and petals with an orange-throated lip. The orange disc in the throat is circular, edged in white, and there is lavender or purple across the bottom edge on the lip. The color pattern of the lip is distinctive to the species.

Alba forms, which are rare in most *Cattleya* species, are not as rare in *C. eldorado*, and the alba form is the one most often pictured in orchid books. The alba forms also have some of the largest and best-shaped flowers in the species—another unusual characteristic for a *Cattleya*. One of the first albas discovered was so outstanding, it was actually described by A. Ducos in *L'Illustration Horticole* in 1876 as a new species and given the name *C. virginalis*. This was, of course, later corrected to *C. eldorado* 'Virginalis', but it reflected the unusually fine appearance of the flowers over the ordinary *C. eldorado*. In 1882 another beautiful alba was described as a new species, *C. wallisii*, by none other than the botanist H. G. Reichenbach. Perhaps the most impressive *C. eldorado* alba ever discovered, the clone 'Crocata', was pictured in Sander's magnificent book, *Reichenbachia*, as an example of an unusually large and well-shaped flower borne on a larger-than-normal plant.

Though quite rare, semialba forms of *Cattleya eldorado* are attractive because the white petals seem to accentuate the white fringe around the orange disc in the lip. Albescens and concolor forms of *C. eldorado* are also much more common than in other *Cattleya* species. The extensive color range of *C. eldorado* includes coeruleas, medium lavenders, and even dark lavender flowers, some of which are quite beautiful. The bright orange disc in the lip again seems to accentuate and enhance the beauty of these darker forms. Linden often wrote of the remarkable hues and tones of color in *C. eldorado* flowers. He thought that no two plants were colored alike, and a group of flowering plants produced a kaleidoscope effect. Some of the best pictures published of *C. eldorado* flowers in recent years are in Francisco Miranda's excellent book *Orchids from the Brazilian Amazon* (1996).

Cattleya eldorado is one of the smaller-growing *Cattleya* species. The pseudobulbs are usually only 3 to 5 inches tall (plus a 4- to 6-inch-tall leaf), and a robust flowering-size plant is often comfortable in a 4-inch clay pot. Most flowers of *C. eldorado* are only about two-thirds the size of a *C. labiata* and have relatively narrow petals, but the back sepal normally stands upright, giving the flower a pleasing appearance. *Cattleya eldorado* produces three to five flowers on a flower spike, and the flowers have excellent lasting qualities, staying in bloom for five to six weeks, sometimes beating *C. trianaei* for longevity. They also have a very appealing sweet fragrance.

In the early days of *Cattleya* breeding, *C. eldorado* was hybridized with many of the other *Cattleya* and *Laelia* species, but the results did not stimulate hybridizers to continue with it to any great extent. *Cattleya eldorado*'s hybrid with *C. bicolor* (*C.* Iridescens) and its hybrid with *C. dowiana* (*C.* Lady Ingram) have produced some interesting colors, and a few hybrids have been made using these two parents. Generally, however, the species has not been too popular for hybridizing because of its narrow petals and smaller size. *Cattleya eldorado* and *C. superba* (syn. *C. violacea*) interbreed in the wild to produce the natural hybrid *C. brymeriana*.

Cattleya eldorado is, without doubt, the rarest of the *Cattleya* species in cultivation in the United States today. Jones and Scully in Miami, Florida, sold meristems of a lavender concolor clone in the 1980s, and this is about the only plant seen in modern collections—and even this has become scarce. While *C. eldorado* was a darling of the 1880s and 1890s, it seems to have been eclipsed by other large-flowered species like *C. labiata* and *C. trianaei* after the turn of the century. These other species were more spectacular in size and shape, and more abundant commercially than *C. eldorado*. They were also more suited for exhibitions. A single *C. mossiae* plant, with four or five 8-inch flowers on a spike, was eye-catching by itself, while *C. eldorado* usually made a good display only as a group of plants.

Although *Cattleya eldorado*, to our knowledge, is not available from commercial growers in the United States, it is for sale from several Brazilian orchid firms. Seedlings of sib crosses are not too expensive, but flowering-size plants and good color forms can cost a king's ransom and are not for the weak of heart or pocketbook.

An old saying reminds us that, "All that glitters is not gold," but, if it is a large-flowered *Cattleya* species growing wild along the Negro River in Brazil, and if it glitters in lavender, orange, pink, and white in the sunlight, it may well be worth its weight in gold. So the fabled land of El Dorado has, after all, produced something more than mythical gold. It has produced the solid-gold *Cattleya*—*C. eldorado*.

Culture

Cattleya eldorado was looked upon as a difficult species to grow when it was first imported into Europe in the 1870s, and it apparently took growers some time to learn its requirements. Because *C. eldorado* is a native of the hot tropical forests at sea level in

Very fine varieties of *Cattleya eldorado* like this rich dark clone can be very expensive and sell for several thousand dollars each.

Brazil, it requires more heat than the typical mountain cloud-forest *Cattleya* species like *C. warscewiczii*, *C. trianaei*, and *C. mendelii*. A night temperature of 68° to 70°F is more to its liking than the normal 58° to 60°F night temperature of most other *Cattleya* species. *Cattleya eldorado* also likes a clear-cut rest period after flowering.

This species will begin growing in the late winter and early spring in the United States. As the new growth matures, you should see buds forming in the sheath, and the plant should flower in early summer. After it flowers, it will begin to root and can be repotted at this time. After repotting, just enough water should be given to the plants to draw the emerging roots down into the potting medium. If this watering is done carefully, the plants should be well rooted by the time they start to grow again. *Cattleya eldorado* benefits from a hot, humid atmosphere when it is actively growing and needs lots of sun and moving air at all times of the year. *Cattleya eldorado* will sometimes flower twice a year, once in July and again in December under greenhouse conditions in the United States.

Cattleya mendelii Dombrain
Floral Magazine, plate 32. 1872

A visit to the gardens at Manley Hall was a wonderful experience. Forty-four greenhouses traveled the spectrum of the whole plant kingdom—with winding walks and waterfalls as in a rich tropical valley of ferns, or stepping stones for walkways that connected a wonderland of artificial lakes filled with aquatic plants. Everything luxuriated in palms, cycads, and beautiful-leaved plants, but there was also a greenhouse full of flowering azaleas surrounded by beds of pansies.

Orchids were the specialty at Manley Hall, and the collection was a showcase of the finest orchid species and varieties of the day. The *Cattleya* species were particular favorites and, when a representative of *The Gardeners' Chronicle* visited Manley Hall in the spring of 1871, he commented with admiration on a large dark *C. mossiae* 'Manley Hall' with 16 flowers. When *The Floral Magazine* visited Manley Hall the following year, it wrote about a magnificent new *Cattleya* species that would excite the interest of the horticultural world for decades to come.

Manley Hall was the estate and residence of Samuel Mendel, Esquire, "the Cotton God" of Manchester, England. Mendel was a true friend of horticulture who opened his gardens and greenhouses free to the public. He was also a good customer of the orchid firm James Backhouse and Sons of York and, when Backhouse received a shipment of a new *Cattleya* species from its collector in South America, Mendel purchased the plants for his collection.

The excitement of owning a new, unnamed *Cattleya* species was almost too much for poor Samuel Mendel, who instructed his superintendent, Mr. Petch, to awaken him at any hour of the night when the flowers began to open. Petch obligingly called Mendel at 4 A.M. when the great event occurred, and Mendel rushed to the greenhouse in dressing gown and slippers, and is reported to have stood for a long time in awe of the new discovery.

In its 1872 article on a visit to Manley Hall, *The Floral Magazine* called the new *Cattleya* species *C. mendeli* (with one *i*), a name given to the magazine by Petch. Who

actually named the plant, however, is still a mystery, because Backhouse sold the plants
to Mendel as just an unknown *Cattleya* species.

Cattleya mendelii was first imported into England in 1870 by two British orchid
firms, Hugh Low and Company of Clapton and James Backhouse and Sons of York. It
first flowered in 1871 in the collection of John Day of Tottenham from plants imported
by Low. It was Backhouse's plants, however, in the collection of Mendel that received all
the publicity, the recognition, and the name.

It is difficult to know who to credit with the first botanical description of *Cattleya
mendelii* because the species was accepted by horticulturists so quickly that it became a
well-established species before anyone formally described it. *The Floral Magazine* essentially wrote a news item about it in 1872 (plate 32) and included a black-and-white picture of a pseudobulb, a leaf, and one flower with a description of the flower's color. The
picture clearly shows the distinctive features of the flowers, and the article is usually
given as the first publication for the species. As a news item, however, the article had no
author, so for want of one, Backhouse's name is often used even though he never named
the species.

Another common reference gives the year 1870 for the first botanical description in
the 6th edition of *The Orchid-Grower's Manual*—a truly grand *faux pas* that originated
with Veitch in his *Manual of Orchidaceous Plants*. Unfortunately for Veitch, the 6th edition wasn't published until 1885—15 years after *Cattleya mendelii* was supposed to have
been described in it. The 4th edition, published in 1871, did not even mention *C.
mendelii*, and the 5th edition, published in 1877, described *C. mendelii*, but not as well
as *The Floral Magazine* had done five years earlier.

An old variety of *Cattleya mendelii* from the late 1800s shows the richness and fine shape of the plants
available at that time. This flower was almost 8 inches across.

Low sent the first flowers of *Cattleya mendelii* to botanist H. G. Reichenbach in 1871, who apparently considered them a fine form of *C. trianaei* at the time and thus did not describe them as a new species. Reichenbach did eventually publish a proper description in Sander's *Reichenbachia* in 1888, crediting himself with the name, but Jean Linden had already published a fine description three years earlier in 1885 in his *Lindenia*, spelling the name "*mendeli*" as *The Floral Magazine* had done.

Since the past is always a little cloudy even on the clearest of days, the best that can be said now is that *Cattleya mendelii* was accepted by everyone with such immediate enthusiasm and eagerness that no one bothered with the technicalities. It was simply a case of the customers saying, "Just sell me a plant."

Cattleya mendelii was unquestionably the premier *Cattleya* of its day. Orchidists everywhere considered it the most beautiful *Cattleya* species ever found. *The Gardeners' Chronicle* called it "the most showy of the favorite genus." Reichenbach called it "a glorious flower," and Linden wrote, "Just to see its flowers is breathtaking!" Watson, in his 1890 book *Orchids: Their Culture and Management*, made the remarkable observation that "not one of its numerous varieties could be called poor."

The old English growers who supervised orchid production at the large American estates during the 1940s were always praising *Cattleya mendelii*. They talked about its beautiful contrasting colors—very pale lavender sepals and petals against a rich purple lip. They spoke about its very wide petals and large, 8-inch flowers, and how well the flowers were presented on the plants. These English growers were in their mid-60s during the 1940s, so they themselves were young men learning about orchids in the 1890s when the *Cattleya* species were the gems of the orchid world. *Cattleya mendelii* for them was obviously a crown jewel.

With such glowing recommendations, we spent a lot of time looking for a fine lavender *Cattleya mendelii*, but never found one that really matched the claims of these English growers. It wasn't until we were leafing through Sander's famous old book *Reichenbachia* that we found what they had been talking about. There, on page 59 of volume I (series 2), was *C. mendelii* 'Measuresiana'—big, bold, bright, and beautiful. It was everything the English growers had said it was (see photo on page 22). It was a magnificent plant for which you might consider mortgaging the house. R. A. Rolfe, editor of *The Orchid Review*, described it with absolute abandon: "Owing to the exceeding great beauty of this variety, the *Reichenbachia* is adorned by one of the finest paintings that ever left the pencil of a painter in any age."

The many *Cattleya mendelii* that we have seen over the years have been charming spring-blooming plants. They had medium-sized 5- to 6-inch flowers with relatively good shape. Their sepals and petals were very pale lavender, sometimes white, and the lip varied from pale to rich dark lavender. Most clones had a distinctive striping that radiated down the center of the lip. These plants were even grown for cut flowers in the early days of the cut-flower industry, but were rapidly replaced by darker lavender species like *C. mossiae* as florists' tastes turned to darker flowers. None of these pale lavender plants, however, were the wide-petaled giants of the 1880s and 1890s. If such splendid forms had existed, we wondered what happened to them.

It is clear today that the first specimens of *Cattleya mendelii* imported into Europe in the late 1800s were of an unusually fine strain. Because of this, they were the collector's favorites and the hybridizer's first choice in breeding. These plants were the parents of many of the early *Cattleya* hybrids, including some of the most outstanding hybrids ever produced.

The early *Cattleya mendelii* hybrids often had very large, round flowers. *Brassocattleya* British Queen (*Bc.* Digbyano-Mendelii × *C.* Lord Rothschild) was one such hybrid that had enormous flowers with wide, overlapping petals. One of the parents, the primary cross *Bc.* Digbyano-Mendelii, itself received four First Class Certificates and two Awards of Merit from the Royal Horticultural Society for its fine flowers. Many of the other primary hybrids of *C. mendelii* also had large, round flowers, particularly *C.* Atlantic (*C. mendelii* × *C. trianaei*) and *C.* Armainvillierensis (*C. mendelii* × *C. warscewiczii*).

Eileen Low, one of the foremost *Cattleya* breeders of all time, could not say enough good things about *C. mendelii*. She felt the species contributed both good shape and good carriage to its hybrids, an unusual combination and one that is sorely needed in many of our modern complex *Cattleya* hybrids. She felt *C. mendelii* increased the size and improved the shape of *Cattleya* hybrids without unduly affecting the color of the other parent. *Cattleya mendelii* was the parent used to increase the size and shape of *C. intermedia* 'Aquinii' to produce the splashed-petaled *C.* Suavior 'Aquinii' in 1930. It was the parent of the best red-colored primary hybrid, *Sophrocattleya* Thwaitesii (*C. mendelii* × *Sophronitis coccinea*), which had better shape, size, and a clearer red color than *Sophrocattleya* Doris (*C. dowiana* × *Sophronitis coccinea*).

Cattleya mendelii is famous for its many pale lavender varieties like this one which has only a trace of color in the lip.

The delicate coloring of the sepals and petals of *Cattleya mendelii* contributes significantly to the flower's beauty by magnifying the lovely color of the labellum, whether it is an intense rich purple or a pastel shade of lavender. The Royal Horticultural Society in London has given 16 First Class Certificates and more than 30 Awards of Merit to this species, and most flowers exhibited had this beautiful contrast between the lip and the sepals and petals.

A considerable number of plants awarded have had white sepals and petals and lavender labellums, and *Cattleya mendelii* has more semialba clones than any other *Cattleya* species. Despite the large number of semialba clones, however, very few true albas have been found. The two best-known albas were both imported by Low. The first one, *C. mendelii* 'Bluntii' FCC/RHS (1885), was named for Low's collector who found the plant. The other, *C. mendelii* 'Stuart Low' FCC/RHS (1910), was an 8-inch giant with wide petals that is usually considered the finest alba clone of the species. Surprisingly, 'Stuart Low' was still available commercially as late as 1950. Another famous old clone that is still found in private collections is the lovely semialba *C. mendelii* 'Thule' AM/RHS (1912), which has a pale pinkish tint to the lip that gives it an enchanting appearance.

Relatively few dark petaled clones of *Cattleya mendelii* have been found, and these have seldom been as beautiful as those with pastel sepals and petals and a contrasting darker lip. The species also has forms with flowers of relatively thin substance, which adds to their delicate beauty.

Cattleya mendelii is native to Colombia, where it grows at an altitude of 2500 to 3500 feet in the Eastern Cordillera. Plants imported in the late 1800s were reported to

Cattleya mendelii 'Carlos Arango' is one of the best modern-day varieties of the species.

have come from an area lying between Pamplona and Bucaramanga, often growing on exposed precipices and bare rocks.

The history of the species, however, is painfully clear. Frederick Sander complained that, in the 1880s, his collectors in Colombia could send him 200 cases of *Cattleya mendelii* when he asked for them, but by 1890, they could only send him one or two cases, and sometimes they even had to buy plants collected and cultivated by native Colombians as their own garden plants.

The grand old strain of *Cattleya mendelii* that made the species famous and contributed so much to early *Cattleya* hybrids disappeared because the native habitat was literally stripped of all the plants, even down to the few specimens that adorned the houses of those who lived there. The old lavender clones of *C. mendelii* that were in cultivation slowly disappeared, as the fashion for dark petaled *Cattleya* hybrids emerged and they could no longer be replaced from the jungle. The grand old monarch simply vanished, and only the colored parchments from the past remain to remind us of its majesty. Will it ever appear again? Perhaps. But we have waited 100 years already for this to happen. We can only hope that somewhere, in an obscure corner of the vast Colombian rainforests, the genes of that magnificent strain of *C. mendelii* still linger and, with still more time, these giants of the past may reappear to grace the orchid world as they did in the late 1800s, during the Golden Age of the *Cattleya* species. Until then, we can still enjoy the few *C. mendelii* that remain in cultivation, for they are among the loveliest of the large-flowered *Cattleya* species that exist anywhere. They are a grower's delight and a collector's treasure.

Culture

Cattleya mendelii is one of the easiest species to grow. It is a vigorous grower and a reliable producer of three or four flowers per flower stem each spring. It is more resistant to rot than most other *Cattleya* species and roots freely. *Cattleya mendelii* normally flowers in April and May in the United States and remains in bloom for several weeks. It begins its new growth in midsummer and completes the growth by late autumn. It can make two growths a season under good growing conditions. When the new growth is completed, *C. mendelii* will rest until buds begin to form in the sheath in February or March. The plants should be watered less during the winter months to avoid damaging the roots. Plants grow and flower best with a good amount of sun and air. They benefit from normal *Cattleya* temperatures of 58° to 60°F at night and 80° to 85°F during the day. *Cattleya mendelii* is one of the least troublesome plants I know and is often recommended for beginning orchid growers. Although the *C. mendelii* available today are not the giant, round flowers of the past, they are still some of the loveliest large-flowered cattleyas you can find.

Cattleya percivaliana O'Brien
Gardeners' Chronicle, n.s., 20: 404. 1883

We cannot imagine Christmas without *Cattleya percivaliana*. Its aromatic fragrance and deep, rich purple coloring are as much a part of our holiday as bayberry candles, pine cones, and the aroma of fresh-baked mince pie.

It wasn't too many years ago that you could buy flowering plants of *Cattleya perci-valiana* at the local florist shop for Christmas. They sold for about $10 a plant in flower and were more popular than poinsettias in some areas. The supply, however, was always limited to those plants with flowers that were too small to be used as cut-flowers for Christmas corsages.

Cattleya percivaliana was a late arrival on the orchid scene compared with most of the other important *Cattleya* species. It took 46 years after the discovery of *C. mossiae* and more than 20 years after the discovery of *C. trianaei*, *C. warscewiczii*, and *C. lued-demanniana* before someone found *C. percivaliana*. By the time it appeared, the orchid world was more than ready to receive it. Growers were desperate to find a *Cattleya* to fill the flowering gap between *C. labiata*, which finished blooming in November, and *C. tri-anaei*, which did not begin flowering until January. *Cattleya percivaliana* flowered dur-ing this empty December period, and orchidists everywhere responded with excitement and pleasure. Frederick Sander proclaimed elatedly that "with the discovery of *C. per-civaliana* and *C. gaskelliana*, we now have cattleyas flowering the whole year." It was all very wonderful.

The glow, however, did not last long. As the newly discovered species began flower-ing in hundreds of greenhouses throughout Europe and the United States, people soon discovered that, despite its good shape, rich dark coloring, and desirable flowering sea-son, *Cattleya percivaliana* produced flowers that were only half the size of the other large-flowered species. The disappointment was intense, and Sir Trevor Lawrence, pres-ident of the Royal Horticultural Society, chastised Frederick Sander publicly for mis-

The typical *Cattleya percivaliana* has 4^1/$_2$-inch flowers with a dark purple lip and a dark orange throat. It can produce a grand display of flowers even in a 5-inch pot.

leading his customers with such high praise for the plant. In disgust, Lawrence simply referred to *C. percivaliana* as "mossiae minor."

Cattleya percivaliana was discovered by William Arnold, a collector for Sander, when he was traveling in a remote area of Venezuela. Arnold wrote to Sander in December 1881 saying he had stumbled upon a beautiful *Cattleya* that he believed to be new and was sending 20 cases of plants back to England and 10 cases to Sander's associate company in the United States. When the plants arrived, Sander coaxed his friend, botanist H. G. Reichenbach, to write a botanical description of the plant so the Sander's firm could begin selling it as a new *Cattleya* species.

Reichenbach, with some reluctance and considerable philosophical comment, formally presented *Cattleya percivaliana* to the horticultural world in the 17 June 1882 edition of *The Gardeners' Chronicle* (p. 796). In his description, Reichenbach lamented that he had only 20 dried flowers, two non-flowering plants, and a few notes from Frederick Sander on which to base a description and place *C. percivaliana* in the botanical scheme of things. Reichenbach ended his lament by saying, "If a young botanist had the time and means, he might do a grand work traveling for the purpose of studying *C. labiata*," and with this melancholy observation, Reichenbach described *C. percivaliana* as "*Cattleya labiata* var. *percivaliana*." Sander was furious. By calling *C. percivaliana* a variety of *C. labiata*, Reichenbach had cut the commercial value of Sander's plants in half.

The following year James O'Brian, writing in *The Gardeners' Chronicle*, raised *Cattleya percivaliana* to species rank, and Sander paid *C. percivaliana* the ultimate compliment by making it the first *Cattleya* pictured in his famous orchid book, *Reichenbachia*. Reichenbach named *C. percivaliana* to honor R. P. Percival of Birkdale, Southport, England. Percival was an enthusiastic private grower of orchids, a hobbyist, described by his friends as "the genial Birkdale orchidist."

Unlike many people whose names appear in orchid nomenclature, Percival took his namesake orchid seriously. When Reichenbach was criticized for writing too many nice things about *Cattleya percivaliana*, Percival sent Reichenbach a bouquet of flowers from his best clones to reassure Reichenbach that *C. percivaliana* was indeed a lovely thing. Percival exhibited *C. percivaliana* at flower shows everywhere and in 1884 received two First Class Certificates from the Royal Horticultural Society, one for a large, richly colored clone, and another for an alba clone.

As a *Cattleya* species, *C. percivaliana* is distinct and easy to identify. Frederick Sander, its greatest promoter, felt no one could mistake it for any other species and "a boy could pick it out blindfolded in a greenhouse." Saying this, Sander must have assumed the boy would smell it, because the fragrance is unique; you have only to smell it once to be able to identify it from then on. Usually the fragrance is described as "spicy" and most people like it. But, not everyone does, and it is the only *Cattleya* species about which there is any doubt that the fragrance is pleasant and desirable.

Another important identifying feature of *Cattleya percivaliana* is its lip color. The throat of the lip typically is an intense deep orange color that seems to underlay even the deep purple of the lower labellum. Sander described this color as having "extraordinary richness," and Reichenbach likened it to "a Persian carpet in which dazzling colors prevail." The lip color is an important reason why *C. percivaliana* was used in early hybridizing, but unfortunately, the color did not produce the same effect in the hybrids as it did in the species itself, so most *C. percivaliana* hybrids were not too successful. Even its natural hybrid with *C. mossiae*, *C.* Peregrine, is not an exciting event in this respect.

The only primary hybrid of *Cattleya percivaliana* that has received significant recognition and is really noteworthy is *C.* Leda (*C. percivaliana* × *C. dowiana*). *Cattleya percivaliana* has good shape and rich dark color. Add to this *C. dowiana*'s well-known effect of intensifying the color of other purple *Cattleya* flowers, and *C.* Leda becomes not only a beautiful flower in its own right, but also a promising parent for dark purple hybrids. *Cattleya* Leda is a parent of such famous dark crosses as *Brassocattleya* Hartland (*Bc.* Hannibal × *C.* Leda) and *Laeliocattleya* Hyperion (*Lc.* General Maude × *C.* Leda). Its cross with *Lc.* Cavalese, *Lc.* Bloody Mary, gives a good description of the purple-red color it can produce in its hybrids.

Cattleya percivaliana was not much of a success in the cut-flower market of the 1930s to the 1950s because a single flower was too small to make a good corsage. Only a few fine clones with large flowers, like *C. percivaliana* 'Summit' FCC/AOS, were grown for cut flowers by such growers as Lager and Hurrell, who had at least 200 plants of the variety for Christmas cut flowers in the late 1940s.

As a pot plant, however, *Cattleya percivaliana* was ideal. It was a relatively small plant that produced two or three flowers per lead. A plant in a 5-inch pot made a beautiful display for the holiday season.

Although *Cattleya percivaliana* is thought of as one of the smaller of the large-flowered *Cattleya* species, there have been clones that had a 7-inch petal spread, but these have been fairly uncommon. The typical flower is about 4½ inches across, compared with 6 or 8 inches across for the typical *C. mossiae*.

A fine clone of *Cattleya percivaliana* was named 'Grandiflora' AM/RHS (1916), but that term is applied today to any large-flowered clone, particularly those with good shape and a wider-than-normal lip.

Cattleya percivaliana produces some of the better-shaped albas of the *Cattleya* species, and John Lager had one that he considered as good for shape and size as his famous lavender 'Summit'. His alba, however, had no clonal name and was apparently lost after his death. In addition to R. P. Percival's alba that received an FCC/RHS in 1884, the clone 'Lady Holford' received an FCC/RHS in 1913, and the unawarded clone 'Christmas Cheer' is a real gem.

The most famous semialba is *Cattleya percivaliana* 'Charlesworth' FCC/RHS (1913), which has a classic deep reddish-purple lip that makes a striking contrast against the white sepals and petals. The commonly available semialbas today, like *C. percivaliana* 'Jewel', lack the intense lip coloration of 'Charlesworth', but are still a nice addition to any Christmas arrangement.

The lavender forms of *Cattleya percivaliana* have lips that vary in color from almost black-purple to medium orange-purple, and there are, of course, pale lavender albescens and concolors. The lip is usually narrow except in the Grandiflora forms. The most famous lavender variety is undoubtedly 'Summit', which has a more square shape than most other clones of *C. percivaliana*. Even the very dark, narrow-lipped *C. percivaliana*, however, are wonderful flowers.

Cattleya percivaliana 'Summit' FCC/AOS is one of the largest and best-shaped forms of the species ever found. It was discovered by the famous American plant collector John Lager, who named it for the city in New Jersey in which his orchid firm, Lager and Hurrell, was located.

Cattleya percivaliana 'Christmas Cheer' is one of the best-shaped modern alba varieties of the species.

If we could ask Santa Claus to bring all our orchid friends one holiday gift, it would be a plant of *Cattleya percivaliana*, filled to the brim with a dozen rich purple flowers—a plant that could stand on their coffee tables by their Christmas trees and welcome holiday guests like an outstretched hand of the genial R. P. Percival of times gone by.

Culture

Cattleya percivaliana is one of the easiest members of the *Cattleya* genus to grow and is normally a vigorous, trouble-free plant. It begins growing in late winter to early spring in the United States and will usually make two growths in succession. Both growths will flower at the same time in late November into December. A sturdy, well-established plant will stay in flower at least four weeks.

This species grows in nature at relatively high altitudes from 4000 to 6000 feet. It is often a lithophyte found on rocks and receives considerable exposure to the sun. Under greenhouse conditions at sea level in the United States, however, it will require at least 30 percent shade in the summer to prevent the leaves from burning. *Cattleya percivaliana* requires lots of sun and air to obtain the best growth and the most flowers. Repotting should be done in the spring before the plant is in active growth.

Because of its vigorous growing habit and small size, *Cattleya percivaliana* makes a great exhibition plant if potted on into the next larger pot without disturbing the rootball. Under these circumstances, you can have a plant in a 6-inch pot with 10 to 12 flowers—and you can have it for Christmas.

The semialba *Cattleya percivaliana* 'Jewel' makes a wonderful pot plant for Christmas.

Cattleya gaskelliana Reichenbach fil.
Gardeners' Chronicle, n.s., 19:243. 1883

It must have been fun to be an orchid enthusiast and live in London in the 1880s. You could see a new display of orchids two or three times a week. You could see the displays even if you only worked in London, because they were usually held from 11 A.M. to 2:30 P.M. weekdays—during your lunch break.

The shows were held at one of several auction houses that specialized in selling orchid plants. Like any good business establishment, these auction houses or "rooms," as they were called, found it easier to sell plants when the customers could see the flowers than when there was just a pile of nondescript pseudobulbs. Most auctions featured lots of flowering plants all lined up and named, including the finest and newest species of the day. You were always welcome at the auction even if you did not plan to buy a plant. The philosophy was: the more people in the rooms, the more excitement the auction generates and the better the overall prices.

One of the busiest auction houses was Stevens Rooms, run by J. C. Stevens at 38 King Street, Covent Garden. One of Mr. Stevens's larger suppliers of orchids was Frederick Sander, and when Sander's collector Seidel sent him a new *Cattleya* species in 1883, Sander offered the plants for sale at auction at Stevens Rooms. Sander labeled the plants *C. gaskelliana* in honor of a good customer, Holbrook Gaskell, Esquire of Woolton, near Liverpool, "a gentleman," Sander said, "who by great diligence has acquired one of the finest collections of orchids in the North of England."

Sander's *Cattleya gaskelliana* first appeared in Stevens Rooms at a Thursday auction the first week in March 1883. It was accompanied by two live cut flowers and one flower on a growing plant. *The Gardeners' Chronicle* described *C. gaskelliana* in a news item on 10 March 1883, the week after the auction, comparing it favorably to *C. mendelii, C. warneri,* and *C. gigas* and saying the chronicle considered it "a distinctive and pretty new plant." Heinrich G. Reichenbach had also mentioned it in *The Gardeners' Chronicle* of 24 February 1883, when he commented briefly on a flower Sander had sent him saying, "It was distinct in colour from anything I saw before." The auction, however, did not go well, and Sander received only ordinary prices for his plants. Buyers were not convinced the species was really new.

As *Cattleya gaskelliana* limped onto the horticultural stage in 1883, it was adrift with no real botanical description and little recognition in horticultural circles. *The Gardeners' Chronicle* did not even mention it in January 1884 in its tribute to the important new plant introductions of 1883. As the spring of 1884 appeared and faded, however, orchid growers took note of one important characteristic of the new *Cattleya* species—its flowering season. *Cattleya gaskelliana* filled the only remaining gap in the year-round flowering cycle of the large-flowered species.

There had always been one large-flowered *Cattleya* species in bloom every day of the year except late May and early June. Then *C. gaskelliana* appeared with its late-May-into-June flowering season and, as Sander observed, "We now have *Cattleya* flowers all year-round." By the summer of 1884, *C. gaskelliana* had changed from an ugly duckling into a swan. The floodgates opened and *C. gaskelliana* flowed into every orchid collection in Europe and established itself firmly as an important member of the large-flowered *Cattleya* species. The Royal Horticultural Society awarded *C. gaskelliana* three First Class Certificates and six Awards of Merit, and the horticultural press wrote about it often.

Cattleya gaskelliana had a number of fine qualities to recommend it to orchid growers. It was easy to grow and very free flowering, and had large 7-inch flowers with a nice fragrance and lovely delicate substance. It had been imported in large quantities, so it was readily available and was not too expensive to acquire. Its flowering season made it a must for all *Cattleya* lovers, because without it, there were no *Cattleya* flowers after *C. mossiae* finished blooming in mid-May until *C. warscewiczii* bloomed in mid-June.

Native to Venezuela, *Cattleya gaskelliana* grows as an epiphyte and lithophyte from 2300 to 3300 feet above sea level in the eastern coastal mountain range, the Cordillera de la Costa. It occurs in three Venezuelan provinces, northeastern Anzoátegui, southern Sucre, and northern Monagas. Its natural habitats vary from tropical, humid cloud forests to somewhat drier areas where it is forced to grow on rocks in nearly full sun. Unfortunately, it has been collected almost to extinction in some areas and is no longer as plentiful as it once was.

Most *Cattleya gaskelliana* flowers are light lavender in color with a slightly darker lip that often has a saddle-shaped purple blotch or splash in the center. Very few really dark forms have been found. John Lager of Summit, New Jersey, had a fine dark *C. gaskelliana* his father had bought during the 1930s for $250—a huge sum for a *Cattleya* plant during the Great Depression. The only other really dark clone we have seen belonged to

The typical *Cattleya gaskelliana* has a floriferous pale lavender flower with a similar or slightly darker lip and a splash of purple on the tip.

Lawrence and Edith Myers in Elkins Park—also in the 1940s. The Myers' clone was con-color dark purple with wide petals, good form, and beautiful thin substance.

Cattleya gaskelliana has some nice semialba clones, and some good coerulea-type clones like the distinctive 'Blue Dragon'. The species contributed significantly to the development of "blue" *Cattleya* hybrids, beginning with the famous *C.* Ariel 'Coerulae' (*C. gaskelliana* 'Coerulescens' × *C. bowringiana* 'Lilacina') made by Sir Jeremiah Coleman in 1915.

The alba clones of *Cattleya gaskelliana*, however, were the most outstanding and had the greatest impact on the breeding of fine hybrids. Without this species, there would have been no *C.* Suzanne Hye or *C.* Bow Bells—and how many fine white *Cattleya* hybrids would we have today without *C.* Bow Bells as a parent? *Cattleya* Bow Bells is a cross between a primary hybrid of *C. gaskelliana, C.* Suzanne Hye (*C. gaskelliana* alba × *C. mossiae* alba), and *C.* Edithiae (*C.* Suzanne Hye × *C. trianaei*), so there is a lot of *C. gaskelliana* in *C.* Bow Bells. The other double parent, *C. mossiae,* is not noted for having alba clones with good shape, while *C. gaskelliana* has several fine white clones, so *C. gaskelliana* may be the most important contributor to the outstanding shape of *C.* Bow Bells. The American Orchid Society has given two awards to alba clones of *C. gaskelliana:* 'Magic White Key' HCC/AOS and 'White Heritage' AM/AOS.

Because it had such thin substance, and because it flowered when greenhouses were often overheated by an intense June sun that usually shortened the life of its flowers, *Cattleya gaskelliana* was not always popular with cut-flower growers in the United States. Its flowering season, however, was so important that large numbers were

The saddle-shaped purple splash on the tip of this semialba is distinctive to many plants of *Cattleya gaskelliana.*

Cattleya gaskelliana 'Blue Dragon' is one form of this species that has contributed significantly to breeding modern coerulea-type hybrids.

grown—even filling entire 30-by-100-foot greenhouses during the 1940s. As *Cattleya* hybrids were developed to provide late-May and early-June flowers, however, *C. gaskelliana* became one of the first victims of the hybrid rage, and it virtually disappeared from both commercial and hobbyist greenhouses. By 1960, there were almost none left in cultivation in the United States. *Cattleya gaskelliana* became another tragic loss in the history of the magnificent large-flowered *Cattleya* species. Although wild-collected plants of *C. gaskelliana* are seldom imported now, the species is still available as sibling crosses from Venezuelan growers, and a few of the fine old varieties are offered now and then by specialists in the *Cattleya* species.

Each new generation of *Cattleya* Bow Bells hybrids reminds us that *C. gaskelliana* is truly the queen bee par excellence of the alba *Cattleya* hybrid, continuously recycling its genes and lending them to each new generation of larger and ever-more beautiful white hybrids—from *C.* Bob Betts to *C.* Pearl Harbor to *C.* Tiffin Bells to *C.* Mary Ann Barnett. *Cattleya gaskelliana* has contributed much to coerulea-type *Cattleya* hybrids, and there is undoubtedly more to come as the popularity of blue cattleyas continues. Above all, however, *C. gaskelliana* is a very rewarding plant to grow itself with its abundance of delightfully fragrant flowers that have a glistening delicate substance and charming pastel colors. If you want *Cattleya* species in flower every day of the year, of course, *C. gaskelliana* is one of those must-have orchids you need to make it happen.

Culture

Cattleya gaskelliana is a vigorous, easy-to-grow, free-flowering plant. It will normally begin growing in the United States in early February and complete its growth by mid-

May. It should be watered sparingly until the new growth is about 3 inches long. Then water should be increased until it is receiving heavy waterings as the growth matures. Always remember to allow the medium to dry out, however, between waterings; otherwise, if the roots are kept too wet, they may rot and die.

This species is one of the cattleyas that produces flowers as the growth is maturing. In other words, it does not produce a growth and then rest for a few months before flowering as do *Cattleya mossiae* and *C. trianaei*. Like most other *Cattleya* species, *C. gaskelliana* needs lots of sun and air to grow and flower well. The night temperature should be 58° to 60°F and the day temperature 80° to 85°F.

Cattleya gaskelliana normally produces three to five flowers on a flower stem in mid-May in the United States. The flowers do not stay in bloom as long as *C. trianaei* or *C. schroederae* and three weeks is normal. Once in flower, the plants should be kept in the coolest part of the greenhouse so the flowers will last as long as possible. After blooming, the plants will sometimes make a second growth, which, unlike *C. warscewiczii*, does not seem to diminish its flower production the following year. Repot the plants only when you see new roots starting from the lead pseudobulb.

Cattleya lawrenceana Reichenbach fil.
Gardeners' Chronicle, n.s., 23: 338. 1885

Orchids were a passion for the new president of the Royal Horticultural Society as he took office in March 1885. His estate at Burford Lodge in Dorking, England, with its 12 greenhouses, was written up frequently in the horticultural press, and it was often said he had the best private orchid collection in Britain. His mother, Louisa, had been an active gardener and botanist, and the new president credited her with stimulating his love for orchids. They were her passion, too.

The Royal Horticultural Society was in great distress when the new president took office. It had considerable debt and not enough income to cover its expenses. It was clearly in crisis, and the 54-year-old president would have his hands full just keeping it alive.

James John Trevor Lawrence was a handsome man, with a reassuring smile and a polished manner. He was known to the horticultural world as "Sir Trevor Lawrence," but to his orchid friends he was just "Sir Trevor." He was accomplished at many things. He had spent 10 years as a medical doctor in India and 17 years as a member of Parliament. He had inherited the title of baronet from his father, a former president of the Royal College of Surgeons, and his estate was a horticultural Mecca. His grower, J. C. Spyers, was so skilled at raising orchids that Burford Lodge was often the only place in Britain where many rare old orchid species could be found still growing vigorously decades after their first importation.

Despite the magnitude and seriousness of the Royal Horticultural Society's problems, it was soon evident they were no match for its inspiring new president, and before long, the gracious and charming Lawrence had turned the Society around and started it moving forward as one of the great horticultural societies of the world. Lawrence remained president for an amazing 28 years, until just before his death in 1914. Along the way, a grateful horticultural world gave him the Victoria Medal of Honor, the Veitch Memorial Gold Medal, and innumerable orchid awards. The orchid world immortalized him by naming *Paphiopedilum lawrenceanum* and the lovely *Cattleya lawrenceana* in his honor.

In his formal description of *Cattleya lawrenceana* in 1885 in *The Gardeners' Chronicle* (23: 338), an admiring botanist, H. G. Reichenbach, wrote,

> At last we have a *Cattleya* bearing Sir Trevor's excellent name. Of course, it ought to be an extra good plant and so it is. . . . I regard it a very good fortune to inscribe such a plant to such an orchidist as Sir Trevor.

Cattleya lawrenceana was discovered in 1884 by Frederick Sander's collector, Seidel, who sent many plants back to England. The first shipment perished, but the second arrived safely and was auctioned at Stephens Rooms, London, on 26 March 1885. Sir Robert Schomburgk had encountered *C. lawrenceana* during an expedition to survey the Venezuela-Brazil-Guyana border in 1842, but it was not recognized as a new *Cattleya* species until Seidel's 1884 importation.

At the time of its discovery, *Cattleya lawrenceana* was considered an unusually lovely new species that was distinctly different from the typical large-flowered labiata-type *Cattleya*. Like *C. labiata*, *C. lawrenceana* has a single leaf at the top of the pseudobulb, but the pseudobulbs are much more slender than those of *C. labiata* and most have a characteristic red hue. Although the flowers of *C. lawrenceana* can reach the size of a typical *C. labiata*, they are normally only two-thirds the size and have an unusually narrow tubular labellum. Because of this distinct labellum, *C. lawrenceana* is one of the

The typical *Cattleya lawrenceana* has pale lavender sepals and petals with a rich dark purple lip and produces five to eight flowers on a spike.

few members of the genus *Cattleya* that botanists have never disputed as being a genuine and distinct species.

Cattleya lawrenceana has one of the broadest ranges of color forms of any of the *Cattleya* species. The typical *C. lawrenceana* flower is pale to medium lavender in color with a dark rose-lavender lip. There are also very rare alba and semialba forms, pastels, dark lavenders, and even dark, rich flammea types. Reichenbach flamboyantly compared the rich color of *C. lawrenceana*'s lip to the "end of the tail of a heathcock," which is like our telling you it has the color of the tail feathers of a Delaware Blue Hen—only a few local readers would know what the state bird looks like. What Reichenbach tried to say was that, at its best, *C. lawrenceana* has a deep, rich, almost glowing royal purple labellum.

Although the flowers are only medium size, they are presented very individually on the flower stem, making *Cattleya lawrenceana* one of the most enchanting species in the genus. *Cattleya lawrenceana* 'Diane', with its delicate pale lavender concolor flowers, is one of the most beautiful cattleyas we know. It does not have wide petals, round shape, or heavy substance, but it needs none of these qualities to be beautiful. *Cattleya lawrenceana* normally produces five or six flowers on a flower spike and, when really well grown, can even give as many as eight.

Native to the Gran Sabana area of eastern Venezuela, where Venezuela borders Brazil and Guyana, *Cattleya lawrenceana* has been found on all sides of this border, but Venezuela is its principal habitat. The plants grow in forested areas, usually near streams or rivers, and are most abundant at elevations between 1200 and 4000 feet above sea level. The most famous home of *C. lawrenceana* is at the foot of the twin table moun-

Cattleya lawrenceana has a wide variety of color forms which even extends to the brilliant flammea type shown here.

tains, Mt. Roraima and Mt. Kukenan, two picturesque plateaus in Roraima that rise almost vertically some 8000 feet. These mountains are so distinct that a woodcut was made of Mt. Kukenan to accompany the 1885 article in *The Gardeners' Chronicle* that introduced *C. lawrenceana* to the orchid world.

Cattleya lawrenceana is the first *Cattleya* species for which concern was expressed for its survival at the time off its discovery. One writer in 1885 expressed "regret at the probable extinction in their native homes of such plants as this by their wholesale collection for market." The famous Venezuelan orchidist G. C. K. Dunsterville showed concern in 1973 and added the acid comment, "When we speak of *Cattleya lawrenceana*, the word *is* may have to be changed to *was*." Venezuelan orchidists today continue to sound the alarm for *C. lawrenceana* as this lovely species disappears from more and more of its native habitats. Even the Venezuelan government's establishment of the huge Gran Sabana National Park in *C. lawrenceana*'s prime area has not stopped the collection of plants by local people who sell them to local tourists.

This species has had a limited but confused history in hybridizing. *Sander's List of Orchid Hybrids* in 1946 shows us that, in the early days of hybridizing, *Cattleya lawrenceana* was crossed with a number of other *Cattleya* and *Laelia* species, three *Brassavola* species, and *Sophronitis coccinea* (syn. *Sophronitis grandiflora*). There were also 17 other hybrids made from these primary crosses up to 1946. Unfortunately, *Sander's List* shows no hybrids with *C. lawrenceana* after 1946 for the next 38 years because, for some strange reason, it suddenly considered *C. lawrenceana* synonymous with *C. labiata*. This is astonishing, of course, considering how different *C. lawrenceana* is from the

Cattleya lawrenceana 'Diane' has pale lavender concolor flowers and is one of the most beautiful varieties of the species in cultivation.

other large-flowered cattleyas. Finally, in 1984 Sander's began listing *C. lawrenceana* as a separate species, but we find only three crosses made since then. Although *C. lawrenceana* seems to intensify the purple coloring in its hybrids, the end result does not seem to recapture the tantalizing charm of the original.

Cattleya lawrenceana is one of the rarest *Cattleya* species in cultivation in the United States today. The few plants we have were acquired many years ago, and we have seen only a scattering of plants for sale in the last 50 years. Fortunately, it is still possible to obtain plants from Venezuelan orchid growers that have been raised from seed in commercial nurseries.

G. C. K. Dunsterville called *Cattleya lawrenceana* the "Queen of the Guayana." The native Venezuelan Indians near Mt. Roraima called it by a name that means "blossom of the wood." We always think of *C. lawrenceana* as the Little Charmer. Its haunting color tones and abundance of cute and unique flowers make it a captivating ambassador of springtime, and it is always gratifying to see a *Cattleya* named for someone who really deserves the honor.

Culture

Cattleya lawrenceana is one of the more difficult species to grow well. It requires careful watering and a warmer night temperature than most other large-flowered cattleyas. It should be put in the warmest part of the greenhouse, along with *C. dowiana*, where night temperatures do not fall below 65°F, and be allowed to dry out completely between waterings to assure the roots do not rot.

Alba, semialba, and albescens forms of *Cattleya lawrenceana* are very rare. Only a few have been found in the wild since the species was first discovered in 1884.

Typically, *Cattleya lawrenceana* begins growing during the summer in the United States, and it completes its new growths during October and November. It then rests until it flowers in early spring. It does not respond well to repotting, and the whole root-ball should be moved on into the next larger pot whenever possible. Like all cattleyas, *C. lawrenceana* should receive lots of sun and moving air. It grows best for us when it is slightly under-potted; a 5-inch clay pot is large for most plants. *Cattleya lawrenceana* is one of our favorite cattleyas and is well worth the care needed to grow it well.

Cattleya schroederae Rolfe
Orchid Review 3: 268. 1895

Baron J. H. W. von Schröder had one of the finest orchid collections in Europe and he loved cattleyas. The largest and grandest greenhouse on his estate near Windsor was built just for cattleyas, and his appetite for fine *Cattleya* species was insatiable. At The Dell, as he called his estate, he wanted only the best and nothing less would do. The baron was a good customer of the English orchid firm Sander's, so when Sander's orchid collector in Colombia, William Arnold, found a new *Cattleya* species in 1886, the first person Frederick Sander thought of was the baron.

When the newly collected plants arrived, Baron Schröder obligingly bought most of them, and Frederick Sander sent the first flowers to the botanist H. G. Reichenbach, with the suggestion that Reichenbach describe them as a new *Cattleya* species. When Reichenbach procrastinated in writing the description, Sander sent more flowers and pushed Reichenbach to visit his greenhouses to see the plants. Yet Reichenbach still did nothing.

Then, on Easter Sunday 1887, the baron himself sent a fine flower of the new plant to Reichenbach, and within a few days Reichenbach wrote a description on page 152 of *The Gardeners' Chronicle* of 16 April 1887. Reichenbach dedicated the "gorgeous" new flower with great satisfaction to Baroness Schröder, "who is so well known as an enthusiastic lover of orchids."

Reichenbach's description of the new plant, however, did not come out quite the way Sander had planned it. Reichenbach described the new plant as "*Cattleya* (*trianaei*) *schroederae*," so the plant was suddenly not a new species, just a new form of a previously described species, *C. trianaei*. Sander, however, was convinced the plant was not *C. trianaei*. Its bright, delicious fragrance was distinctive and different from the subtle fragrance of *C. trianaei*. Its petals and lip were more frilly and crisped, and it was a more vigorous grower. It also produced more flowers on a stem than *C. trianaei*. Sander felt it had to be a new species.

Being an inventive businessman, Sander decided to take the matter into his own hands. In doing so, he joined the increasing chorus of horticulturists of the late 1800s who felt the only way to put the large-flowered cattleyas in their proper botanical places was to do the job themselves. James O'Brien, one of the most prominent and skilled horticulturists of the day, had done this with *C. percivaliana* in 1883. Now, Frederick Sander plunged into the fray with *C. schroederae*. He referred to it wherever he could as simply "*Cattleya schroederae*," whether it was in letters, speeches, or a glamorous plate in his own book *Reichenbachia*. Sander asked botanist R. A. Rolfe to write the botanical description for *C. schroederae* in *Reichenbachia*, not Heinrich Gustav Reichenbach. In plate 37 of the new series volume 1 (1892), Rolfe gave numerous reasons why *C. schroederae* was not a variety of *C. trianaei*, and although he left it as "*C. labiata* var. *schroederae*," he had caught Sander's message for change. Three years later in 1895, Rolfe made *C. schroederae* a full-fledged species (*Orchid Review* 3: 268).

Cattleya schroederae has always been considered a feminine flower. Its lovely pale lavender color is often described as "overlaid with pink pearl," and it has a tantalizingly sweet fragrance. Reichenbach certainly thought it was feminine when he named it for Baroness Schröder, because he named a bold dark purple variety of *Cattleya trianaei* for the baron (*Cattleya trianaei* 'Schroederiana').

Despite its feminine appearance, however, *Cattleya schroederae* had only a limited presence as an adornment for women in the cut-flower market of the 1930s to the 1950s. *Cattleya schroederae* lacked the wide range of color found in *C. trianaei*, and yet it competed with *C. trianaei* for the late-February to early-March flower sales. Most varieties of *C. schroederae* looked more or less the same, and no woman wanted to look like all the other women at a dance or reception, at least not in the United States.

Cattleya schroederae's beautiful shape, however, made it the perfect model for a fine exhibition plant. Here its free-flowering nature, frilly petals and lip, and pleasing fragrance were definite assets. *Cattleya schroederae* produced three to five flowers on a spike, unlike *C. trianaei* that had only two or three. *Cattleya schroederae* can have seven flowers on a spike if exceptionally well-grown and can produce a magnificent speci-

The typical *Cattleya schroederae* has pale lavender sepals and petals with a yellow or orange disc in the throat, and the inflorescence bears three to five flowers.

men. One such plant was even pictured in the June 1903 issue of *The Orchid Review* and the March 1953 *American Orchid Society Bulletin.*

As a result of its excellent shape, *Cattleya schroederae* garnered nine First Class Certificates from the Royal Horticultural Society in the first 20 years following its discovery, despite the color similarity of the various clones exhibited. R. A. Rolfe, editor of *The Orchid Review*, considered *C. schroederae* alba the finest white *Cattleya* species in existence in 1893.

The American orchid collector, John Lager, found *Cattleya schroederae* to be the most abundant *Cattleya* species in Colombia during his explorations there in the early 1900s. During one trip, Lager discovered two of the finest and eventually most famous varieties of *C. schroederae* on the mountain slopes above the Casanare River.

The first clone, *Cattleya schroederae* 'Hercules', was a beautiful, round alba form with an orange throat. It was so fine that Lager used its picture to adorn the stationery of his own orchid company, Lager and Hurrell in Summit, New Jersey. The flower was also pictured in the September issue of the first volume of the *American Orchid Society Bulletin* in 1932. Lager sold a division of 'Hercules' to a private collector and the plant eventually found its way to the English orchid firm Stuart Low, which exhibited it in 1925 in London where it received an Award of Merit from the Royal Horticultural Society. The American Orchid Society (AOS) also gave 'Hercules' an AM in June 1932 when it was exhibited by the second president of the AOS, Fitz Eugene Dixon.

The second variety Lager named *Cattleya schroederae* 'Summitensis' for his nursery in New Jersey. This was a large semialba flower with an intense reddish-orange throat

Alba forms of *Cattleya schroederae* are relatively rare. This unnamed variety shows the fine shape for which the species is famous.

and a purple lip. 'Summitensis' had a fine round shape and was also sold to a private collector. It was later acquired by Major George L. Holford (Sir George Holford of Westonbirt fame) who exhibited it under the name 'The Baron'. As 'The Baron', it received an FCC/RHS in 1908 and, right or wrong, the clone 'Summitensis' has been known as 'The Baron' ever since.

No really dark clones of *Cattleya schroederae* exist, but 'Pitt's Variety' FCC/RHS (1901) did have sepals and petals of a medium lilac color, and you can occasionally find a clone today, like 'Severn's', that approaches this color. The rich orange color in the throat of *C. schroederae* is typical for the species, and it is present in most varieties. A few forms have lemon-yellow and pale yellow throats, however, in keeping with the natural color variability of any *Cattleya* species.

Cattleya schroederae has made significant contributions to *Cattleya* hybridizing. The very pale coloring in the sepals and petals has allowed hybridizers to retain the beautiful colors of an art-shade *Cattleya* while improving the shape and increasing the size of these flowers. One of the earliest successful crosses was *Laeliocattleya* Elinor (*C. schroederae* × *Laelia* Coronet), which retained most of the brilliant reddish-yellow and orange shades of *Laelia* Coronet (*L. cinnabarina* × *L. harpophylla*) while producing an acceptably shaped flower. The round shape of many large, exhibition, pale lavender *Cattleya* hybrids today often comes from *C. schroederae*, not just *C. trianaei*.

The biggest problems Reichenbach had in classifying *Cattleya schroederae* were in its growth and flowering habits and its flowering season, which are virtually the same as a late-flowering *C. trianaei*. *Cattleya schroederae* begins growing in the spring when a late

Most *Cattleya schroederae* have relatively pale colored lips, but an occasional variety like the one shown here can have a rich, almost red-purple color.

C. trianaei would, and its growth matures with *C. trianaei* in late summer. It then rests for several months, like *C. trianaei*, before sending up flowers. The pseudobulbs of *C. trianaei* and *C. schroederae* look virtually the same, and one can easily be mistaken for the other. The flowers of *C. schroederae*, like those of *C. trianaei*, are also among the longest lasting of the *Cattleya* species (five weeks is normal), and both *C. trianaei* and *C. schroederae* are well known for their fine, round varieties. From Reichenbach's point of view, *C. schroederae* seemed nothing more than a pale lavender strain of *C. trianaei*. One had to grow the plants for a season or two to see the differences, and Reichenbach's friends, like Frederick Sander and Baron Schröder, did not give him the luxury to do this.

It is interesting to note that during the heyday of the cattleya as a cut flower, the rich dark purple-colored cattleyas were the preferred flowers for corsages in Great Britain and the United States, while the pale lavender flowers, like *Cattleya schroederae*, were preferred in Germany. When Reichenbach named *C. schroederae* for a baroness with the German name Schröder, he apparently knew more of what he was doing than he is often given credit for.

With a delicate, pink-pearl coloring and sweet fragrance, *Cattleya schroederae* is an enchanting maiden of the realm of the *Cattleya* species—a sumptuous flower that takes you from winter into springtime with the soft touch of a beautiful baroness.

Culture

Cattleya schroederae makes a good beginner's plant because of its ease of culture. It will start growing in early spring in most of the United States and, like *C. trianaei*, will complete a growth by late June. If you continue to provide good growing conditions *C.*

The dorsal, or back, sepal of most *Cattleya schroederae* tends to curl over as shown in this flower.

schroederae will normally make a second growth that will be completed by the end of August. The plant will then rest until buds begin to form in the base of the sheath in late December. Because of the short days at this time of year, the buds grow slowly and the flowers will not open until late February or early March. Both the first and second growths will usually flower at the same time.

When the plant is dormant from September until February, it should be watered sparingly—just enough to keep the pseudobulbs from shriveling. Overwatering the plants while they are dormant can kill the roots and shorten flower life. Fertilize the plants only when they are actively growing from March through August. Never fertilize them when they are dormant because this can sometimes lead to a toxic accumulation of salts in the pseudobulbs that can kill the plant. Fertilizer damage is often mistaken for fungal or bacterial rot, which it closely resembles.

Cattleya schroederae is one of the most rewarding of the *Cattleya* species to grow because it will stay in flower five or six weeks if kept cool (55°F) and dry. Like all cattleyas, it produces the best growths at 85°F day and 60°F night temperatures with lots of sunshine and moving air. A thorough watering should be given when it is actively growing, but the medium should be allowed to dry out before a second watering is given. *Cattleya schroederae* seedlings are usually rapid growers and seem to reach flowering size sooner than most of the other large-flowered *Cattleya* species. Seedlings grow better with a night temperature of 65°F than with the usual 58° to 60°F prescribed for adult plants.

Cattleya rex O'Brien
Gardeners' Chronicle, 3d series, 8:684. 1890

James O'Brien was one of the most famous horticulturists of the late 1800s and was an expert on orchids, particularly the large-flowered *Cattleya* species. He was secretary to the Royal Horticultural Society's Orchid Committee, advisor to the editors of *The Gardeners' Chronicle*, and frequently assisted H. G. Reichenbach in his botanical deliberations. When Her Majesty Queen Victoria awarded the first Victoria Medals of Honor in Horticulture (VMH), she presented one to O'Brien.

O'Brien was a pioneer in reclassifying the large-flowered *Cattleya* species, insisting they should be individual species and not varieties of *C. labiata*. He often took his case to horticulturists outside England, and, on one of his visits to Jean Linden of Horticulture Internationale in Brussels in the autumn of 1890, he happened upon the first flowering of a new *Cattleya* species from Peru that Linden had recently received from the orchid collector Eric Bungeroth.

The plant O'Brien saw in Linden's greenhouse was a marvelous specimen. It had tall pseudobulbs and a long flower spike with six flowers standing in an upright position in the manner of *Cattleya warscewiczii*. The flowers themselves were 7 inches across and had unique cream-colored sepals and petals, and a lip of various shades of crimson, in netting and marbling that almost defied description. Linden himself was so impressed with the flower and the gorgeous flower spike that he had his artist paint them, and published the picture in *Lindenia* the following year.

Rather than see this magnificent new *Cattleya* species subjected to years of indecision from botanists like its predecessors, O'Brien decided to describe the species himself and wrote a botanical description on page 684 of *The Gardeners' Chronicle* of 13 December 1890. He gave the new species the grand name *Cattleya rex.*

Cattleya rex was one of the last large-flowered cattleyas to be described, but it was not really a stranger to the orchid world. Jean Linden had seen *C. rex* as a young man during his travels through South America in the 1840s. The famous orchid collector Gustav Wallis had also seen it in the 1870s. Several plant collectors over the years had even tried to extract it from its hideaway in the western Peruvian Andes, but the plants never survived the hard trip through the mountains to the Peruvian coast, down the west coast of South America, through the Straits of Magellan, and across the Atlantic Ocean. Shipping the plants in the opposite direction, down the tributaries of the Amazon River on a long, circuitous route to the east coast of Brazil was equally hazardous and unsuccessful. It finally took Eric Bungeroth, one of the re-discoverers of the lost *C. labiata*, to transport a group of *C. rex* plants he had collected through the hot, steamy jungles of Peru, along the wandering little watery fingers of the Amazon, to the port of Manaus, where they ultimately sailed from Brazil to England.

Even Bungeroth, however, failed to enjoy the full fruits of his success, for, although the plants arrived in Liverpool, England, very much alive, many of them froze to death as the shipping boxes languished in the unheated dock warehouse. The loss of the plants broke Bungeroth's spirit because this new *Cattleya* was to have been his crowning achievement. With a heavy heart, he abandoned collecting and never ventured into the jungles again in search of *C. rex.*

The typical *Cattleya rex* has flowers with cream-colored sepals and petals and a dark crimson lip with a gold throat. It normally produces five or six flowers on a bloom spike.

Of the plants that survived the freezing, some were sold to Horticulture Internationale in Brussels. The plant that Linden pictured in *Lindenia* and that O'Brien described in *The Gardeners' Chronicle* was the first of that group to flower. Except for this one 1890 shipment, no one successfully imported *Cattleya rex* for the next 50 years.

It was not until 1940 that a reasonable number of *Cattleya rex* finally reached the outside world. In 1940 Harry Blossfeld, a Brazilian orchid grower, armed with Eric Bungeroth's notes, attacked the Peruvian jungle with an intense passion to succeed, and emerged some months later with almost 800 plants. It took a gold-mining project to open up the area where *C. rex* grew, and the new technology of the airplane to get *C. rex* back alive to Lima, Peru, and then to São Paulo, Brazil.

Harry Blossfeld sold his *Cattleya rex* through advertisements in issues of the *American Orchid Society Bulletin* of the early 1940s. You could buy a package of five plants for $37.50, a handsome sum back then, and most orchid hobbyists on the east coast of the United States acquired a plant or two at that time. If you were a beginning orchid grower, a friend might give you a backpiece or even a plant of *C. rex*, and this species was one of the first cattleyas many young hobbyists learned to grow during the 1940s.

Cattleya rex is one of the easiest large-flowered cattleyas to recognize because it has one of the more uniform color patterns. Most plants of *C. rex* have white sepals and petals with an undertone of yellow that gives them a cream-colored appearance. The lip pattern is unique and is made up of varying shades of crimson in an irregular netting and marbling that often coalesces into an almost solid crimson lip. Jean Linden described the labellum of *C. rex* with great admiration. He said:

> Throughout the whole orchid family there exist but few gems comparable to the labellum of this species, in which the purple combined with gold is modified into a crimson of the hue of Spanish wine, and the marbling and veins are of an exquisite elegance.

Despite the similarity of most flowers, of course, *C. rex* still has the normal color types for which all the large-flowered *Cattleya* species are famous. There is a very rare alba form, a semialba, and a pale pastel delicata. There are forms of *C. rex* with solid crimson lips, and a few clones with splashes of yellow in the sepals and petals.

Not all flowers of *Cattleya rex* are 7 inches across, as were the flowers that O'Brien and Linden saw. Harry Blossfeld seems to have imported a number of plants that were in the 6- to 7-inch range, but most *C. rex* flowers are closer to 4 or 5 inches across—at least in cultivation in the United States and Europe today. These smaller flowers have sometimes been a disappointment to collectors, but the plant makes up for this with the large number of flowers it produces on a flower spike. *Cattleya rex* is one of the most floriferous of the large-flowered *Cattleya* species and will normally produce five or six flowers on a spike. There are records of plants with as many as 9 and 10 flowers.

When *Cattleya rex* was introduced, it added a new dimension to the breeding of yellow cattleyas. Prior to that time, *C. dowiana*, with its yellow sepals and petals, was considered the only yellow species among the large-flowered cattleyas. But the yellow flower color was so recessive that it rarely appeared in hybrids of *C. dowiana*. When the cream-colored *C. rex*, however, was crossed with *C. dowiana*, the resulting hybrid, *C.* Triumphans, had yellow-petaled flowers, so in reality, there are two yellow large-flowered *Cattleya* species, *C. dowiana* and *C. rex*.

Cattleya Triumphans was a sensation when it first flowered, and it received its share of First Class Certificates and Awards of Merit from the Royal Horticultural Society in England. Because of the scarcity of *C. rex* during the late 1800s and early 1900s when breeding with the *Cattleya* species was at its peak, *C.* Triumphans became the primary vehicle for *C. rex* breeding. *Cattleya* Triumphans is a vigorous grower with large flowers borne well on a tall flower spike, and it imparts these excellent qualities to its hybrids. It also imparts the full, or entire, lip to its hybrids, which avoids the lip and flower distortions that sometimes result from cut-lip yellows.

Because *Cattleya rex* was in such short supply for so many years, the full extent of its breeding potential has never been explored. While *C. dowiana* has been used to make hundreds of crosses, only a handful were made with *C. rex*. This is unfortunate, because *C. rex* is superior to *C. dowiana* in several important qualities. The flowers of *C. rex* last more than twice as long as those of *C. dowiana*, and *C. rex* is much less susceptible to rot. *Cattleya rex* produces more flowers on a spike than does *C. dowiana* and its flowers have better form. While we know a great deal about the inheritance of the yellow color in *C. dowiana*, relatively little is known about the inheritance of yellow color from *C. rex*.

Like *Cattleya dowiana* in Costa Rica, *C. rex* grows near the top of huge tropical trees that often tower some 70 feet in the air and have trunks 2 feet or more in diameter. The native Peruvians Harry Blossfeld hired to collect *C. rex* in 1940 refused to climb these gigantic trees, so the trees had to be cut down—which took two men at least half a day

Most varieties of *Cattleya rex* are similar in color, but this rare 'Purple Flare' has an unusual purple stripe along the center vein of the petals.

per tree and produced an ecological disaster. Only a few plants of *C. rex* grow on each tree, and many of these were crushed and destroyed when the trees struck the ground or hit adjacent trees as they fell. It was a costly project to collect *C. rex*, not only in the number of lost plants, but also in the loss of the giant hardwood trees. Even Blossfeld expressed sadness at the destruction of so many splendid trees. Time, unfortunately, has only made the ecological problems worse, as present-day coffee, tea, and corn growers use the modern slash-and-burn technique to clear land, and the giant trees themselves have become a cash crop. For *C. rex*, however, survival may be better than ever as Peruvian orchid lovers rescue large numbers of plants that would otherwise be destroyed by the fires and escort them to a safe haven in orchid nurseries. As sibling crosses are produced from these plants, we will hopefully see a lot more of *C. rex* in the future.

Among the large-flowered cattleyas, *Cattleya rex* has been much glamorized, and Linden's portrait of the first *C. rex* is one of the most striking pictures in *Lindenia*. Even today, Angela Mirro's great watercolor of *C. rex* is so outspoken in its praise of *C. rex* that it spent the entire spring of 2000 on display at the Smithsonian Institution in Washington, D.C. (see photo on page 198).

Cattleya rex is one of the golden treasures of the Incas that neither the Spanish conquistadors nor the voracious Victorian plant hunters successfully conquered. Like the Incas themselves, who survived in the protection of their mighty mountains, *C. rex* still reins supreme from its towering trees in its isolated haunts in the Peruvian jungle, and now, aided by its many friends, it may finally be able to pass on its full legacy to the orchid world.

A good example of a fine *Cattleya rex* is this unusually large and bold variety 'Grande'.

Culture

Like most of the large-flowered *Cattleya* species, *C. rex* is relatively easy to grow. It will send out a new lead in late winter or early spring in the United States and complete the growth from late May to late June. Buds will appear in the sheath before the growth is completed, and the plant should be in flower by mid-July to early August. After flowering, *C. rex* will rest until it begins growing again in late winter. Like *C. dowiana*, *C. rex* benefits from lots of sun during the winter months, and the more sun it receives, the more flowers it will produce. It should receive a night temperature of 60°F and a day temperature of 80° to 85°F.

Cattleya rex will usually send out a new flush of roots about the time it begins new growth, and the best time to repot it is when this flush of roots appears. Under greenhouse conditions, *C. rex* will usually produce a 10- or 12 inch-tall pseudobulb, and five or six flowers on a flower spike. Unlike *C. dowiana*, which often lasts only a week or so in flower, *C. rex* flowers will normally last three weeks or more.

Some people have described *Cattleya rex* as difficult to establish, but we have not found this to be true. When we acquire *C. rex* plants, even imported plants, we wash off all the old medium and immediately pot them in sphagnum moss in the smallest pots possible. We do not allow any room for the plant to make a new growth since the purpose here is to encourage the plants to root, not grow. Once a plants is well-rooted in the small pot, the whole root-ball is eased out and moved into the next larger pot, one that will allow room for one new growth. At this point, you can add your standard medium in front of the sphagnum root-ball, and the plant should grow normally. When using sphagnum, it is important not to pack it tightly so there is a good air exchange to stimulate root growth. You should also avoid using more than a 4-inch pot so the sphagnum will not stay too wet too long. If you must go to a 5-inch pot because of the size of the plant, you will have to take care in watering the sphagnum so it will not stay too wet. Clay pots are preferred over plastic pots because they allow a better air exchange with the medium.

Cattleya jenmanii Rolfe
Kew Bulletin 20:85. 1906

Rumors about a new large-flowered *Cattleya* species that lurked in the dense jungles around the Gran Sabana in the southeastern corner of Venezuela were beginning to find their way into orchid circles in Venezuela in the mid-1960s. How a new species could appear at this late date was beyond understanding. Venezuela had been the hunting ground for cattleya collectors for more than 120 years, beginning with the discovery of *C. mossiae* in 1836, and virtually no area of Venezuela had been left untouched. Most orchidists dismissed the idea as "ridiculous."

Then, in 1968 and 1969, a few plants were brought from the jungle that were not quite like the *Cattleya* species with which everyone was familiar. They looked like a poor variety of *C. labiata*, but the flowers had a sweet scent reminiscent of *C. gaskelliana*. A couple of plants found their way to the famous Venezuelan orchidist G. C. K. Dunsterville, who wrote an article about them in the British publication *The Orchid Review* in

October 1969. The article was titled "Orchid Puzzlements" and it created an aura of intrigue and excitement around a shadowy purple image from the Venezuela interior. Dunsterville had no name for the new *Cattleya* and referred to it only as "*Cattleya guayana*"—Guayana being the broad area of Venezuela where the plants were believed to exist.

In December 1971, after two years' investigation, Dunsterville wrote a more comprehensive article for the United States publication *The Orchid Digest*, which featured a color photograph and botanical drawings of the new *Cattleya* species. Dunsterville had also asked Leslie Garay at the Orchid Herbarium of Oakes Ames at Harvard if the species had ever been described before. Garay made the remarkable discovery that the species had indeed been found back in 1906 and described at that time by Robert Allen Rolfe, editor of *The Orchid Review*, who named it *C. jenmanii*. It even sported a proper botanical description in Latin, a rare thing for a large-flowered *Cattleya* species.

Rolfe had described the species in *Kew Bulletin* 20 and *The Orchid Review* of July 1906. He named the species in honor of "the late Mr. G. S. Jenman, the government botanist in Georgetown, British Guiana," who had sent plants to a Miss Sinnock of Downford, Hailsham, Sussex, England. It was Sinnock's plants and flowers that Rolfe used for his description. Unfortunately, Rolfe must not have thought too much of the new species because he did not bother to mention it in 1907 as one of the important plant events in 1906, and nothing much was heard of *Cattleya jenmanii* after that.

The first published pictures of *Cattleya jenmanii* would not inspire many *Cattleya* lovers to try to acquire a plant. Like the earliest plants of *C. labiata*, they were poorly

The typical *Cattleya jenmanii* has flowers with medium lavender sepals and petals and a dark purple lip with a pale lavender edge. The flowers are about 5 to 5$^1/_2$ inches across and usually four or five on a bloom stem.

grown, inferior clones. They had virtually nothing to recommend them to the horticulturist over any of the established large-flowered *Cattleya* species. Eventually, however, good clones were found that were quite beautiful and distinctive, and these have helped define the character of the species as we know it today.

Cattleya jenmanii is basically a dwarf-pseudobulb member of the large-flowered cattleyas, and this compact habit, along with the strong, wonderful fragrance and free-flowering nature, are the most distinguishing features of the species. *Cattleya jenmanii* has the same general color patterns in its lavender flowers as *C. labiata*, and some clones can easily be mistaken for *C. labiata*. There are also clones that look similar to *C. gaskelliana*. *Cattleya jenmanii*, however, is easily distinguishable from *C. labiata* by its single sheath, because *C. labiata* normally has a double sheath. *Cattleya jenmanii* also usually has smaller flowers than *C. labiata*, and it flowers at the end of the *C. labiata* season. While *C. jenmanii* has a wonderful fragrance, similar to that of *C. gaskelliana*, it can be separated from *C. gaskelliana* by its flowering habit. Under greenhouse conditions in the United States, *C. gaskelliana* flowers as the pseudobulb is still maturing, while *C. jenmanii* completes its new growth and, like *C. labiata*, rests for a few months before sending up flowers. *Cattleya gaskelliana* also flowers in June in the United States, while *C. jenmanii* normally blooms in the late autumn.

Some authors have dismissed the single-sheath versus double-sheath difference between *Cattleya jenmanii* and *C. labiata* because *C. labiata* will occasionally produce a single sheath (or no sheath at all), and *C. jenmanii*, on rare occasion, has been known to produce a double sheath. The idea that a double sheath is not a basic characteristic of *C. labiata*, however, is absurd, and has tended to confuse a clear difference between *C. jenmanii* and *C. labiata*. More than 99 percent of all *C. labiata* plants have double sheaths, and the few that have a single sheath or no sheath are natural anomalies. A single-sheathed *C. labiata* is no different from a *C. labiata* with two lips; these phenomena do occur due to culture or mutation, but they are certainly not basic characteristics of the species. There is no doubt today that *C. jenmanii* is a separate and distinct species, giving Venezuela six proud large-flowered *Cattleya* species—*C. mossiae*, *C. gaskelliana*, *C. lueddemanniana*, *C. lawrenceana*, *C. percivaliana*, and *C. jenmanii*.

In its native Venezuela, *Cattleya jenmanii* grows between 1300 and 3600 feet above sea level in relatively dense forests. The temperature in these areas varies from about 60° to 85°F. *Cattleya jenmanii* grows both as an epiphyte on tree branches and as a lithophyte on rock outcroppings. Two biotypes come from somewhat separated areas. One type has light- to medium-lavender flowers with relatively good shape and large size. The other type produces smaller, more poorly shaped flowers, but with much richer color. In nature, *C. jenmanii* is reported to flower twice a year, once from February to April and again from September through October. In cultivation in the United States, however, it is normally only an autumn bloomer.

Cattleya jenmanii has all the normal color forms of the large-flowered *Cattleya* species. It has some beautiful alba varieties, attractive semialba clones, good lavender clones, and even beautiful coeruleas.

One of the endearing qualities of *Cattleya jenmanii* is its free-flowering nature. It normally produces five flowers on a flower stem, and even on a weak or poorly established plant, it will often struggle and produce three flowers regardless of the damaging effect on the plant. *Cattleya jenmanii* is known to produce as many as seven flowers on a flower spike.

Because it was not discovered until 1906, *Cattleya jenmanii* is not mentioned or pictured in any of the famous old orchid books like *Reichenbachia, Lindenia,* or *The Orchid-Grower's Manual.* It was mentioned in the 1927 edition of *Sanders' Orchid Guide* as a "rare and handsome species of the labiata section." Sander's is the only company that made an effort to use *C. jenmanii* in hybridizing, and in 1954 the firm flowered a hybrid between *C. jenmanii* and *C. percivaliana,* which was the first cross ever registered for this species. Sander's thought so much of the cross, it named it *C.* David Sander. Since then, no other *C. jenmanii* crosses have been registered despite the more than 30 years that have passed since the species's rediscovery in 1969. Before the appearance of *C. jenmanii,* the Gran Sabana of Venezuela was known as the home of *C. lawrenceana,* so it was no surprise when a natural hybrid between *C. jenmanii* and *C. lawrenceana, C. gransabanensis,* turned up in the area.

It seems strange that it took more than six decades to rediscover *Cattleya jenmanii* after it was described in 1906. It is as though King Arthur's famous magician, Merlin, had waved his magic wand and cast a spell over the species that put it to sleep for the next 60 years. In its magic sleep, *C. jenmanii* missed the Golden Age of the *Cattleya* species with its plundering Victorian plant hunters, and it escaped the attention of the cut-flower merchants, who ravaged the jungles during the 1930s and 1940s to fill huge commercial greenhouses, only to see the plants discarded by the tens of thousands in the

Like the other large-flowered *Cattleya* species, *C. jenmanii* has both alba and semialba varieties. A typical semialba is shown here.

1960s. When the spell was broken, *C. jenmanii* awakened to an age of environmental conservation—lucky orchid. But, even *C. jenmanii* is not immune to native poachers, who sell the plants to tourists who cannot take them out of the country legally, so Venezuelan growers have had to rescue plants and produce sibling crosses to guarantee the species's survival.

Let us hope that, like Merlin, *Cattleya jenmanii* will grow younger instead of aging as the years go by, and it will blossom everywhere orchids are grown into one of the jewels of the large-flowered *Cattleya* species. It is certainly a worthy member of the new age of the *Cattleya* species. *Cattleya jenmanii* has almost no history as a parent in hybridizing yet many attractive qualities, from its small plant size and relatively large flowers to its wonderful fragrance. It is indeed a delightful addition to our modern gallery of favorite *Cattleya* species—late in arriving, but worth the wait.

Culture

Cattleya jenmanii is a traditional *Cattleya* species where culture is concerned. It requires the normal temperature range of 60°F at night and 80° to 85°F during the day. It benefits from lots of sun and moving air and needs only a modest dry period during the cold winter months in temperate areas like the United States. It is not particularly subject to rot, but water should not be left on the leaves and new growths at night or on cloudy days. Repot *C. jenmanii* only when new roots begin to appear on the newest pseudobulb. Any of the standard mediums, such as bark mixes used for cattleyas, are suitable. In the United States, *C. jenmanii* will normally complete its new growths in early summer and flower in late autumn just after the last of the *C. labiata* have bloomed.

FIVE

The Orphanage—
The Brazilian Laelia/Cattleyas

THE LARGE-FLOWERED group of *Cattleya* species would not be complete without the six large-flowered Brazilian species that have been botanically classified for so many years as laelias. These species have all the physical characteristics of the large-flowered cattleyas both in their vegetative and floral parts and have proved to be genetically more compatible with the large-flowered *Cattleya* species in hybridizing than even the cut-lip or bifoliate group of *Cattleya* species where deformed flowers can occur in the hybrids.

Since it was shown quite clearly in the June 2002 *Lindleyana* (pp. 96–114) that these Brazilian species do not belong with the Mexican laelias for whom the genus *Laelia* was named, the Brazilian species now live in a botanical orphanage waiting for a new name and a foster home. These large-flowered Brazilian species have eight pollinia instead of the usual four, but this is a trivial difference when all the similarities with the large-flowered cattleyas are considered, and there is certainly no justification for establishing a new and separate genus for them. Three of the species were originally described as cattleyas, and we feel they all belong in the genus *Cattleya* and have treated them that way in this book.

Table 4. Large-flowered Brazilian species that resemble the large-flowered *Cattleya* species.

SPECIES	YEAR	PUBLICATION WHERE FIRST DESCRIBED
C. crispa	1831	Lindley, *Genera and Species of Orchidaceous Plants*, p. 116
C. perrinii	1838	Lindley, Edwards's *Botanical Register* 24, plate 2
C. lobata	1848	Lindley, *Gardeners' Chronicle* 8: 403
C. grandis	1850	(Lindley & Paxton) A. A. Chadwick, new combination. Based on *Laelia grandis* Lindley & Paxton, *Paxton's Flower Garden* 1: 60
C. purpurata	1854	Beer, *Praktische Studien an der Familie der Orchideen*, p. 213
C. tenebrosa	1891	(Rolfe) A. A. Chadwick, new combination. Based on *Laelia grandis* Lindley & Paxton var. *tenebrosa* Rolfe, *Gardeners' Chronicle*, 3d series, 10: 126

Cattleya crispa Lindley
Genera and Species of Orchidaceous Plants, p. 116. 1831

In 1826 the Horticultural Society of London received an orchid plant from Sir Henry Chamberlayne of Rio de Janeiro, Brazil. The Society put the plant in its stove house at Chiswick Garden where the plant flowered the following year. The plant produced a flower spike with five unusual flowers that had a striking crisping along the edges of the petals and lip that was different from anything seen before. The botanist John Lindley studied the plant and flowers and decided it belonged in his new genus *Cattleya* and called it "*Cattleya crispa*, the curled-petaled cattleya."

While *Cattleya crispa* did not have flowers as large and well formed as *C. labiata*, the flowers were much larger than those of the other *Cattleya* species known at the time and the plant had more flowers on an inflorescence than any *Cattleya* known. The new *C. crispa* was soon found to be the easiest *Cattleya* to grow and the most free-flowering, producing from 5 to 10 flowers on a spike in midsummer in Europe.

The popularity of the new species grew as more plants found their way to Europe, and in 1831 Lindley summarized the genus *Cattleya* in his *Genera and Species of Orchidaceous Plants*; the first species listed on page 116 was *C. crispa*. In 1836 Joseph Paxton included *C. crispa* in his *Magazine of Botany* (5: 5), and in 1842 Curtis's *Botanical Magazine* published a detailed botanical description (plate 3910), calling it the "crisp-flowered cattleya," along with a picture of a stunning five-flowered spike of flowers. The *Botanical Magazine* said that *C. crispa* "may be among the most beautiful of a highly beautiful genus."

One of the most beautiful varieties of *Cattleya crispa* is 'Candidissima'.

Cattleya crispa was one of the most showy and popular of the large-flowered *Cattleya* species of the mid-1800s, so, when botanist Heinrich Gustav Reichenbach lifted it out of the genus *Cattleya* in 1853 and put it in Lindley's new genus *Laelia*, no one paid any attention to the change. The plant continued along happily in orchid circles as *Cattleya crispa*. As late as 1877, 24 years after Reichenbach made the change to *Laelia*, B. S. Williams in the 5th edition of his ever-present *The Orchid-Grower's Manual* listed the plant as *C. crispa* so all the growers would know what plant he was talking about. Warner and Williams were much less considerate in the second volume of their 11-volume masterpiece, *The Orchid Album*, published in 1883 when they described a fine variety of *C. crispa* in plate 81. They said quite bluntly that they did not accept the change to *Laelia*: "We follow the original description of the species of the late Dr. Lindley, by retaining it in *Cattleya*." It is interesting to note that although he established the genus *Laelia*, Lindley never described *C. crispa* as a *Laelia* in any of his works even though it had eight pollinia. Williams still showed *crispa* under *Cattleya* in the 7th and last edition of *The Orchid-Grower's Manual* published in 1894 and the whole horticultural world knew it only by that name.

The storm clouds began to gather around *Cattleya crispa*, however, when Veitch published the first volume of his *Manual of Orchidaceous Plants* in 1887. Veitch unfortunately ignored his own common sense and his vast experience growing the *Cattleya* species and accepted the botanical outline set out by George Bentham and Joseph D. Hooker in their *Genera Plantarum* for the purpose of his book. Veitch made no reference to *crispa* under the genus *Cattleya* and included it only under the genus *Laelia*. Veitch's *Manual* was considered by many to be the most authoritative work on orchids in the 1890s and it doomed *C. crispa* to the genus *Laelia* over the dead bodies of a lot of knowledgeable horticulturists. The ironic part of this story is that Veitch himself did not believe *crispa* belonged in the genus *Laelia*. He said in his *Manual* that

> the two genera (*Cattleya* and *Laelia*) pass into each other by gradations so small as to render a separating character difficult, if not impossible to be found. . . . and it is, therefore, much to be regretted that the distinguished authors of the *Genera Plantarum* should have thought fit to still kept them distinct.

Veitch considered *crispa* a *Cattleya* to his dying day.

Cattleya crispa is not as popular in the United States now as it was in the early days of orchids in Europe and it is difficult to find a plant in many orchid collections today. Many varieties have very narrow petals that sometimes reflex, or fold backward, which is not considered fashionable in orchid circles. Because it produces such a grand display of flowers, however, this species is still a lovely orchid and very rewarding to own.

The species grows naturally in the Brazilian state of Rio de Janeiro where it is found growing on the branches of large trees and sometimes rock outcroppings where natural forest still exists. It likes considerable sun, but its leaves and pseudobulbs do not normally show any purple tinting. Unlike *Cattleya lobata*, *C. crispa* is not found on vertical rock faces. It has relatively few color forms compared with most of the other large-flowered *Cattleya* species, and most varieties of *C. crispa* have white to light lavender-pink sepals and petals with a darker lip. The lip color can be very dark at times, and the lip is sometimes curled and pointed at the tip on poor varieties. The flowers average about 6 inches across and have a particularly nice fragrance.

Cattleya crispa was one of the favorite orchids of the first hybridizer of cattleyas, John Dominy. Despite the uncertainty of his records, Dominy is believed to have crossed *C. crispa* with several cattleyas, including the large-flowered species *C. dowiana* and *C. mossiae.* A cross between *C. crispa* and *C. warscewiczii* called *Laeliocattleya* Nysa, which was registered by Veitch in 1891, produced a variety 'Superba' that was considered by Veitch (1906, p. 205) to be "one of the finest products of orchid hybridizing."

As late as 1923, the second president of the American Orchid Society, Fitz Eugene Dixon, thought so much of his cross between *Cattleya lueddemanniana* and *C. crispa* that he named it for his good friend and orchid authority, John E. Lager. As round flower shape became an overriding standard for fine *Cattleya* hybrids, however, *Cattleya crispa* ceased to be an important parent for breeding and it has seldom been used to make cattleya alliance hybrids since the 1950s.

Cattleya crispa today is like a sleeping giant—a giant that dominated the early days of orchid growing when cattleyas were new to European horticulture and people tended to accept nature's standards more than their own. In the early 1800s, *C. crispa* was pictured and written about more than the great large-flowered *C. mossiae*, because it was so easy to grow and produced such a beautiful head of flowers. It was eclipsed in the mid-1900s by the craze for big, round *Cattleya* hybrids, and the species has largely disappeared from cultivation in most collections. It now waits for a new generation of

Most plants of *Cattleya crispa* have white or pale lavender-pink sepals and petals, but the lip can be a variety of colors, including a pink 'Carnea.'

orchid growers who have a broader view of beauty than just round flowers to waken it from its slumber.

Culture

Most of the large-flowered *Cattleya* species are easy to grow, but *C. crispa* is undoubtedly the easiest. It grows well in clay pots in any standard cattleya mix. It begins a new growth in late summer in the United States and completes the growth by late autumn or early winter. If conditions are warm and sunny, it will often make a second growth and after a short rest, flower in late spring. *Cattleya crispa* likes an abundance of moving air and requires lots of sun if you want the best flower production; it should produce between 5 and 10 flowers on a spike. *Cattleya crispa* is quite resistant to rot and we have never had any trouble with this species from fungus or bacterial diseases. The flowers will normally last three weeks or more, and the plant makes an attractive exhibition piece because of its showy display.

Cattleya perrinii Lindley
Edwards's *Botanical Register* 24, plate 2. 1838

Cattleya perrinii was apparently grown in Europe for several years before John Lindley described it as a new species of *Cattleya* in 1838 in the *Botanical Register* (plate 2). It must have been available in reasonable numbers because all the important orchid collections of the 1830s had plants, and several people sent Lindley plants and flowers for him to use in writing a botanical description—including botanist James Bateman. Lindley named the species for Mr. Perrin, the gardener to Richard Harrison who had sent him the first specimens. *Cattleya perrinii* was a typical large-flowered *Cattleya* from Brazil with nice medium-lavender blooms about 6 inches across and tall *Cattleya*-like pseudobulbs, and it became one of the most popular cattleyas of the late 1830s.

Everything went well for the new *Cattleya* species until 1842 when Lindley summarized the 10 known species of his genus *Laelia* in the *Botanical Register*. To everyone's surprise, Lindley added one new species, *L. perrinii* to the list. All the laelias described previously had come from Mexico and Guatemala, but because it had eight pollinia, the Brazilian *Cattleya perrinii* was included by Lindley as *L. perrinii*. It was the first time a Brazilian species had been put in the genus *Laelia* and it created a problem. *Cattleya perrinii* was not like the other laelias. It had very different plant characteristics and resembled the *Cattleya* species much more than it did the Mexican laelias. Lindley's eight-pollinia concept was so simple, however, and so easy for a botanist to use when describing a new species, that it became the botanical standard for laelias, and *Cattleya perrinii* remained *Laelia perrinii* for the rest of the 19th century and all of the 20th century. *Cattleya perrinii* did not leave the genus *Laelia* until modern science showed it simply did not belong there.

Cattleya perrinii is native to the Brazilian states of Rio de Janeiro and Espírito Santo where it can be found growing in somewhat shaded areas in the mountain forests. It grows at an altitude of 1200 to 3000 feet above sea level. There are a number of color forms that are typical of the large-flowered *Cattleya* species, including lavenders, albas, semialbas, and coeruleas. *Cattleya perrinii* is an autumn bloomer in the United States and Europe and was considered a valuable species because of its flowering season until *C. labiata* was re-discovered in 1889. Once *C. labiata* returned with its longer-lasting flowers that were much larger and better shaped, *C. perrinii*'s importance as an autumn-bloomer diminished and the plant largely disappeared from *Cattleya* collections.

Because it was a common plant in cultivation in Europe in the 1850s and 1860s, *Cattleya perrinii* was one of the parents used by John Dominy to make some of the first *Cattleya* hybrids. In March 1867, Dominy's cross between *C. perrinii* and *C. crispa*, *Laeliocattleya* Pilcheriana, flowered for the first time, and Dominy's successor, John Seden, made a number of crosses between *C. perrinii* and large-flowered cattleyas like *C. gaskelliana*, *C. dowiana*, and *C. labiata* during the late 1880s. *Cattleya perrinii*'s very narrow petaled flowers and their short longevity of only a week or two, however, caused hybrid-

Lithograph of *Cattleya perrinii* from *The Orchid Album*

izers to lose interest in the species after that, and we find very little done with *C. perrinii* in hybridizing during the 20th century.

Cattleya perrinii is not widely grown by orchid collectors in the United States today, although a few commercial companies still offer plants for sale now and then.

Culture

Cattleya perrinii requires similar growing conditions to most of the mountain-inhabiting large-flowered *Cattleya* species. It needs a good amount of sun, lots of moving air, and a night temperature of 60°F. *Cattleya perrinii* needs regular heavy watering while it is actively growing, and after flowering, water should be reduced to just enough to keep the pseudobulbs from shriveling too much. Watering must always be done with care during the cold winter months in northern climates to avoid rotting the roots.

Cattleya lobata Lindley
Gardeners' Chronicle 8:403. 1848

When he saw the first plant of *Cattleya lobata* in 1847 in the commercial greenhouses of the British orchid firm of Loddiges, botanist John Lindley thought it was probably a variety of *C. labiata*. It had the same general size and look as *C. labiata* and the plant was very similar. The lip, however, had a somewhat different color pattern, and Lindley finally decided, after studying it for a second season, that it should be described as a new species. He wrote a botanical description of the plant in *The Gardeners' Chronicle* of 1848 (8: 403) and a black-and-white woodcut of the flower accompanied the description. Lindley referred to the new species as "the lobed cattleya" alluding to the "excessive lobing of the petals and lip," and he looked at *C. lobata* much as he looked at *C. mossiae*—as a distinct type of *C. labiata*.

Lindley had taken a lot of criticism from horticulturists after he condemned William Jackson Hooker's decision to make *mossiae* a *Cattleya* species in 1836, so he was reluctant to call the new species "*Cattleya labiata* var. *lobata*" as he had done with *C. mossiae*. There was no doubt in his mind, however, that the new species was a *Cattleya*.

Although Lindley himself had named *Cattleya labiata* in 1821, it apparently never occurred to him how confusingly similar the names *C. labiata* and *C. lobata* were. The two species had already been confused earlier when the British naturalist George Gardner in 1836 found *C. lobata* clinging to the rugged cliffs of the Organ Mountains in the Brazilian state of Rio de Janeiro. Gardner had announced to the world he discovered the lost *C. labiata*—a confusion that led to a wild stampede of orchid hunters into the state of Rio de Janeiro to find it. Despite John Lindley's attempts during the 1850s to make the small, trivial difference between four and eight pollinia into a large-enough difference to justify establishing his new genus *Laelia*, the orchid world called *lobata* a *Cattleya* for the next 50 years. The 7th edition of *The Orchid-Grower's Manual* describes only *C. lobata* as late as 1894. There is no *Laelia lobata* anywhere to be found. What happened next, however, was nothing short of bizarre.

James Veitch was one of the most respected horticulturists and orchid experts of the late 1800s. He was particularly knowledgeable on the genera *Cattleya* and *Laelia* because these were the most popular orchids of the day, and his commercial firm, Veitch and Sons, grew thousands of these plants for sale to collectors. Veitch was a strong advocate for returning the laelias to the genus *Cattleya* because, like most horticulturists of his time, he saw no meaningful difference in the plant's structural or growth characteristics. The Mexican laelias might have shorter and more rounded pseudobulbs and longer flower stems, but the Brazilian large-flowered laelias were so similar to the large-flowered *Cattleya* species that they were botanically indistinguishable. Because he was considered such an authority on orchids, however, Veitch felt he had to organize his book, A *Manual of Orchidaceous Plants*, on the accepted botanical classifications of the time even though in the case of the laelias, he did not agree with it. Veitch followed the botanical outline of Bentham and Hooker in their *Genera Plantarum* and inadvertently stumbled into being the first person to transfer *Cattleya lobata* to the genus *Laelia*. It is ironic that Veitch, the one man more than any other who felt *lobata* should be a *Cattleya*, is given credit today for the first botanical description of it as a *Laelia*.

The story does not end here, however. As the year 1999 rolled into the millennium 2000, the new field of DNA analysis showed conclusively that the Brazilian laelias like *lobata* are botanically different from the Mexican laelias for which the genus was named (*Lindleyana* 15 (2): 96–114). While this was an old idea revisited, it suddenly had the blessing of modern science and it opened a Pandora's box for the Brazilian laelias. *Lobata* cannot continue to be called *Laelia lobata* botanically. It needs a different name. The best name, of course, is *Cattleya lobata*, the name it was originally given by John Lindley and a name that puts it in the genus where it has always belonged.

The typical *Cattleya lobata* has four or five flowers about 6 inches across, an attractive form, and a medium lavender color.

Cattleya lobata is a lovely orchid, yet it has always had a difficult time gaining the recognition it deserves. Because it is a sun-loving plant, even to the extreme, it was dubbed "the *Cattleya* that never flowers" by growers in the overcast climate of northern Europe where clouds, rain, and umbrellas are the order of the day. Given the right culture and plenty of sun, it is a free-flowering plant. Its relatively short pseudobulbs somewhat resemble its fellow Brazilian cattleya and neighbor *C. warneri*, although it is considered more closely allied to *C. crispa*.

Like most of the large-flowered *Cattleya* species, *C. lobata* has a variety of color forms. There are beautiful shades of lavender, from pale albescens to dark purple. There are semialbas and enchanting true albas and everything in between. *Cattleya lobata* has a pleasant fragrance and is quite floriferous. It will normally produce four or five flowers on a spike like *C. warneri* and *C. labiata*.

Native to a limited area of Brazil from the vicinity of Rio de Janeiro southward to the state of São Paulo, *Cattleya lobata* is often found growing on rocks facing the ocean and fully exposed to the sun. Because of the difficulty of collecting it, the species has never been in abundant supply on the commercial market, and as a result, it was not attractive to the major orchid companies of Europe during the 1800s. The most famous of all orchid books, *Lindenia* and *Reichenbachia*, produced by Linden and Sander respectively, have no paintings of it under either the name *Cattleya lobata* or *Laelia lobata*. *The Orchid-Grower's Manual* tells us that it was seldom seen at horticultural shows, but blames this on its shy blooming. The scarcity of the plant, however, was probably also important.

Like all the large-flowered *Cattleya* species, *C. lobata* has many color forms, including this lovely coerulea variety.

Cattleya lobata has occasionally appeared in the literature under the name *Laelia boothiana* because the botanist H. G. Reichenbach in 1853 actually described it as a *Laelia* before anyone else. Since Lindley described it first in 1848 as *Cattleya lobata*, the species name *lobata* has priority over the species name *boothiana*, so botanically *Laelia boothiana* has never been a correct name for this orchid.

Among the lovely clones of *Cattleya lobata* are several which have received awards from the American Orchid Society. Perhaps the most beautiful is a pale lavender-pink concolor named 'Jeni' AM/AOS. An alba, 'Horich', also received an HCC, as did a rose-lavender, 'Future Look'.

Cattleya lobata has not been used extensively in hybridizing, although it would seem to be a suitable parent for breeding with its lovely coloring, floriferousness, and relatively small plant. In the late 1800s and early 1900s, it was crossed with many of the large-flowered *Cattleya* species, including *C. labiata*, *C. trianaei*, *C. mendelii*, *C. mossiae*, and *C. dowiana*. It was also crossed with the Brazilian *C. crispa*, *C. tenebrosa*, and *C. purpurata*. The resulting hybrids, however, were not as attractive as other *Cattleya* and *Laelia* crosses and little breeding was done after that.

In the wild *Cattleya lobata* hybridizes with *C. crispa* to produce the natural hybrid *C. wyattiana* (syn. *Laeliocattleya wyattiana*) and with *C. intermedia* to produce *C. Amanda* (syn. *Laeliocattleya* Amanda).

Like a production of smoke and mirrors in a magic show, *Cattleya lobata* first appeared as *C. labiata*; then it appeared as *C. lobata*. Then it became *Laelia lobata*, ushered there by a man who never thought it should be a *Laelia*. It is a perfect case of now-you-see-it-now-you-don't. This lovely, misunderstood flower, ignored by many grow-

One of the most beautifully colored varieties of *Cattleya lobata* is the pale lavender-pink 'Jeni' AM/AOS.

ers because of its reputation as a shy bloomer, has shown a tenacity to survive in its native habitat under some of the most rugged natural conditions, yet after a century and a half it still struggles to retain its place in the artificial world of botanical nomenclature. We have now welcomed it back to the place John Lindley originally prepared for it—a place with the large-flowered *Cattleya* species.

Culture

Cattleya lobata has the reputation of being difficult to bloom, but we have not found this to be true. It likes a good amount of sun and should be placed in the sunniest location in the greenhouse. It should not receive so much sun, however, that its leaves turn excessively yellow. The normal light green leaf color recommended for all *Cattleya* species is fine, along with normal cattleya temperatures of 58°F at night and 85°F during the day.

Some people suggest growing *Cattleya lobata* on cork slabs to give it more aeration, but it does well for us in clay pots. We do not recommend growing any of the large-flowered *Cattleya* species on slabs because their roots dry out too fast and the pseudobulbs invariably shrivel even when the plants are actively growing. This tends to retard growth, unless you soak the slabs every day.

Some growers suggest allowing *Cattleya lobata* to grow over the edge of the pot because they have observed the plant produces its best growths then. The same thing can be accomplished by putting the plant in a larger pot so the second and third years' growth will be able to root in the pot instead of in the open air. Most plants resent being cut up and repotted and will produce a growth and flowers the year after they are repotted that are not as good as they will be in the next two or three years. Newly repotted plants need a little tender loving care after repotting. Pot the plants only when they begin sending out new roots from the front pseudobulb. Always use clay pots because clay pots breathe while plastic pots do not. Spray the plants frequently, but water them only lightly. Give them just enough water to encourage the new roots to go down into the potting medium. Increase the water slowly until the roots fill the pot. Overwatering a newly repotted plant is a sure way to produce a water-logged medium that will rot the new roots.

Cattleya lobata is a tough plant. It is quite resistant to rotting and will take a lot of cultural abuse, but if you take care of it, it will reward you with a reliable production of four or five lovely flowers every year. It normally flowers in April and May in the United States and will stay in bloom about a month.

Cattleya grandis (Lindley & Paxton) A. A. Chadwick, new combination
based on *Laelia grandis* Lindley & Paxton, *Paxton's Flower Garden* 1:60. 1850

Cattleya grandis has been one of the rarest of the large-flowered *Cattleya* species in cultivation ever since it first flowered in the collection of Mr. Morel in Paris in 1850. The 17 December 1864 issue of *The Gardeners' Chronicle* noted that the species had virtually disappeared from orchid collections over the previous 10 years, and the *Chronicle* was relieved to learn that the British orchid firm Hugh Low and Company had received an importation of new plants and had re-introduced it. By 1880, however, the species had disappeared again, and Warner and Williams in their book *The Orchid Album* observed that it was a plant that "is little known, and which is extremely rare." The species continued to be uncommon in orchid collections throughout the 20th century despite its free-flowering nature and attractive flowers, and it is still hard to find in modern-day collections.

Flowers of the typical *Cattleya grandis* have yellow sepals and petals with a touch of light bronze in them. They are narrow and tend to curl or twist and sometimes reflex. The lip is very distinctive, with magenta-colored veins radiating out of the otherwise creamy white trumpet. The flowers have an entire lip structure and present a lovely, delicate appearance with a thin substance that characterizes the best look-but-do-not-touch feeling of a fine large-flowered *Cattleya* species. *Cattleya grandis* produces four or five 5-inch flowers on a flower spike and blooms in late spring in the United States. Unlike most of the large-flowered *Cattleya* species, *C. grandis* flowers are not noticeably fragrant.

Although botanist John Lindley originally described the species as *Laelia grandis* in *Paxton's Flower Garden* in 1850 (1:60), Joseph Dalton Hooker in 1866 in Curtis's *Botanical Magazine* felt it was "indistinguishable from *Cattleya*" and even questioned the significance of the eight-pollinia difference Lindley had used to separate it from the genus *Cattleya*. Like so many orchid experts, however, after presenting good reasons for putting *grandis* back in the genus *Cattleya*, Hooker called it *Laelia grandis* and went on to other things.

The typical *Cattleya grandis* has yellow sepals and petals suffused with light bronze. The petals are narrow and tend to reflex. The lip is an unusual creamy white color with magenta veins radiating from the throat.

Because of its scarcity and the fact that many orchid growers had never seen the plant, *Cattleya grandis* was often confused with other Brazilian species during the 1800s, particularly the yellow-flowered *Laelia xanthina* which had similar looking plants but very different flowers. It was even confused with *C. purpurata* during the 1850s.

Cattleya grandis is native to the state of Bahia in southern Brazil and is considered to be a warm-growing member of the large-flowered Brazilian species. It grows in the upper branches of tall trees where it is exposed to considerable sunlight. It is considered a rare plant even in its native country. The species has relatively few color variations and the ones that do exist are limited to differences in the intensity of color in the sepals and petals and the amount of purple veining in the lip.

In the wild *Cattleya grandis* hybridizes with *C. warneri* to produce *Laeliocattleya albanensis*, and with *C. amethystoglossa* to produce *Lc.* Pittiana, both of which have been artificially produced commercially. *Cattleya grandis* was crossed with a number of the other large-flowered *Cattleya* species in the early days of breeding, but because its petals tend to reflex like *C. crispa*, it has not been too popular a parent since then. The dominance of its yellow color is largely unknown.

Culture

Cattleya grandis is in the group of cattleyas that require higher-than-normal night temperatures. For the plant to grow well, the night temperature should be at least 65°F, and it will even do well at 70°F at night. Day temperatures should be 80° to 85°F. Although it is considered a high-light plant, *C. grandis* grows well for us at normal light levels for species like *C. warneri*. It should receive lots of moving air like other *Cattleya* species. *Cattleya grandis* begins growing in the United States in late summer and will complete its growth during the late fall and, after a rest period, flower in the spring. It is normally a vigorous grower and produces four or five flowers on a flower spike that will last three or four weeks.

Cattleya purpurata Beer
Praktische Studien an der Familie der Orchideen, p. 213. 1854

Cattleya purpurata is without doubt one of the finest of all cultivated orchids. In addition to its large, showy flowers, it has one of the widest range of color forms and more named varieties than any other *Cattleya* species. This says a lot when you realize that named varieties of *C. mossiae* and *C. trianaei* number in the many hundreds.

The large flowers of *Cattleya purpurata* are 6 to 8 inches across, and usually four or five of them are on a flower spike. The lavender color in the lip can be a brilliant royal purple often mixed with tones of red. This color can even appear in the sepals and petals to produce a flame-colored flower in flammea types. Many lovely semialba varieties exist that often have strikingly dramatic dark purple lips and present a gorgeous contrast in color. Semialba forms also include flowers with pink to reddish lips, and lips that are dark slate-blue. Although there are a number of pale lavender albescens varieties, there are also a few true albas that are quite beautiful.

This species does not have the wide petals of a *Cattleya trianaei* and tends to pass its narrow petals on to its hybrids. It more than makes up for this, however, by imparting the brilliant, rich colors of its labellum to the lips of its hybrids, and it is the chief contributor to the intense deep purple in the lips of many of our modern hybrids. There are some particularly good coerulea forms of *C. purpurata*, and some of the best coerulea hybrids come from this species.

Cattleya purpurata has been one of the most widely used parents in making *Cattleya* hybrids over the years, and more than 90 percent of the so-called laeliocattleyas in *Sander's List of Orchid Hybrids* have *C. purpurata* in their ancestry. The species is one of the parents of the most famous primary hybrid in orchid history, *Laeliocattleya* Canhamiana (*C. purpurata* × *C. mossiae*). This cross, which blooms in June in the United States, was the wedding flower of the cut-flower days, and literally tens of thousands of plants were grown during the 1940s to satisfy the demand for these flowers. The semialba variety was the wedding orchid itself and it was pictured in advertisements in magazines and newspapers and even in full color on the cover of the *American Orchid Society Bulletin* for December 1946, followed by four full-color pages of the flowers in bridal bouquets, travel corsages, hair swirls, and even on a graduation diploma. Canhamiana shows the dominance of *C. purpurata*'s magnificent lip color which made the semialba form so appealing. There have been many named varieties of this cross over the years, but the best we have seen is an old clone named 'King George', which has superior shape and a particularly large and beautiful lip.

Santa Catarina in southern Brazil is home to *Cattleya purpurata*, which is also the state flower of Santa Catarina. The species is extremely popular with local Brazilian

Cattleya purpurata has one of the widest ranges of color forms among the large-flowered *Cattleya* species, including the typical lavender type.

orchid growers, and rare varieties can sell for thousands of dollars each. Whole orchid shows are dedicated to *C. purpurata* and, with its many color forms, it is a collector's dream.

Today *Cattleya purpurata* is only known in the orchid world as *Laelia purpurata.* It was pictured in the famous old orchid books *Lindenia* and *Reichenbachia* under this name, and it appears in modern works like L. C. Menezes's book entitled, *Laelia purpurata*. In addition, when used as a parent in hybridizing, the name *L. purpurata* is used by the Royal Horticultural Society's orchid registrar, and both that society and the American Orchid Society record their awards to this species under this name. The history that led to this phenomenon is fascinating.

The genus *Laelia* was established by the botanist John Lindley in 1831 based on the Mexican species *L. grandiflora* (*L. speciosa* today). In his book *Genera and Species of Orchidaceous Plants* in which he described the genus *Laelia* on page 115, Lindley divided the tribe Epidendreae into three groups based, rather simplistically, on their number of pollinia (two, four, or eight). He put the genus *Cattleya* into the four-pollinia group with genera like *Epidendrum* and *Broughtonia*, and *Laelia* went into the eight-pollinia group with genera like *Phaius* and *Bletia*. This did not affect the large-flowered *Cattleya* species at the time because none of them grew in Mexico. When Lindley re-described his *Cattleya perrinii* as *Laelia perrinii* in 1842, however, he introduced a different type of plant into his genus *Laelia* without apparently realizing it. The plant did not come from Mexico; it came from Brazil and its pseudobulbs and flower spikes were like the typical South American large-flowered *Cattleya* species, not the Mexican laelias. Lindley's deci-

Cattleya purpurata produces some truly lovely bright pink lips like this 'Carnea Longwood' variety.

sion to put the eight-pollinia Brazilian species *lobata* into the genus *Cattleya* in 1848 after just putting the eight-pollinia *perrinii* into the genus *Laelia* shows his misunderstanding of the difference between the Mexican and Brazilian species. Lindley had also put the Brazilian species *crispa* in the genus *Cattleya* in *Genera and Species of Orchidaceous Plants* back in 1831 at the same time he described *Laelia* as a new genus despite its eight pollinia.

Lindley was not the only botanist describing the new species from Brazil. Other botanists had also received plants of *purpurata* and were assigning the species to the genus *Cattleya*. In the same year Lindley described *Laelia purpurata*, French botanist Antoine Charles Lemaire described the same plant as *Cattleya brysiana*. In 1854, in his book *Praktische Studien an der Familie der Orchideen*, Beer called it *C. purpurata* and put it right back in the same genus Lindley had just taken it out of. It was like a game of botanical checkers.

Despite the reservations of many orchid authorities, however, Bentham and Hooker's *Genera Plantarum* with Veitch's support sealed the fate of the large-flowered Brazilian species in the 1890s, and kept them out of the genus *Cattleya* for all of the 20th century. No one would challenge the classification despite its atrocious logic because even a child of three or four could tell the difference between four and eight. It finally took modern science in a new millennium to separate Brazil from Mexico.

Cattleya purpurata is one of the great *Cattleya* species of all time. Without it, our modern purple and semialba *Cattleya* hybrids would be quite different and we would have missed a lot of beauty that this wonderful species has added to these hybrids. The

Some of the best coerulea hybrids began with *Cattleya purpurata* varieties like 'Werckhauseri'.

species is easy to grow and has an abundance of beautiful flowers and many fascinating varieties. We feel no orchid collection should be without it.

Culture

Cattleya purpurata has the same cultural requirements as the other large-flowered *Cattleya* species. It benefits from lots of sun and moving air and a temperature between 58° and 60°F at night and 80° to 85°F during the day. It usually begins sending up new growths in late summer and early autumn in the United States, and these growths will be completed by mid-January or early February. Buds will begin to form in the sheath after a short rest period, and the plants will flower from late May into June depending on the variety.

Give *Cattleya purpurata* a few weeks of rest after it flowers by minimizing the watering, but do not let the pseudobulbs shrivel too much. Once the plant begins to grow, it requires lots of water, particularly as the growth elongates beyond 6 inches. *Cattleya purpurata* can develop some really large pseudobulbs, often exceeding 20 inches from the base of the pseudobulb to the tip of the leaf, if grown well.

Cattleya tenebrosa (Rolfe) A. A. Chadwick, new combination

based on *Laelia grandis* Lindley & Paxton var. *tenebrosa* Rolfe, *Gardeners' Chronicle*, 3d series, 10: 126. 1891

Robert Allen Rolfe was one of the giants of the orchid world during the late 1800s. One of the most knowledgeable and hardworking botanists of his time, he was ultimately recognized for his accomplishments with Britain's highest honors, including the Victoria Medal of Honor and the Veitch Memorial Medal. He established *The Orchid Review* in 1893 and was the magazine's primary author and editor until shortly before his death in 1921.

Rolfe was unique among his peers because he seemed almost happy at times to admit he was wrong about a botanical description, the location of an orchid habitat, or some other important fact pertaining to orchids. He wrote the first account of the discovery of *Cattleya labiata* in the November 1893 issue of *The Orchid Review* only to change it in 1900 and again in 1907. By the time he finished, he had shown conclusively that his original 1893 account was close to 100 percent wrong.

Rolfe seems to be the only botanist of the 1800s who was interested in *Cattleya tenebrosa* which he called a *Laelia*. In 1889 the Liverpool Horticultural Company sent him a flower that he described in *The Gardeners' Chronicle* of 1 June 1889 as a larger and darker-than-normal form of *Laelia grandis*—a species Lindley had described in 1850 on page 60 of *Paxton's Flower Garden*. Based on Rolfe's description of the 1889 flower, however, it was undoubtedly a *Cattleya tenebrosa*, but Rolfe felt it was just an "individual variation" (of *L. grandis*) and therefore hardly worth describing as a "variety."

Two years later in 1891, A. H. Grimaditch of Clapton Square, Liverpool, sent Rolfe a flower and a pseudobulb from a plant that Rolfe described as "*Laelia grandis* var. *tenebrosa*," on page 126 of *The Gardeners' Chronicle* for that year. Grimaditch said the plant had come from a new district in Brazil. The flowers were large and copper-bronze, and the sepals and petals were flat, not twisted as in the typical *L. grandis.* This time Rolfe considered it "no trifling variation" and described it as a "geographical variety."

Linden published a painting of the flower in his famous *Lindenia* (plate 290), with Rolfe's accompanying comments. The flowers were quite impressive and, when they were later exhibited by Lord Rothschild at a Royal Horticultural Society meeting, they received a First Class Certificate. Sander also included a painting of a large plant in the company's magnificent book, *Reichenbachia,* where Rolfe again wrote the description. Sander's firm also received an FCC/RHS on its plant, but felt it had "many distinct peculiarities in growth, form, and colouring and it is quite probable that we shall ultimately regard it as a species." Again Rolfe called it "*Laelia grandis* var. *tenebrosa.*"

Rolfe made it a point to look at other plants of his "*Laelia grandis* var. *tenebrosa*" in several collections over the next season, and in 1893 he decided he had been wrong in describing it as a geographical variety. It was really a new species, and in the May 1893 issue of *The Orchid Review,* he called it just "*L. tenebrosa.*" He said,

> *Laelia grandis* has smaller flowers, with nankeen-yellow, very undulate sepals and petals, and a white lip, beautifully veined throughout with radiating rose-purple veins; while *L. tenebrosa* has larger flowers with broader and flatter sepals and petals and a bronze or almost coppery hue, and a large deep purple lip with a lighter margin.

Rolfe felt the differences were constant, and his description of the differences are very much the way we view the species today. The one thing Rolfe overlooked in his writings,

The typical *Cattleya tenebrosa* is a vigorously growing, floriferous plant with four or five bronze-colored flowers on a flower spike.

of course, was that the new species belonged in the genus *Cattleya*, not *Laelia*, and it should have been called *Cattleya tenebrosa*.

Plants of *Cattleya tenebrosa* were never available commercially in large numbers, and except for a brief period in the late 1800s, this species has been scarce in cultivation compared with other large-flowered cattleyas. *Cattleya tenebrosa* comes from a small area in southern Brazil, where it is now considered to be virtually extinct. It grew originally on large trees in relatively dense forests. Most plants available today come from sib crosses or meristems from old jungle plants still in existence.

While there are still some good large varieties in cultivation, like 'Rainforest' FCC/AOS, we have to go back to the old paintings of the late 1800s to see how fine the species can be. *Lindenia* contains three such paintings, and they are most impressive. They show a rainbow of colors from rich, clear bronze through reddish purple, through yellow in the sepals and petals with contrasting purple lips—some with a distinct white edge. The largest flowers measure 7½ inches across. Although not shown in *Lindenia*, there are varieties with deep bronze sepals and petals and a deep, solid purple lip and some like 'Walton Grange' FCC/AOS-RHS, with clear yellow sepals and petals with a white lip with purple markings. There is also a variety with green sepals and petals and a white lip that is sometimes referred to as an alba.

In its primary hybrids, *Cattleya tenebrosa* tends to impart a brightness that enriches the color and almost makes it glow. This species is one of the most important parents of many of our yellow and art-shade hybrids. Its hybrid with *Cattleya dowiana* made by Charlesworth and Company in 1901 is the famous *Laeliocattleya* Luminosa that was

Cattleya tenebrosa has a variety of bright rainbow colors, including yellows, yellow-orange, and yellow-green.

the main building block for many of these early hybrids. The hybrid of *C. tenebrosa* with *C. warneri* is the famous *Lc.* Gottoiana, a parent of important early purple hybrids like *Lc.* St. Gothard, which is in the background of most of our famous modern lavender hybrids like *Brassolaeliocattleya* Norman's Bay, *Blc.* Memoria Crispin Rosales, and *Lc.* Princess Margaret.

In the late 1800s, when *Cattleya tenebrosa* was most abundant in European collections, there were also some outstanding varieties of *C. warneri* in cultivation, which may account for the impressive *Laeliocattleya* Gottoiana used in early breeding. Gottoiana is also a naturally occurring hybrid, and some beautiful clones were imported from Bahia, Brazil, in 1882—one of which received a First Class Certificate from the Royal Horticultural Society—so early breeders had several fine varieties of the hybrid available for breeding which may account for its early extensive use as a parent. The hybrid was named for E. Gotto of Hampton, England.

Cattleya tenebrosa is considered by orchid breeders to be dominant for color, large size and deformity-free flowers, as well as excellent plant vigor. It has an entire lip structure, like the labiata-type cattleyas, and it imparts an unbelievable richness to the flowers of its hybrids. Its only negative character may be its narrow petals. It is certainly one of the grandest of Brazil's orchids and has been recognized for its excellence with seven American Orchid Society Awards of Merit and two First Class Certificates.

Like the fine, old varieties of so many of our large-flowered *Cattleya* species, most of those of *Cattleya tenebrosa* have been lost to cultivation and appear only in the rich coloring of our *Cattleya* hybrids. *Cattleya tenebrosa* today is like the elusive pot of gold at the end of the rainbow. It is there—but it is not there. Of the sib crosses still being made, there is always hope that some of the old genes may still be present in the plants and re-appear to unlock the grandeur of the past.

Culture

Cattleya tenebrosa is a vigorous, easy-to-grow plant and one that most beginning orchid hobbyists should be able to grow well. It needs the same growing conditions as most other large-flowered *Cattleya* species, including a day temperature of 80° to 85°F, night temperatures of 60°F, and lots of moving air. Like its Brazilian neighbor, *C. warneri*, it prefers slightly less sun than the sun-loving *Cattleya* species of Colombia and Venezuela, like *C. warscewiczii* and *C. lueddemanniana*.

When actively growing, *Cattleya tenebrosa* requires frequent watering and should not be allowed to become completely dry. It should be kept on the dry side, however, after flowering until it begins to grow again. *Cattleya tenebrosa* normally begins growing in the early autumn in greenhouses in the United States and will complete its new growth by midwinter. It will then rest for several weeks and flower in late spring to early summer depending on the variety. A well-grown plant should produce four or five flowers on a flower spike, and the flowers should last in bloom at least three weeks. The flowers will last longer if they can be kept out of the intense sun and heat of a summer greenhouse. We usually put them on a cool, non-air-conditioned porch.

SIX

Fiddling with Nature— The *Cattleya* Hybrids

Jo H N D O M I N Y, foreman for the horticultural establishment of James Veitch and Son, Exeter, England, is credited with making the first *Cattleya* hybrid in 1852. Since the structure of the tropical orchid flower was so different from the more common greenhouse flowers of Europe, horticulturists during the mid-1800s were not really sure how to make an orchid hybrid and Dominy himself needed help. As James Veitch described it on page 99 in his family history, *Hortus Veitchii*,

> Mr. John Harris, a surgeon of Exeter, who possessed an acquaintance with botany, first suggested to Dominy the possibility of obtaining hybrid orchids, and explained to him the structure of the orchid flower and the purpose of pollination. As soon as an opportunity presented itself, Dominy lost no time in turning the suggestion to practical account.

In 1852 Dominy pollinated some *Cattleya* flowers, and the following year he pollinated some *Calanthe* orchids. Since calanthes grow from seed to flower in much less time than cattleyas, the first orchid hybrid to actually flower was a *Calanthe*. In 1856 *Calanthe dominii* was proclaimed the first orchid hybrid produced in cultivation.

This seems a great injustice to cattleya lovers, of course, because Dominy made the cattleya crosses first, and after their normal seven-year maturation period, two *Cattleya* hybrids flowered in 1859 to the excitement of everyone. The excitement soon turned to frustration, however, when Dominy was asked what *Cattleya* species he had used to make the crosses. Although Dominy was a good hybridizer, he was not a good record keeper and he kept no written record of the parents for either of his 1859 cattleya crosses. The first cross, which flowered in August 1859, was given the charming name *C. hybrida*, and the parentage was variously reported as *C. granulosa* and *C. harrisonae*; *C. granulosa* and *C. loddigesii*; *C. guttata* and *C. intermedia*; *and C. guttata* and *C. loddigesii*. Veitch, in whose nursery it was raised, said the parents were "probably *C. guttata* and *C. intermedia*," but the knowledgeable editor of *The Orchid Review* (1 [1893]: 4), Robert Allen Rolfe, said, "The characters of the plant, however, leave little room for doubt that *C. guttata* and *C. loddigesii* were the parents." With this background, the best that can be said about the first *Cattleya* hybrid is that it was a cross between two bifoliate *Cattleya* species.

The second *Cattleya* hybrid, which flowered in November 1859, was described by John Lindley on page 948 in *The Gardeners' Chronicle* of 1859 and given the name *C.*

Dominiana. Lindley said the hybrid was a cross between *C. labiata* and *C. intermedia*, but he compared the flower's size, color, and column characteristics to *C. mossiae*. Rolfe went even further, saying *C.* Dominiana was a cross between *C. maxima* and *C. intermedia*—a big difference from *C. labiata* and *C. mossiae*. Lindley and Rolfe at least agreed that it was a hybrid between *C. intermedia* and a large-flowered *Cattleya* species, so we will leave it at that.

In 1863 two more of Dominy's cattleya crosses flowered. The first bloomed in July and was named *Cattleya* Aclandi-Loddigesii but was exhibited under the name *C. hybrida* when it won a First Class Certificate and a Silver Banksian Medal from the Royal Horticultural Society. Since Dominy's first *Cattleya* hybrid had been named *C. hybrida*, the cross was eventually renamed *C.* Brabantiae for the Duchess of Brabant who became Queen of the Belgians. The hybrid has the distinction of being the first *Cattleya* hybrid Dominy made where everyone agreed on the names of the parents.

The second of Dominy's 1863 cattleya crosses to flower was exhibited at the Royal Horticultural Society on 9 September 1863 and awarded a Second Class Certificate that year and a First Class Certificate the next. The hybrid was named *Laeliocattleya* Exoniensis, and Veitch felt "the parents were probably *Laelia crispa* (syn. *Cattleya crispa*) and *C. mossiae*." Rolfe, however, felt the large-flowered *Cattleya* was *C. labiata* not *C. mossiae*. The hybrid was considered one of the most beautiful Dominy had made, and it had the distinction of being the first *Laeliocattleya* hybrid.

The fifth *Cattleya* hybrid was named *C.* Devoniensis, and it was awarded a First Class Certificate by the Royal Horticultural Society on 11 October 1864 even though the parents are completely unknown.

Things seemed to go from bad to worse as the years went by and in August 1866 John Dominy's hybrid, *Cattleya* Manglesii, was not only subjected to the embarrassment of questionable parents (*C. mossiae* and *C. harrisonae* or *C. lueddemanniana* and *C. loddigesii*), but botanist H. G. Reichenbach even gave Dominy's assistant, John Seden, credit for making the cross. Dominy's record keeping remained in disarray until the end of his breeding efforts and his last hybrid, *Laeliocattleya* Dominiana (not to be confused with *Cattleya* Dominiana) which bloomed in 1877, was a cross between *C. dowiana* and, as Rolfe observed, "some laelia." The *Laelia* was *L. purpurata* (syn. *Cattleya purpurata*) according to Veitch, and *L. crispa* (syn. *Cattleya crispa*) according to Rolfe.

Since the cross between *Cattleya dowiana* and *Laelia crispa* was eventually registered under the name *Laeliocattleya* Pallas in 1894, *Lc.* Dominiana is now *C. dowiana* × *L. purpurata* regardless of what Dominy actually used for parents. John Dominy, however, went down in orchid history as the first hybridizer of cattleyas and he produced a number of interesting hybrids using "probable" parents. Fortunately for everyone, Dominy's successor at Veitch, John Seden, was not only a prolific orchid breeder, but also a good record keeper and Seden's crosses were well documented.

James Veitch and Son monopolized the breeding of orchid hybrids until about 1880 when other breeders, both private growers and commercial firms, began to experiment with orchid hybrids. Veitch remained the leader in Europe, however, for the rest of the century largely due to the efforts of John Seden.

Seden was probably the most outstanding orchid breeder of the late 1800s and he produced some of the most famous primary hybrids of the large-flowered *Cattleya* species ever made. He started his career with Veitch in 1861 working under John Dominy in the orchids and stove plants which gave him his introduction to the techniques of orchid hybridizing. His breeding was not limited to cattleyas, however, or even orchids, and he produced a wide variety of hybrids of common greenhouse pot plants like gloxinias and begonias and some of the best varieties of tree fruit of the early 20th century.

In recognition of his outstanding work in hybridizing, in 1897 Seden was chosen as one of the original recipients of the Victoria Medal of Honor. Among his outstanding accomplishments in cattleya breeding were the primary crosses *Cattleya* Enid, *C.* Empress Frederick, *C.* Fabia, *Brassocattleya* Digbyano-mossiae, *Laeliocattleya* Canhamiana, and *Lc.* Callistoglossa which together formed the basis for most of the large purple *Cattleya* hybrids for the next 75 years. Seden also bred the first *Sophrocattleya* hybrid, *Sc.* Batemaniana, from *Sophronitis coccinea* and *Cattleya intermedia*.

Raising orchid hybrids in the 1800s was the least successful part of orchid growing because of the rudimentary methods of planting orchid seed used at the time. The seed was usually shaken from the seed pod onto a finely divided medium like milled peat which had been boiled to kill any pathogens, and covered with a clean piece of burlap or coarse canvas and germinated in a hot greenhouse at 80°F. Sometimes the seed was shaken on the surface of the pot containing the pod parent where it was invariably washed away when the plant was watered.

Growers were often lucky to have any plants at all survive to flowering, and most crosses saw only a dozen or so seedlings reach maturity. Veitch tells us that only a single plant of *Laeliocattleya sedenii* survived to maturity, and other crosses produced as few as two plants. Since growers were not experienced in storing orchid pollen, most early hybrids were crosses between plants that flowered at the same time. This is why we see so many early crosses between two bifoliate *Cattleya* species or a bifoliate and a large-flowered *Cattleya* instead of the more promising potential of two large-flowered *Cattleya* species.

Unfortunately for the early hybridizers, each of the large-flowered *Cattleya* species bloomed at a different time of the year and only a few of them had overlapping flowering periods. If you wanted to cross them, you had to be able to hold pollen for weeks or even months. The first hybrid between two large-flowered *Cattleya* species did not appear until 1889, almost 30 years after Dominy's first bifoliate *Cattleya* hybrid. The cross was made by Sir H. S. Leon of Bletchley Park, England, and was called *C.* Maggie Raphael. The parents were *C. dowiana* and *C. trianaei*, two plants that had flowering periods half a year apart, so the pollen had to be held close to six months to make the cross. Once growers discovered you could hold pollen this long, however, large-flowered cattleyas soon became the most popular orchid hybrids produced, and breeding these hybrids moved from a snail's pace to that of a frightened jackrabbit.

The number of *Cattleya* hybrids that were bred during the 20th century is so large that it would be impossible to look at even one percent of them in this book. A few, however, have had such an impact on cattleya hybridizing that they are worthy of some individual discussion and, in the following pages, we will try to cover the most famous of these. The hybrids will be grouped according to color because color in most cases is an important element in their success. We have also used the terms *Laeliocattleya*, *Brassocattleya*, and *Brassolaeliocattleya* in the text to conform to the present nomenclature of the International Registration Authority for Orchid Hybrids in England even though some of the hybrids had large-flowered Brazilian *Cattleya* species like *C. purpurata* as a parent.

White *Cattleya* Hybrids

Many white *Cattleya* hybrids were produced from the large-flowered *Cattleya* species during the early 1900s, but only a few of these hybrids were really noteworthy. *Cattleya* Mrs. Myra Peeters alba (*C. warneri* alba × *C. gaskelliana* alba), made by Peeters in 1904, gave a number of large, fairly well shaped flowers. The original cross of *C.* Lady Veitch (*C. warneri* alba × *C. lueddemanniana* alba) made by Sander in 1915 from two unusually fine varieties produced some large round flowers like the clone *C.* Lady Veitch 'Superbissima', which had wide petals that overlapped. For the most part, however, the quality of large white *Cattleya* hybrids was relatively poor and the plants themselves were not particularly good growers.

All this changed in April 1945 when the British orchid company Black and Flory registered the cross *Cattleya* Bow Bells. Clint McDade, the owner of Rivermont Orchids in the United States, had bought a large number of *C.* Bow Bells seedlings from Black and Flory before the cross was registered and, when he exhibited five of the plants at the September 1945 meeting of the trustees of the American Orchid Society, *C.* Bow Bells became an orchid sensation. One plant, *C.* Bow Bells 'Purity', received a First Class Cer-

Cattleya Bow Bells 'Anne Chadwick' Best of Show Orlando 1960

tificate and the whole group of five plants, four of which were flowering for the first time, was awarded a rare American Orchid Society Silver Medal for excellence. In 1948 *C.* Bow Bells received another unprecedented compliment at the Miami Orchid Show when two individual plants were awarded First Class Certificates. This was only the beginning, however, and before the American Orchid Society judges were finished with *C.* Bow Bells, they had given it 49 awards, including 16 Awards of Merit and 5 First Class Certificates.

McDade described *Cattleya* Bow Bells as a "botanical phenomenon among orchid plants" because all the seedlings of the cross produced strikingly similar flowers of outstanding shape on short vigorously growing plants. Most white *Cattleya* crosses produced only a few really good varieties out of the whole seed pod, but with *C.* Bow Bells, most of the plants were fine. *Cattleya* Bow Bells was a relatively simple cross between a primary hybrid, *C.* Suzanne Hye (*C. gaskelliana* × *C. mossiae*) and a secondary hybrid, *C.* Edithiae (*C. trianaei* × *C.* Suzanne Hye). The *C.* Edithiae was the famous clone 'White Empress' that had received a First Class Certificate from the Royal Horticultural Society in 1914 and had often been used in hybridizing but with only mixed results. The *C.* Suzanne Hye, however, was simply the best white that Black and Flory had ever seen.

Pedigree of *Cattleya* Bow Bells

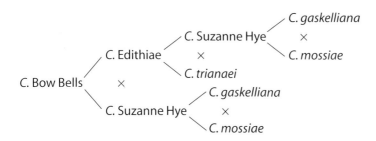

The story of *Cattleya* Bow Bells, of course, is not just the tale of a fine white *Cattleya*, for *C.* Bow Bells has a touch of romance intermingled with its history. This hybrid was named for the bells of St. Mary-Le-Bow church in the financial district of London. The church was a legend in the city for it is said that you were not a true Cockney or Londoner unless you were born within the sound of Bow bells. During the Second World War the church had been badly damaged by Hitler's bombers and it was still in need of repair when the photo on page 166 was taken in 1955. There is no doubt that when Black and Flory named their hybrid *C.* Bow Bells, it helped to call attention to the church and aided in collecting funds to rebuild it.

Cattleya Bow Bells is also the sad story of the magnificent *C.* Suzanne Hye parent that was used to make the cross. Black and Flory considered the plant to be so outstanding and so valuable that when England was threatened with a German invasion, they carefully packed up the plant and sent it to the United States for safe keeping only to see the ship on which it was carried sunk by a German submarine and the plant lost forever.

Although *Cattleya* Bow Bells was essentially a triploid genetically and triploids are notorious non-breeders, some plants of *C.* Bow Bells were diploids and tetraploids that did breed. The finest varieties were tetraploids and these began to be used to make new hybrids. *Cattleya* Bow Bells soon became the best white parent in the world, and the cattleya bells rang for years with *C.* Empress Bells, *C.* Angel Bells, *C.* Laura Bells, *C.* Signal Bells, *C.* Sleigh Bells, *C.* Vesper Bells, *C.* Tiffin Bells, *C.* Tribells, *C.* Princess Bells, and more than a few "bows."

The most famous of *Cattleya* Bow Bells crosses, *C.* Bob Betts, was also the first *C.* Bow Bells cross to flower in the United States. The hybrid was registered by McDade in 1950 as *C.* Bow Bells crossed with *C. mossiae* var. *wagneri*. Bob Betts was McDade's grower at the time, and the cross was an attempt to extend the *C.* Bow Bells flowering season from the fall and winter into spring when white cattleyas were in greatest demand for cut flowers. *Cattleya* Bob Betts turned out to be almost better than its parent and, if the American Orchid Society judges loved *C.* Bow Bells, they adored *C.* Bob

Sign on side of war-damaged St. Mary-Le-Bow church, London, 1955

Betts. *Cattleya* Bob Betts soon became the most awarded white cattleya in the history of the Society's judging with over 66 quality awards.

Other *Cattleya* Bow Bells crosses which came later also received a good number of American Orchid Society awards, but none came even close to rivaling *C.* Bob Betts. Remakes of *C.* Bob Betts by other orchid growers strangely never produced the fine quality flowers of McDade's original cross, prompting endless speculation on just what parents McDade actually used to make the cross. Regardless of the intrigue that sometimes surrounds their parentage, however, there is no doubt that *C.* Bow Bells and *C.* Bob Betts were unique among white *Cattleya* hybrids and together they raised the standard of excellence for these hybrids to such a high level that there was little room left to increase the quality of white *Cattleya* hybrids after that. Many more white hybrids based on *C.* Bow Bells and *C.* Bob Betts were made, but they were seldom as good, and rarely better than the two originals.

Cattleya Bow Bells and its hybrids have so dominated white cattleya breeding for so many years that a few fine white non–Bow Bells hybrids were somehow lost in the shadows and we do not hear much about them today. One of these was *C.* Joyce Hannington, which interestingly enough was also registered as a new hybrid in 1945 and, like *C.* Bow Bells, was basically a triploid with a few tetraploid clones. *Cattleya* Joyce Hannington was taller growing than *C.* Bow Bells, more floriferous, and at its best was certainly the equal of *C.* Bow Bells for quality of flowers. Even though it received 18 awards from the American Orchid Society, including 7 Awards of Merit and a First Class Certificate, the complexity of the cross (*C.* Barbara Dane × *C.* Snowdon) did not give the high percentage of fine plants that *C.* Bow Bells gave and for that reason *C.* Joyce Hannington was not as popular a parent as *C.* Bow Bells or *C.* Bob Betts.

Cattleya Bob Betts 'Wilbur Davis' HCC/AOS

Cattleya Dorothy Mackaill

As if to prove that 1945 was a magical year for white hybrids, H. Patterson and Sons introduced their beautiful white *Cattleya* Dorothy Mackaill that year. This hybrid was an even simpler cross than *C.* Bow Bells. It was just *C. mossiae* alba crossed with *C. Edithiae* alba. The flowers had thinner substance than those of *C.* Bow Bells but had very nice shape and usually came in June. *Cattleya* Dorothy Mackaill was an important cut flower for Patterson because it supplied the lucrative June wedding market, and the company made no particular effort to exhibit it or otherwise publicize it. Like *C.* Joyce Hannington, *C.* Dorothy Mackaill eventually faded from the white *Cattleya* market as *C.* Bow Bells and *C.* Bob Betts thrived and took over.

Semialba *Cattleya* Hybrids

One of the most beautiful color combinations in the large-flowered cattleyas is the form which has white sepals and petals and a lavender lip. The combination was referred to as a "white with colored lip" cattleya for more than 100 years, but in recent times the term "semialba" has been coined to describe it. All of the large-flowered *Cattleya* species, including the large-flowered Brazilian Laelia/Cattleyas, have semialba forms except the yellow-toned species like *C. dowiana* and *Laelia grandis* (syn. *Cattleya grandis*). The color of the lip in these semialbas can vary from a pale tinge of lavender to a solid rich, dark velvety purple, but the most popular semialbas have dark purple lips. The effect produced by the deep purple lip against a background of pristine white petals is particularly dramatic, and most of the orchids named for the first ladies of the United States have had this color combination.

Semialba *Cattleya* species are almost as rare in nature as the all-white alba varieties

Brassolaeliocattleya Laura Bush

and in a few cases are even more rare. Many of the fine semialba varieties are among the most famous plants in the history of the *Cattleya* species and, because of their rarity, they survived the rigors of the last century and are still available in private and commercial collections today. Some of the most famous of these include *C. mossiae reineckiana* 'Young's Variety', *C. warscewiczii* 'Frau Melanie Beyrodt' ('F.M.B.'), *C. trianaei* 'Trenton', *C. schroederae* 'The Baron', *C. lueddemanniana* 'Stanleyi', *C. labiata* 'Cooksoniae', and *C. labiata* 'Mrs. E. Ashworth'.

The large-flowered Brazilian species, *Cattleya purpurata* (syn. *Laelia purpurata*), is also quite important in semialba breeding because of its intensely dark purple lip color which it readily imparts to its offspring. Because *C. purpurata* has a large number of semialba varieties, however, the individual clones did not receive the recognition they deserved, and most of the fine varieties of the past century were not named.

Like the alba form in cattleyas, the semialba is genetically unique and both parents must have the gene for semialba if it is to manifest itself in the offspring. In other words, if you cross an alba cattleya or a lavender cattleya with a semialba, you will get a lavender hybrid, not an alba or a semialba. You will only get a semialba cattleya if you cross it with another semialba. The only exception to this is the yellow *C. dowiana aurea* which acts like a semialba when crossed with a semialba. A few lavender *Cattleya* hybrids carry the genes for semialba even though they do not show it and, when two of these lavenders are crossed, an occasional semialba plant can appear among the seedlings of an otherwise lavender cross. This was particularly noticeable in hybrids like *Laeliocattleya* DeLoris Ziegfeld where two excellent semialba varieties appeared among the hundreds of fine dark purple flowers of the cross.

The most famous semialba *Cattleya* hybrid of all time is *Laeliocattleya* Canhamiana alba which is a primary cross between semialba varieties of *C. mossiae* and *Laelia pur-purata* (syn. *C. purpurata*). The cross was not famous because of its fine varieties, how-ever, but because of the time of year it flowered. It was an unusually vigorous grower and prolific bloomer that flowered during the month of June in the United States when white cattleya flowers were scarce and demand for bridal orchids was high during the cut-flower era of the 1930s to the 1950s.

Although it is a semialba, it was called *Laeliocattleya* Canhamiana alba because there were no real alba forms of the hybrid available at the time, but there were lavender forms and calling it a "white with colored lip" was too cumbersome for everyday use. Literally tens of thousands of *Lc.* Canhamiana alba plants were grown during the heyday of cut-flower cattleyas. Thomas Young Orchids alone had more than 10,000 plants in just one greenhouse, and it had more than one greenhouse filled with this hybrid. The cross was so famous during this period that it appeared in newspapers and magazines throughout the United States as the June wedding flower and it became the most featured cattleya orchid of all time.

The purple form of *Laeliocattleya* Canhamiana was originally bred at James Veitch and Sons Royal Exotic Nursery in Chelsea, England, in 1872. The cross was noteworthy at the time because it took 13 years from seed to flower. When it finally did flower, it was described by botanist H. G. Reichenbach as a new hybrid in the 4 July 1885 issue of *The Gardeners' Chronicle* and named for Charles Canham, an outstanding grower and fore-man at Veitch's nursery. Reichenbach had nothing but praise for the hybrid, except for its 13-year gestation period, and said, "The lip is tinted with such fine dark velvet pur-ple that you may scarcely find finer in the vegetable kingdom."

Laeliocattleya Canhamiana alba

The semialba form of *Laeliocattleya* Canhamiana was produced by Sander and Company at St. Albans, England, in 1902 from *Cattleya mossiae reineckiana* and a semi-alba form of *C. purpurata*. The company thought so much of the hybrid that it originally registered it as a separate cross under the name *Lc.* Canhamiana Rex. There were apparently no true alba varieties of *C. purpurata* in cultivation during the 1800s and into the mid-1900s to enable breeders to produce an all-white *Lc.* Canhamiana hybrid, but these varieties are available today and all-white forms of *Lc.* Canhamiana have been produced in recent years. Although there is now a true alba form of *Lc.* Canhamiana as well as a semialba, the semialba will probably always be referred to as *Lc.* Canhamiana alba because of its remarkable place in orchid history.

Laeliocattleya Canhamiana alba was widely used in breeding semialba *Cattleya* hybrids, and there are crosses with virtually all of the large-flowered *Cattleya* species. Some of its more significant hybrids are its cross with *C. warscewiczii*, which produced *Lc.* Britannia alba, a parent of one of the most beautiful semialba hybrids of the 1940s, *Lc.* Jane Dane. The semialba's affinity for the female gender continued unabated as *Lc.* Canhamiana was bred back on *Lc.* Jane Dane to produce *Lc.* Ethel Merman, and with *C.* Priscilla to produce *Lc.* Lily Pons. *Laeliocattleya* Lily Pons crossed with *C.* Ardmore alba produced our favorite Mother's Day semialba, *Lc.* Olive Chadwick (mother and grand-mother respectively). *Cattleya mossiae reineckiana* crossed with *Lc.* Canhamiana was also a favorite semialba hybrid with the Sander family. The cross was named *Lc.* Isabel Sander, and Sander used it to breed a line of notable semialbas, including *Lc.* Sally Sander and *Lc.* Erica Sander.

After *Laeliocattleya* Canhamiana alba, the most important semialba is probably the

Laeliocattleya Jane Dane alba

primary cross between semialba varieties of *Cattleya mossiae* and *C. warscewiczii* called *C.* Enid alba. Here again, there was no true breeding alba *C. warscewiczii*, so the semi-alba became the alba in everyday usage. *Cattleya* Enid was originally made in the lavender form by John Seden of James Veitch and Son in 1896. Like *Lc.* Canhamiana, the cross became famous as the semialba during the cut-flower days of the 1940s and 1950s when H. Patterson and Sons began remaking the hybrid with two outstanding parents, *C. mossiae reineckiana* 'Young's Variety' and *C. warscewiczii* 'F.M.B.' Patterson remade the cross over and over again using the same two parents because the results were so tremendous and the demand was so great for both cut flowers and plant sales.

Although both *Cattleya mossiae reineckiana* 'Young's Variety' and *C. warscewiczii* 'F.M.B.' have only the normal diploid number of chromosomes, some of the remakes of *C.* Enid produced a few tetraploids which had large beautifully shaped flowers. These were so fine that the American Orchid Society gave awards to 16 of them, including 8 Awards of Merit and 2 First Class Certificates. The high quality of Patterson's *C.* Enid alba is a testament to the success that can be achieved in breeding using outstanding varieties of the large-flowered *Cattleya* species. You do not need complex crosses to produce fine hybrids. By selecting the very best varieties of the species, even primary hybrids can be outstanding and awardable.

Because *Cattleya mossiae* and *C. warscewiczii* have very different growth and flowering habits, *C.* Enid has an irregular flowering period and can bloom at any time of the year, occasionally even twice a year. The unreliability of its flowering season was really its only drawback, for otherwise it was a marvelous hybrid. *Cattleya* Enid formed the basis for many of the fine semialba *Cattleya* hybrids made during the 20th century.

Laeliocattleya Shelly Compton 'Touch of Class'

Cattleya Enid alba crossed back on *C. mossiae reineckiana* 'Young's Variety' produced the excellent semialba *C.* Ardmore alba, which gave us outstanding, vigorous growing and flowering semialbas like *C.* Eileen Patterson and *C.* Jacqueline Kennedy. Other important hybrids with *C.* Enid include *C.* Lorna (with *C. warscewiczii*), *Luellocattleya* Cynthia (with *Lc.* Schroederae), and *Lc.* Steven Oliver Fouraker (with *Lc.* Pegi Mayne).

Because of the popularity of the semialba color, many semialba *Cattleya* hybrids have been made over the years and many of the finest varieties of these hybrids have been meristemmed for commercial sale. We have included pictures of some of the best of these varieties to illustrate their beauty.

Laeliocattleya Ecstasy

Laeliocattleya Kittiwake 'Brilliance' AM/ODC

Laeliocattleya Persepolis 'Splendor' AM/AOS

Laeliocattleya Powhatan 'Steven Christoffersen'

Lavender Cattleya Hybrids

The large number of fine lavender *Cattleya* hybrids produced in Europe and the United States during the past century is almost endless, and no single hybrid dominates the landscape like *C.* Bow Bells does. The hybrids developed in many directions, and most modern-day lavenders have a complex parentage with a genealogy that would fill this page. Many of the most advanced hybrids are not really as good as their parents because their flowers are either too crowded on the flower stem or their substance is so thick that it is unnatural and unattractive for an otherwise delicate flower.

Early hybridizers found it relatively easy to make hybrids with large, well-shaped flowers. All they had to do was use fine round varieties of *Cattleya trianaei*, *C. schroederae*, or *C. lueddemanniana* to make their crosses. Shape, however, was not the only desirable quality in a lavender hybrid. Equally important was color, and most *C. trianaei*, *C. schroederae*, and *C. lueddemanniana* hybrids had flowers with predominantly pastel shades of lavender.

If hybridizers wanted dark purple or bright yellow tones in the lip they needed parents like *Cattleya dowiana* or *C. purpurata*. *Cattleya dowiana* tended to deepen the shade of lavender in its hybrids, give them a strong fragrance and a certain amount of brilliance in color. *Laelia purpurata* gave its hybrids rich, velvety purple lips. Both species, however, had relatively narrow petals which they tended to pass on to their offspring, so when hybridizers used them in breeding, they often started down a long path to recapture the beautiful shape of the pastel-colored hybrids. The desire to produce rich coloration in lavender cattleya flowers, however, led hybridizers to use both *C. dowiana* and L. *purpurata* extensively in making new crosses. *Cattleya dowiana*'s effect in deepening lavender color and enriching the lip with bright yellow made it the most used of all the *Cattleya* species in breeding lavender hybrids by a wide margin.

One of the most spectacular of the early primary hybrids using *Cattleya dowiana* was *C.* Fabia, a cross with *C. labiata*. This cross was vigorous and free-flowering, with fragrant flowers that, at their best, were a dark glowing purple. It was an early autumn bloomer and because it was a primary hybrid, the plants were fairly uniform in the quality of their flowers. Some of them were fine enough that they received Awards of Merit from the Royal Horticultural Society. *Cattleya* Fabia was such a good flower that it was often used in breeding and was the parent of well over 200 lavender hybrids before the century was even half over. Its famous hybrids include *Laeliocattleya* Ishtar and *Lc.* Cavalese, and it was in the background of both parents in *Brassolaeliocattleya* Norman's Bay. When made with really excellent varieties of *C. dowiana* and *C. labiata*, however, *C.* Fabia was an end in itself, with no further breeding needed to produce handsome dark purple flowers. During the 1930s and 1940s whole greenhouses full of *C.* Fabia could be found in the United States for cut-flower production.

Laelia purpurata's (syn. *Cattleya purpurata*) contribution to lavender breeding began with *Laeliocattleya* Callistoglossa, its primary cross with *C. warscewiczii*. *Cattleya warscewiczii* has some unusually large and very dark varieties which, when combined with the intensely dark lip of *Laelia purpurata*, produced a large, often concolor dark purple hybrid, *Lc.* Callistoglossa.

Laeliocattleya Princess Margaret 'Orchidhaven'

Laeliocattleya DeLoris Ziegfeld 'Olive Chadwick'

Laeliocattleya Callistoglossa was first made in 1882 by John Seden of James Veitch and Son and was described by botanist H. G. Reichenbach on page 7 in *The Gardeners' Chronicle* of 21 January 1882. Harry Veitch apologized for the quality of the flowers he sent Reichenbach because they had been produced without a flower sheath. Reichenbach, however, felt no apology was necessary and said, "Even as it is now, it is a fine thing." *Laeliocattleya* Callistoglossa is a tall, strong growing plant that produces an abundance of very large flowers in late spring and early summer. The flowers have relatively narrow petals, but the flower color is a dark and beautiful purple and, as a head of flowers, it is most impressive.

Laeliocattleya Callistoglossa was re-made many times by many growers, but one clone belonging to J. Cypher, which was purchased by Sir George Holford at Westonbirt, was used by Holford's grower, H. G. Alexander, to make the fabled *Lc.* Lustre (*Lc.* Callistoglossa × *Cattleya lueddemanniana*). The best variety, *Lc.* Lustre 'Westonbirt', was one of the most glorified lavender hybrids of the 20th century and has been discussed and applauded for its contribution to breeding by numerous writers. It was such a fine stud plant that it was used extensively in breeding for many years. Its cross with *C.* Peetersii, called *Lc.* Queen Mary, was Sir George's favorite purple hybrid. *Laeliocattleya* Lustre 'Westonbirt' was eventually found to be a tetraploid and was bred with *C.* Fabia to produce *Lc.* Cavalese, a parent of *Lc.* Bonanza, and with *C.* Hardyana to make the magnificent *Lc.* Sargon, which went into *Lc.* Ishtar and *Brassolaeliocattleya* Norman's Bay.

Another important line of lavender breeding started with the unlikely cross between two natural hybrids—*Laeliocattleya* Gottoiana (*Cattleya warneri* × *Laelia tenebrosa*) and *C.* Hardyana (*C. warscewiczii* × *C. dowiana aurea*). The combination produced *Lc.* St. Gothard, which the British orchid firm Charlesworth registered in 1908. At least one variety of *Lc.* St. Gothard, 'The Globe', was particularly fine and received an Award of Merit from the Royal Horticultural Society. *Laeliocattleya* St. Gothard was widely used in breeding lavender *Cattleya* hybrids, including Charlesworth's famous *Lc.* Serbia which appeared in 1915. Another British orchid company, McBean, took *Lc.* Serbia and crossed it back on *C.* Hardyana in 1922 to make *Lc.* Profusion.

Laeliocattleya Profusion was a fine, floriferous hybrid in its own right, but McBean created a truly breakthrough hybrid when it crossed the hybrid with *Cattleya* Clotho, one of the wonderful round, pastel-colored *C. trianaei* hybrids, to make *Lc.* Princess Margaret in 1930. At least a dozen varieties of *Lc.* Princess Margaret have been named, all of them fine and several awarded, but one clone, 'Orchidhaven' (Patterson's #2) was outstanding in breeding fine-shaped *Cattleya* hybrids. *Laeliocattleya* Princess Margaret 'Orchidhaven' was widely used to make such fine dark purple hybrids as *Lc.* DeLoris Ziegfeld and *Lc.* Harold J. Patterson during the 1940s and 1950s. We used it as late as 1990 with a narrow-petaled *C. dowiana* to make *Lc.* Powhatan with great results.

We have included pictures of a few of the famous lavender *Cattleya* hybrids of the past 75 years to show the high quality that has been achieved in these flowers.

Brassolaeliocattleya Norman's Bay 'Low's' FCC/RHS/AOS

Laeliocattleya Cavalese FCC/AOS

Cattleya Dinsmore 'Perfection' FCC/AOS

Brassolaeliocattleya Glad Tydings

Laeliocattleya Bonanza 'Vesuvius' AM/AOS

Brassolaeliocattleya Memoria Crispin Rosales 'Red Robin' AM/AOS

Yellow, Red, Orange, and Art-Shade Cattleyas

Most large-flowered *Cattleya* species have petals that are lavender, white, or a mixture of these colors. The only other colors that occur naturally in these flowers are yellow and yellow-orange, which is very prominent in *C. dowiana* and subdued in *C. rex.* If we include the large-flowered Brazilian *Cattleya* species like *C. tenebrosa,* we can add the color bronze as well. *Cattleya* hybrids, however, come in all colors of the rainbow today except true blue, and there are beautiful large red, yellow, and orange flowers and lovely art shades like peach and salmon. Producing these non-lavender colors in large *Cattleya* hybrids was a real challenge for orchid hybridizers.

The most spectacular yellow *Cattleya* species is *C. dowiana,* but its beautiful yellow color is so recessive that the yellow virtually disappears in its hybrids. Crossing a yellow *C. dowiana* with a semialba form of *C. warscewiczii* gives a hybrid with white sepals and petals but not even a hint of yellow. *Cattleya* hybrids that have yellow-colored petals exclusively from *C. dowiana* are extremely rare and are usually the result of crossing a primary lavender hybrid of *C. dowiana* back on itself. Even then, you may get only one or two yellows out of the whole cross. There are yellow-petaled varieties of *C.* Fabia, *C.* Empress Frederick, *C.* Prince John, *C.* Triumphans, and *C.* Hardyana, but hybridizers have ignored these lovely full-lip plants because of the difficulty of keeping the yellow color in subsequent generations.

Cattleya dowiana hybrids with the pale green *Brassavola digbyana,* like *Brasso-*

Brassocattleya Mrs. J. Leemann 'Low's'

cattleya Mrs. J. Leemann, do maintain the *C. dowiana* yellow, but the beautiful peach or yellow colors of a good *Bc.* Mrs. J. Leemann are usually lost in the next generation of breeding. Because of the extremely recessive character of the yellow color in *C. dowiana*, most hybridizers have used the small, narrow-petaled yellow Brazilian laelias like *L. xanthina* and L. *flava* or a bifoliate *Cattleya* like *C. bicolor* to make yellow *Cattleya* hybrids.

One of the first efforts to intensify and stabilize yellow color in cattleyas was made by James Veitch and Sons when they crossed *Cattleya dowiana* with the small yellow *Laelia xanthina*. They named the hybrid *Laeliocattleya* Ophir when it flowered in 1901. *Laeliocattleya* Ophir had much larger flowers than *Laelia xanthina* and good yellow-colored sepals and petals with a yellow-lavender lip. *Laeliocattleya* Ophir became a popular parent for yellow hybrids despite a tendency of the petals to sometimes reflex slightly. *Laeliocattleya* Ophir was eventually crossed back on *C. dowiana* to produce two of the early successes in yellow breeding, *Lc.* Thyone and *Lc.* President Wilson.

Pedigree of *Laeliocattleya* President Wilson

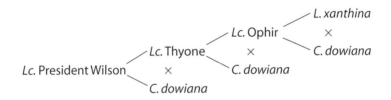

Laelia xanthina

Laeliocattleya President Wilson had good-sized flowers with a soft yellow color, but it was only used to a limited extent in breeding because other lines of hybridizing produced brighter yellow color. *Laeliocattleya* President Wilson received considerable recognition, however, including at least one First Class Certificate from the Royal Horticultural Society. Naming an orchid for U.S. president Woodrow Wilson during the First World War was a popular thing to do, and the yellow *Lc.* President Wilson of 1918 was often confused with the excellent lavender hybrids, *Cattleya* President Wilson (*C.* Fabia × *C. labiata*—1916) and *Brassolaeliocattleya* President Wilson (*Lc.* Lustre × *Brassocattleya* Mrs. J. Leemann—1917). The nomenclature was muddled further when Hassall and Company in London named its cross between *Lc.* Thyone and *Bc.* Mrs. J. Leemann, *Blc.* Thyone.

Another important hybrid of *Laeliocattleya* Ophir was its cross with *Brassocattleya* Mrs. J. Leemann called *Brassolaeliocattleya* The Baroness. The cross was made by Baron Schröder and flowered in 1913. *Brassolaeliocattleya* The Baroness produced both yellow and art-shade cattleyas and was used much more extensively in hybridizing than *Lc.* President Wilson. Its success in breeding may have been related to the relative simplicity of the cross and the neutral color input from *Bc.* Mrs. J. Leemann.

Pedigree of *Brassolaeliocattleya* The Baroness

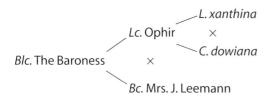

A brighter and deeper yellow with good shape and size was produced by Sander's with its hybrid *Laeliocattleya* Primrose which flowered in 1918. *Laeliocattleya* Primrose started with the bright yellow *Laelia flava* crossed with the well-shaped, large-flowered *Cattleya trianaei* and *C. schroederae*, but *Lc.* Primrose seemed to have little more success than *Lc.* President Wilson as a parent for creating more yellow *Cattleya* hybrids.

Pedigree of *Laeliocattleya* Primrose

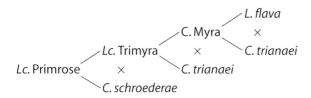

Although Veitch bred several of the early yellow hybrids like *Laeliocattleya* Ophir and *Cattleya* Myra and the orange-colored *Lc.* G. S. Ball (*L. cinnabarina* × *C. schroederae*), it was the British orchid firm Charlesworth and Company that was the real pioneer in developing yellow, orange, and red *Cattleya* hybrids. One of the first of Charlesworth's yellow *Cattleya* hybrids to make a name for itself was *C.* Iris which flowered in 1901. *Cattleya* Iris was a cross between the beautiful, full-lip *C. dowiana* and the long spade-lip *C. bicolor. Cattleya* Iris had a nice yellow color but an atrocious shape, and Charlesworth immediately crossed it back on *C. dowiana* to try to improve the shape. This produced the hybrid *C.* Venus in 1908 which still had so much *C. bicolor* shape left in it that the name "Venus" can only have been given to it tongue-in-cheek

Charlesworth also made a more promising cross in 1901 called *Laeliocattleya* Luminosa which used *Cattleya dowiana* with the full-lip *C. tenebrosa.* This produced a large-flowered hybrid with a normal full-lip in varying bright shades of bronze and yellow-bronze.

Undaunted by Charlesworth's dubious successes with *Cattleya* Iris and *C.* Venus, another British firm, Stuart Low, in 1922 crossed *C.* Venus with *Laeliocattleya* Luminosa and created the infamous *Lc.* Mrs. Medo. *Laeliocattleya* Mrs. Medo received a number of awards because of its strong yellow color but went on to produce a host of yellow hybrids with a dismal history of deformed flowers. The deformities were generally attributed to the incompatibility of the long spade-lip of *C. bicolor* with the full-lips of the other parents.

Even as late as 1952 and the infusion of still more *Laeliocattleya* Luminosa, the advanced yellow hybrid *Lc.* Lorraine Shirai produced mostly *Cattleya* Venus–shaped flowers. The *C.* Iris line of breeding, however, produced the most intense shades of yellow, and it became the preferred route to yellow hybrids despite the loss of the beautiful full-lip in these hybrids.

Toward the end of the 19th century, Charlesworth began making experimental

Cattleya Venus

crosses using the small orange-colored Brazilian laelias, *Laelia cinnabarina* and *L. harpophylla*, and the small red-flowered *Sophronitis coccinea*. The hybrids began flowering right after the turn of the century: *Laeliocattleya* Charlesworthii (*L. cinnabarina* × *C. dowiana*) in 1900, *Sophrolaelia* Gratrixiae (*S. coccinea* × *C. tenebrosa*) in 1901, and *Laelia* Coronet (*L. cinnabarina* × *L. harpophylla*) and *Sophrolaelia* Psyche (*L. cinnabarina* × *S. coccinea*) in 1902. These crosses produced an abundance of small, brightly colored flowers in shades of orange-red. The flower shape left much to be desired except in the *Sophronitis* hybrids, but it was a start toward creating orange- and red-colored *Cattleya* hybrids.

The next step was to cross these small colorful flowers with a round large-flowered *Cattleya* species to put some size into the flowers. The most reliable round breeders were *C. trianaei* and *C. schroederae*, and Charlesworth took its most brilliant hybrid, *Laelia* Coronet, and crossed it with a very pale lavender *C. schroederae*. The resulting hybrid was *Laeliocattleya* Elinor which flowered in 1908. *Laeliocattleya* Elinor was a good small to medium-sized orange, and in the early 1920s H. G. Alexander crossed it with another Charlesworth hybrid, *Brassocattleya* Heatonensis (*Brassavola digbyana* × *C.* Hardyana), to make the first large, clear concolor yellow-orange *Cattleya* hybrid, *Brassolaeliocattleya* Orange Glory. *Brassolaeliocattleya* Orange Glory 'Empress' immediately received a First Class Certificate from the Royal Horticultural Society and *Blc.* Orange Glory 'Worrall' and *Blc.* Orange Glory 'Golden Queen' were still receiving Awards of Merit from the American Orchid Society as late as 1964 and 1965.

Charlesworth had also made a hybrid called *Laeliocattleya* Aureole in 1907 crossing its *C. bicolor* hybrid, *C.* Iris, with *Lc.* Luminosa. Alexander had seen the potential in this hybrid when he worked for Sir George Holford at Westonbirt and bred it with *Sophroni-*

Laeliocattleya Lorraine Shirai

Brassolaeliocattleya Orange Glory 'Empress' FCC/RHS

tis grandiflora (syn. *S. coccinea*) to produce the first true red *Cattleya* hybrid, *Sophrolaeliocattleya* Falcon in 1917. The fine red color of *Slc.* Falcon 'Westonbirt' FCC/RHS was and still is the standard for red color in *Cattleya* hybrids. *Sophrolaeliocattleya* Falcon lacks a number of desirable qualities in its flowers like good carriage and large size, but its color is as red as red can be. It even blooms for us on Valentine's Day, which is almost too much to ask, and then blooms again in the early autumn.

In 1908 Charlesworth bred its *Sophrolaelia* Psyche with the large-flowered primary hybrid *Cattleya* Empress Frederick (*C. dowiana* × *C. mossiae*) to make one of the first successful art-shade *Cattleya* hybrids, *Sophrolaeliocattleya* Marathon. When Charlesworth crossed *Slc.* Marathon with the old *Laeliocattleya* Dominiana (*C. dowiana* × *C. purpurata*), it made one of the most famous purple-red cattleyas of all time, *Slc.* Anzac. The best variety, *Slc.* Anzac 'Orchidhurst' FCC/RHS, was a good medium-size flower with excellent shape and was the parent of many of the purple-red and art-shade *Cattleya* hybrids for many years.

With almost 100 years of breeding behind them, modern growers have continued to make improvements in the size and shape of these flowers, and we have available today many fine quality yellow, orange, red, and art-shade large-flowered *Cattleya* hybrids. Thanks to the modern technology of meristemming, it is possible to produce thousands of plants of the best variety and discard the deformed or poor quality plants of the cross. Some of these modern hybrids have *C.* Iris in their ancestry, but it only shows a little, and occasionally you find one like *Brassolaeliocattleya* Williette Wong 'The Best' that does not show it at all.

Sophrolaeliocattleya Falcon 'Westonbirt' FCC/RHS/AOS, Valentine's Day corsage

Sophrolaeliocattleya Anzac 'Orchidhurst' FCC/RHS

Brassolaeliocattleya Williette Wong 'The Best'

Laeliocattleya Chickahominy 'Olivia'

Brassolaeliocattleya Malworth Sunset 'Orchidglade'

Brassolaeliocattleya Erin Kobayashi 'Lahaina Gold' AM/AOS

SEVEN

Cattleyas in Art

L ONG BEFORE modern photography and printing came along, the watercolor artist made paintings of plants and flowers as a botanical reference to record the details of new and interesting varieties of plants that were being discovered by plant hunters in foreign lands. The pictures were painted to the exact size and shape of the plants and flowers and as close to natural color as watercolor pigments allowed. The watercolors were painted on a vellum-type of hand-made paper, and the paintings were reproduced by engraving and hand-colored for publication in books on botany. The paintings became known as "botanical illustrations," a term that is still used for this type of art. When just the flower alone was painted, the art was sometimes referred to as "flower portraiture," but the technique was the same. Watercolor was chosen as the medium to paint these new horticultural subjects because it was easier to portray fine detail and delicate shades and hues of color with watercolor than with oils.

A number of good watercolor artists appeared in Europe during the late 18th and early 19th centuries to feed the growing demand for the botanical illustrations needed to picture the large influx of newly discovered tropical plants that were finding their way into European gardens and greenhouses. When the first large-flowered cattleya, *Cattleya labiata*, was described by John Lindley in his book *Collectanea Botanica* in 1821, one of these artists, John Curtis, painted the watercolor botanical illustration of the *C. labiata* that accompanied Lindley's description. Curtis painted the plant exactly as he saw it in William Cattley's stove house in Barnet, England, and, in doing so, captured some of the cultural problems in growing cattleyas at the time. Curtis's picture of *C. labiata* showed a plant with flowers that were forced out prematurely by the excessive heat of the stove house. The flowers barely resembled *C. labiata* as we know it under good cultural conditions today (see photo on next page). The picture showed shriveled pseudobulbs from either a lack of roots or the drying, overpowering heat from the stove. This realism, of course, was the great benefit that botanical illustration offered botanists, but it was not always pleasing to the art critics of the day. Only a few artists were able to incorporate a feeling of emotion into these botanical illustrations to raise them to the level of more interpretative art.

One of the most successful early periodicals to use botanical illustrations of new plants was William Curtis's *Botanical Magazine* which began publication in 1787. The first issue had only three plates but, over the years, averaged about 45 plates annually.

Curtis tried to picture "the most ornamental Foreign Plants" in the *Botanical Magazine* and hired three watercolor artists, William Kilburn, James Sowerby, and Sydenham Edwards, to do the paintings. The *Botanical Magazine* was remarkable from a production point of view because from 1787 to 1948 all the paintings, with the exception of a few chromolithographs in the 1921 volume, were colored by hand.

After Curtis died in 1799, the *Botanical Magazine* struggled financially for a while until William Jackson Hooker took over direction and illustration in 1826. Hooker was a superb watercolor artist in addition to being an important botanist and had produced a much more impressive painting of *Cattleya labiata* in volume 2 of his *Exotic Flora* (plate 157) in 1825 than John Curtis had done in *Collectanea Botanica* (see photo on page 192). Hooker did all the illustrations for the *Botanical Magazine* until 1834 when the job took too much of his time and he hired a talented young botanical illustrator,

First illustration of *Cattleya labiata* by John Curtis in *Collectanea Botanica* (1821)

Walter Hood Fitch, to do them. It was Fitch who painted the picture of the two *C. mossiae* flowers (plate 3669) that accompanied Hooker's description of the new species in 1836 (see photo on page 193). Fitch was so accomplished at his trade that he not only painted the watercolors, but also did the lithographs for publication as well, and he is generally considered to be the most outstanding botanical illustrator of the mid-1800s. When William Jackson Hooker died in 1865 and his son, Joseph Dalton Hooker, took over direction of Curtis's *Botanical Magazine*, Fitch continued as illustrator and painted the impressive 10-by-12-inch foldout of three *C. dowiana* flowers for James Bateman's description of *C. dowiana* in 1867 (plate 5618).

During the years when Curtis's *Botanical Magazine* had financial problems, one of the original watercolor artists, Sydenham Edwards, decided to start his own botanical publication and, in 1815, Edwards launched the *Botanical Register*. The *Botanical Register* did not promote itself as a record of foreign plants like Curtis's *Botanical Magazine* but as a picture book of "exotic plants cultivated in British gardens with their history and mode of treatment." It also advised readers that the designs were by Sydenham Edwards. With Edwards's death in 1819, John Lindley continued the publication using other artists and re-described and pictured all three of the large-flowered *Cattleya* species known at the time—*C. labiata*, *C. maxima*, and *C. mossiae*. The quality of the botanical illustrations in the *Botanical Register*, however, did not begin to compare with the excellent watercolors of Walter Fitch in Curtis's *Botanical Magazine*, and Edwards's *Botanical Register* discontinued publication at the end of 1847.

The bright rose-lavender color of the typical large-flowered *Cattleya* species is difficult to duplicate in watercolor, and artists have had varying degrees of success doing this. William Jackson Hooker painted *C. labiata* in 1825 in a pink-lavender color, while

Cattleya labiata by William Jackson Hooker in *Exotic Flora*, plate 157 (1825)

Walter Fitch used only a hint of pink in his *C. mossiae* in 1836. The most unnatural color renditions were those that used blue-purple pigments like some of the paintings in the *Botanical Register* and *The Orchid Album.* These blue-purple tones seem to dominate modern botanical illustrations of dark lavender cattleyas which definitely detracts from their beauty. Shades of yellow and cream can be reproduced with much more accuracy in watercolor than the lavender or purple shades, and artists seem to have few problems with non-lavender colors in cattleya flowers.

Although botanical illustration started as a means of identifying plants for botanical and horticultural purposes, watercolor paintings of flowers soon became popular with wealthy plant collectors who hired artists to paint not only their wives and children in real life, but also their favorite plants and flowers. The interest in watercolor painting blossomed to such a degree and became so pervasive that by the mid-1800s, a proper English young lady was expected not only to speak a little French and play the piano, she was also expected to be able to paint a few flowers in watercolor.

Watercolor paintings, of course, were not well suited to publications like newspapers and weekly periodicals because they were too expensive to make and could not be produced in large enough quantities. The agricultural weekly, *The Gardeners' Chronicle,* printed a continuous stream of flower portraits like the *Cattleya warscewiczii* Sanderiana (as *C. sanderiana*) of 1883 that used wood engraving from black-and-white drawings.

As the increasing interest in plants and flowers developed during the Golden Age of horticulture in Europe, numerous books began to be published showing botanical illustrations of popular, interesting, and beautiful new flowers. These have often been described with a touch of distain by art critics as "sentimental flower books," but they brought together whole groups of plants like roses, camellias, and orchids and put these

Lithograph of *Cattleya mossiae* by Walter H. Fitch from Curtis's *Botanical Magazine,* plate 3669 (1836)

Woodcut of *Cattleya warscewiczii* Sanderiana (as *C. sanderiana*) by W. J. Welch from *The Gardeners' Chronicle,* figure 62 (1883)

plants in good historical perspective for future generations. Some of the most impressive of these flower books were in the field of orchids beginning with James Bateman's gigantic folio, *The Orchidaceae of Mexico and Guatemala,* and culminating with the truly grand orchid books of the late 1800s, *The Orchid Album, Lindenia,* and *Reichenbachia.*

The Orchid Album was essentially a picture book of particularly fine varieties of orchids and was published by the author of *The Orchid-Grower's Manual,* Benjamin Samuel Williams. It was marketed to the elite hobbyists who could afford to buy the best varieties of orchids, and it was embellished with Williams's comments on culture and Thomas Moore's botanical descriptions. It pictured all of the important *Cattleya* species and was sold as an annual volume of 12 monthly installments. Williams said it was designed for "both the drawing room and the library," and it was similar to today's

Chromolithograph of *Cattleya crispa* 'Buchananiana' by John Nugent Fitch from *The Orchid Album,* plate 81 (1883)

glamorous cocktail-table orchid books. The original watercolor paintings and the chromolithographs were done by Walter Fitch's young nephew, John Nugent Fitch, who was considered to be almost as fine a botanical illustrator as his uncle. The 10-by-12-inch size of the *Album* gave Fitch ample room to demonstrate his talents. *The Orchid Album* began publication in 1882 and continued through the production of eleven impressive volumes.

Lindenia was a monthly publication of four chromolithographs of fine, new or rare orchid plants and was published from 1885 to 1906 by Jean Jules Linden, the owner of the Belgian orchid company Horticulture Internationale. The text was in French, but an English-language edition was also eventually produced. The original watercolor paintings for *Lindenia* were painted by seven artists headed by P. de Pannemaeker and the chromolithographs were done by J. L. Goffart and de Pannemaeker. During its 21-year existence, *Lindenia* published 814 beautiful plates of orchids, including many large-flowered *Cattleya* species like the brilliant *C. dowiana* 'Statteriana'. Naturalia Publications in France even republished the *Lindenia* in five volumes in 1993 with English-language text.

Reichenbachia was a four-volume set of books of chromolithographed botanical illustrations of orchids produced on a grand scale with text in English, French, and German. It was published by Sander's of St. Albans, England, from 1888 to 1894. The flowers were presented life-size, and the regular edition was unusually large at 21½ inches high by 16 inches wide. The Imperial Edition was even larger at 29½ by 23½ inches. The

Chromolithograph of *Cattleya dowiana* 'Statteriana' by A. Goossens from *Lindenia*, plate 356 (1892). Courtesy of Naturalia Publications

chromolithographs were produced using as many as 20 inks and the cost to Sander was enormous and almost bankrupted the firm.

Most of the original watercolor paintings for *Reichenbachia* were done by the artist Henry George Moon (H. G. Moon), although a few were painted by artists like A. H. Loorch and W. H. Fitch. Moon was unique among the botanical illustrators of his day because he painted the orchid plants and flowers exactly as he found them, much to the consternation of Frederick Sander. Moon's watercolors showed the orchid plants with all their insect-damaged leaves, and flower and pseudobulb imperfections that other botanical illustrators would smooth out to give a more perfect-looking rendition. Moon also placed the flowers exactly as they grew instead of in more attractive positions, and seldom embellished the color of the flowers even though he hand-touched many of the finished chromolithographs. Moon has been characterized by some reviewers as probably the greatest of all British flower painters, and there is no doubt that Moon produced a good design in many of his paintings and, now and then, a feeling of life and excitement that his contemporaries seemed to lack. His painting of *Cattleya labiata* from the last volume of *Reichenbachia* gives a different feeling to the species than the pictures of any other botanical illustrator of his time.

In 1897 the Royal Horticultural Society in England began having a watercolor artist paint a picture of the plants that received awards from the society. These botanical illustrations enabled the Society to record the details of the awarded flowers before the age of color photography, and their paintings have been an invaluable reference for many of

Chromolithograph of *Cattleya labiata* by H. G. Moon from *Reichenbachia* (1894).

Award painting of *Cattleya warscewiczii* 'Low' FCC/RHS 1910 by Nellie Roberts. Copyright © Royal Horticultural Society, Lindley Library. Used by permission.

Angela Mirro. *Cattleya dowiana aurea* 'Kathleen AM/AOS 2002. Watercolor 29 × 22 inches. Courtesy Angela Mirro, Brooklyn, New York. Private collection.

Angela Mirro. *Cattleya* rex 'Splash Mariza' 2000. Watercolor 29 × 22 inches. Courtesy of Angela Mirro, Brooklyn, New York. Private collection.

the old named varieties of the large-flowered *Cattleya* species and hybrids. More than 20 artists did these paintings over the years, and names like Nellie Roberts and Jeanne Holgate are familiar to most cattleya aficionados. It is fascinating to see that in an age steeped in fine and inexpensive color photography, the Royal Horticultural Society still has its awarded plants hand-painted by a watercolor artist.

Botanical illustrations of orchid plants and flowers are still popular with orchid growers and the American Orchid Society includes at least one original botanical illustration in its monthly magazine, *Orchids*. One modern illustrator, Brooklyn artist Angela Mirro, has produced a number of paintings of large-flowered *Cattleya* species that are particularly appealing to collectors of these orchids. Her paintings of *C. dowiana* 'Kathleen AM/AOS and *C. rex* 'Splash Mariza' have been very popular and are still available as limited edition prints from the artist.

Not all art depicting the classic cattleyas are botanical illustrations, of course. At orchid shows that have competitive classes for orchid art, you often see examples of interpretive art that go beyond the routine picture-perfect reproductions of these flowers. We found a striking pastel of a *Brassocattleya* by American artist Georgia O'Keeffe

Georgia O'Keeffe (1887–1986). © Artists Rights Society, New York. An Orchid. 1941. Pastel on board, 21 3/4 × 27 5/8 inches. Bequest of Georgia O'Keeffe. © The Museum of Modern Art, New York. (556.1990). Digital image © The Museum of Modern Art/Licensed by SCALA/Art Resource, New York.

(1887–1986) on display in the Museum of Modern Art in New York. It was entitled merely "An Orchid" and was painted by O'Keeffe in 1941. The picture captures the *feeling* of the flower's labellum in a way not found in botanical illustrations.

New York artist Anne Link has also used the cattleya as a subject in some of her present-day works. Ms. Link specializes in three-dimensional art from large construction pieces that take up more floor space in an art gallery than a 200-square-foot orchid exhibit in an orchid show, to more traditional wall paintings. She is known for her envi-

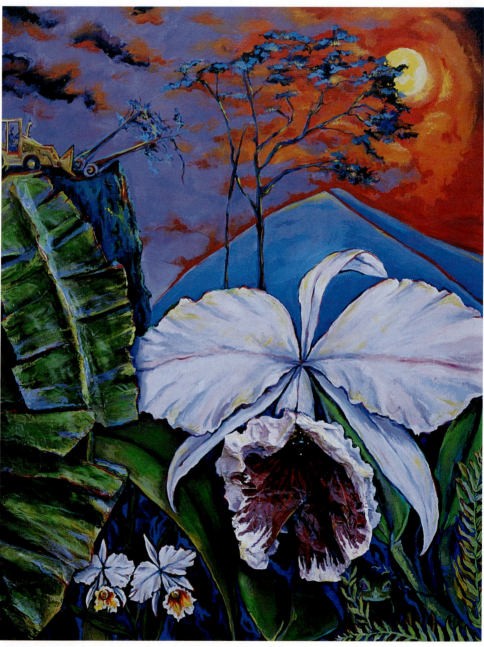

Anne Link. Bulldozer. 2000. Acrylic and papier-mâché on 4-by-5-foot canvas. Courtesy of Anne Link, New York. Private collection.

Anne Link. Serenity. 2004. Acrylic on 30-by-40-inch canvas. Courtesy of Anne Link, New York. Private collection.

Anne Link. Clusters. 2004. Acrylic and papier-mâché on 36-by-42-inch canvas. Courtesy of Anne Link, New York. Private collection.

ronmental themes, and we have pictured our favorite Anne Link cattleya painting—a 4-by-5-foot acrylic canvas entitled "Bulldozer" that shows a huge cattleya flower in a jungle with a menacing bulldozer clearing land in the distance. An angry blood-red sky hangs over a barren hillside to emphasize the violent nature of the things to come. Both the large banana leaves and the lip of the cattleya flower extend several inches beyond the canvas which makes the painting unique among those we have seen.

Ms. Link has also used cattleyas in her non-environmental paintings like "Serenity"—a 30-by-40-inch picture of a purple-and-white cattleya. We find it refreshing to see cattleya flowers incorporated into modern interpretative art like this because the flower's bilateral symmetry makes it a difficult subject to handle in such works.

In "Clusters," Ms. Link has blended three cattleya lips into a design that magnifies nature's invitation to enter this erotic realm. The yellow lobes of the lip resemble ripe pollen sacs waiting to be plucked by a dazzled pollinator—not quite a sentimental-flower-book character—more like a touch of the flower's soul in its endless struggle to perpetuate life.

EIGHT

Growing Your Own Cattleyas

I F YOU HAVE a greenhouse that gets a few hours of sunshine during the day, cattleyas are one of the easiest orchids you can grow. Even if you do not have a greenhouse, you can still grow many varieties of cattleyas by using nature's greenhouse (your own backyard) when the plants are actively growing during the late spring and summer, then flowering them inside your home when they are resting during the fall and winter. If you live in subtropical areas like South Florida and Southern California, or in tropical areas like Hawaii, nature's greenhouse is available to you virtually the whole year.

Nature's Way

Cattleyas are epiphytes, which means they grow on another plant and use that plant for support. They are not parasites, and their roots do not penetrate the host plant or feed on the host's sap even though their roots grow all over the outside of the host plant. In their native habitats, cattleyas usually grow on large trees and their roots cling to the rough bark of the tree to anchor the plants securely. The roots grow in all directions from the cattleya plants as they seek moisture and nutrients for their survival and growth. Cattleya roots have a spongelike outer layer that absorbs any moisture that touches it from falling rain, water running down the tree, or even morning or evening dew. The plants can be drenched by heavy tropical rains several times a day during their active growing season. Cattleyas normally grow fairly high up in trees where they are exposed to a constant flow of air and receive a considerable amount of sunlight. They are protected from too much direct sun by the leaves of the trees which scatter the sun's rays as they penetrate the tree canopy.

A few cattleyas are found growing on rock outcroppings in the jungle where they are sometimes exposed to direct sunlight for most of the day. Direct exposure to the sun like this requires either the cooling effect of strong breezes or the cooler temperatures and thinner air of higher altitudes, or both, to prevent the plants from being scorched by the sun.

Cattleyas are often exposed to dry periods in the wild which can last from a few weeks to several months. During these dry periods, the plants get their moisture from mists and fog in the air and the moisture stored in their large pseudobulbs and thick, fleshy leaves. With all their exposure to wind, sun, heavy tropical rains, and periods of drought, cattleyas are tough plants that are able to handle a wide variety of conditions and still thrive, grow, and produce beautiful large flowers season after season for many years.

Greenhouse Cultivation

Duplicating the conditions found in nature, of course, is not practical for everyday greenhouse cultivation. It is not realistic to put a 30- or 40-foot tall tree in your greenhouse, or expose your orchids to the direct ultraviolet rays of the sun, or water the plants several times a day. Glass and polycarbonate plastics used to cover greenhouses block out ultraviolet rays, few greenhouses can accommodate even a 10-foot tree, and only nature has the time to water plants all day every day.

Some orchid growers in Europe during the late 19th century tried to duplicate outside conditions by removing the glass from their greenhouses during the summer. The additional sun and air the plants received produced better growths and many more flowers, but the efforts were short lived because it was not practical to take all the glass out and put it back every year. Even though we cannot provide raw jungle conditions in a greenhouse, we can come close enough to nature so our plants grow well and produce flowers virtually as well as in the wild.

Temperature

Since cattleyas are tropical plants, their first requirement is a warm, tropical environment. Large-flowered *Cattleya* species and most of their hybrids grow well at daytime temperatures of 80° to 85°F under greenhouse conditions. Temperatures above 85°F, particularly in the 90°F range, tend to retard growth and can significantly shorten the life of cattleya flowers. Night temperatures, however, are not the same for all the species and are just as important as daytime temperatures in growing these plants.

The mountain species like *Cattleya warscewiczii* and *C. trianaei*, which are subjected to hot days and cool nights in the wild, like a night temperature of 58° to 60°F and produce their best growths and largest flowers when grown under these conditions. Most *Cattleya* hybrids also do well at night temperatures around 58° to 60°F.

Species that come from the lower altitudes of the hot Amazon basin like *Cattleya eldorado*, however, prefer warmer night temperatures from 65° to 70°F. *Cattleya lawrenceana* from Venezuela, *C. dowiana* from Costa Rica, and *C. dowiana aurea* from Colombia also do better under greenhouse conditions at these higher night temperatures particularly during the cold winter months. If the temperature in the greenhouse is expected to fall below 65°F at night, it is important to keep this group of warm *Cattleya* species as dry as possible. If they are allowed to stay wet, the combination of cold temperatures and wet roots can lead to pseudobulb rot, a condition that will usually kill the plant once symptoms begin to appear.

Cattleya warneri and *C. lueddemanniana*, because they are actively growing during the winter months in northern greenhouses, are intermediate in their temperature requirements between the warm- and cool-growing groups and seem to do better at a temperature of about 63° to 64°F at night.

Table 5. Nighttime temperature preferences of large-flowered cattleyas

COOL GROUP 58° TO 60°F	INTERMEDIATE GROUP 63° TO 64°F	WARM GROUP 65° TO 70°F
C. gaskelliana	C. jenmanii	C. dowiana
C. labiata	C. lueddemanniana	C. dowiana aurea
C. maxima	C. warneri	C. eldorado
C. mendelii		C. lawrenceana
C. mossiae		
C. percivaliana		
C. quadricolor		
C. rex		
C. schroederae		
C. trianaei		
C. warscewiczii		

Greenhouses normally have microclimates in them and some areas are slightly warmer or cooler than the rest of the greenhouse so it is usually possible to accommodate all the large-flowered *Cattleya* species in a single greenhouse. When it is too cold for the warm group during the winter months in the United States, these plants should be kept as dry as possible to prevent them from developing rot.

Humidity

Like most tropical plants, cattleyas like a reasonable amount of moisture in the air around them, and it is important to create a moist tropical atmosphere in the greenhouse when you grow them. The most common way to provide humidity to the greenhouse is using a hose to spray water on the walls and under the benches in the morning and early afternoon. This requires no special equipment and it is very effective in producing a good level of humidity.

Since relative humidity increases as the temperature falls in the late afternoon, you should avoid spraying water around the greenhouse later than midafternoon so the air does not become saturated with moisture during the night. High humidity at night can cause spotting of flowers and infect young growths with rot. Moisture that does not evaporate from the plant's leaves before this late afternoon temperature drop can also lead to the development of black rot on young cattleya growths (see disease section).

Good levels of humidity can also be produced using fogging machines that can automatically send a dense fog of water into the air throughout the day. These foggers can also be very helpful in lowering the temperature when the greenhouse begins to reach 90°F. A sudden burst of fog can drop the temperature by 5° or 10°F within a few minutes. It is still important, however, when using these fogging machines, to be sure they do not fog in the late afternoon or at night.

Air Circulation

Good air circulation is important to the successful culture of cattleyas and, depending on the size of your greenhouse, you should have one or more fans that keep the air moving all the time. The fans should produce a gentle breeze, not a hurricane wind, and their purpose is to even out the temperature throughout the greenhouse and prevent the accumulation of gases like ethylene around the flowers that can shorten their life. Since you only need a light movement of air, a small, efficient $\frac{1}{32}$ horsepower fan is sufficient. The fan should run continuously, 24 hours a day, 365 days a year.

Sun and Shading

Sunshine is one of the most important elements needed to produce strong growths and many flowers in cattleyas. Without enough sunshine, growths tend to be dark green, slender, and weak in appearance, and the plants flower poorly if at all. An ideal greenhouse is one that receives sunshine all day long, but good success can still be enjoyed from lesser amounts of sun. The color of the cattleya's leaves is the best indicator of whether the plants are receiving the right amount of sun. The leaves should have a light green color like the middle leaf in the photo below. If they are dark green like the leaf on the right, they are receiving too little sun, and if they are yellow or yellow-green like the one on the left, they are receiving too much sun. If the leaves feel warm when you put your hand on them, they are receiving too much sun and should be moved immediately to a more shaded location.

During the winter months in the United States when the sun is at its lowest angle, most greenhouses do not require any shade over the glass or polycarbonate panels to protect the plants. As the sun rises higher in the sky in the late winter and begins to increase in intensity, some light shading will be needed to prevent the leaves of the cattleyas from becoming yellow or warm to the touch. If you live in a northern area where

The color of a cattleya leaf is the best indicator of how much sun the plant is getting. A dark green leaf (right) shows not enough sun, a yellow leaf (left) shows too much sun, and a light green leaf (center) shows the proper amount.

it is still bitter cold outside in late February, put some light shade cloth on the inside of the greenhouse instead of the outside to allow the maximum amount of sun to come through to warm the greenhouse but still give the plants the shade they need. Most greenhouses require at least 50-percent shade by late March until October to prevent cattleyas from becoming too yellow. In some cases even 70-percent shade may be needed by June. Remember that cattleya leaves are thick and fleshy and they absorb more heat from the sun than the thin leaves of common garden plants. This heat can literally cook the cattleyas if you are not careful.

The biggest problem with too much sun is primarily one of overheating the plants. To avoid overheating, greenhouses normally have ventilators on their sides and top to let cooler air in and hotter air out. If more cooling is needed when the outside temperature goes over 90°F, an evaporative cooler can be installed at one end of the greenhouse. An evaporative cooler uses a fan to pull air into the greenhouse through a fibrous pad dripping with cold water. The temperature can also be lowered by spraying a little water over the plants. If money is no object, the greenhouse can be air-conditioned.

There are many ways to shade the outer surface of the glass or polycarbonate sheets that cover a greenhouse. For many years, a whitewash compound was sprayed on the outside of the greenhouse glass. The compound adhered to the glass, but slowly wore off over the summer until it was virtually gone by the time the plants needed more sunshine in the autumn. These whitewashes are not as common today because they are messy to apply and do not always give as uniform a shading as polypropylene or nylon shade cloth. Slatted wood or aluminum roller blinds were often used on wealthy estate greenhouses because they could be raised and lowered throughout the day to let in more or less sunlight as the weather changed. The estates, of course, had full-time gardeners who could do this chore.

Today most growers shade their greenhouses with black shade cloth, which is a loose netting made of polypropylene or nylon. The shade cloth is available through most suppliers of greenhouse products and comes in 10-percent increments (10-percent shade, 20-percent shade, 30-percent shade, and so forth) and can be ordered to fit the exact size of a greenhouse. We have some black polypropylene shade cloth that has been used to shade one of our greenhouses for over 25 years, so shade cloth can be a one-time investment for the hobbyist. When ordering black shade cloth, be sure it has grommets along all the edges at about 3-foot intervals so the shade cloth can be securely anchored to the greenhouse frame. If the shade cloth is not held securely, it can be blown loose and subject your plants to a sudden increase in sunlight that could burn them badly or even kill them.

Watering

One of the most important things you have to learn when you grow any kind of orchid is how to water it properly, and cattleyas are no exception. Regardless of the medium in which the plants are grown, the first rule to follow in watering mature, well-established cattleya plants is to water them thoroughly. This means you should put enough water on the plants to wet the medium completely. When you do this, the water will pour out the bottom of the pot almost as fast as it is poured on the top surface of the medium. It takes about a quart of water to thoroughly wet a 5- or 6-inch pot containing most cattleya mediums, but this is not a precise measure since you will probably be using a garden hose to water them and a little extra water will not harm the plants. What is important is that every corner of the medium is thoroughly wet and all the roots are moistened. A good thorough watering draws the roots down into the pot where they remain moist for a few days. When water is just splashed on the surface of the medium, the medium underneath will remain dry and the roots will stay on the surface of the pot and grow over the sides of the pot seeking water.

Spraying the plants would be fine if you were growing them on the side of a tree in the jungle, but it is bad if you are growing them in pots in a greenhouse because they will seldom get enough water to produce their best growths. In a greenhouse, you want all the roots inside the pot not wandering around the benches and onto other plants. You sometimes see long cattleya roots dangling from the bottoms of pots halfway to the floor under some grower's benches. This shows the plants are not getting a thorough enough watering and it is a good indicator of how well or poorly the grower is doing the watering job.

The second rule in watering cattleyas is to let the plants dry out almost completely before you water them again. You can learn to do this by picking up the pot with one hand and feeling its weight. A newly watered plant is heavy and it becomes lighter as it dries out. Allowing the plant to dry out thoroughly stimulates the roots to seek water and continue to fill the pot. Plants should never be allowed to sit in a soggy, waterlogged medium for any length of time because this condition is a root killer.

Light spraying or splashing water on the surface of a pot causes roots to grow across the medium instead of down into the medium.

How often you have to water your cattleyas depends, of course, on how rapidly they dry out. This will vary depending on the season of the year and the conditions in your greenhouse. Mature cattleya plants usually need to be watered about once a week. Seedlings in small pots, however, dry out more quickly and may have to be watered every day or two.

In the winter when the heating system is producing a lot of dry heat, the plants may have to be watered more often than once a week. Be careful not to overwater, however, during these cold months because the combination of a wet medium and cold temperatures encourages the growth of fungi, some of which can be pathogenic and kill orchid roots and sometimes pseudobulbs. It is a good rule to keep cattleyas a little drier during the winter when temperatures are at a minimum in the greenhouse. The warm-growing group of species like *Cattleya dowiana* should receive a bare minimum of water during this cold period and some people just water lightly around the inside edge of the pot rather than soak the whole pot to keep the medium from becoming too wet.

If you want to be a real expert and get the very best growths and flowers from your plants, you should vary the frequency of watering during their growing cycle. Most cattleya species do better if they are kept dry for several weeks before they normally start growing. This dryness seems to stimulate the plant to develop strong, rather thick and blunt new growing buds. The plant should remain on the dry side until the new growth is at least 3 inches tall.

Many of the early cattleya growers in the 1800s found that if they did not water *Cattleya warscewiczii* until the growths were 4 inches tall, they got the best flower pro-

When a cattleya plant is properly watered, the roots are entirely inside the medium in the pot.

duction, and we have also found this to be true. Once the plants pass the 4-inch stage, they should be given a good thorough watering regularly until their growth is mature and they begin to flower.

After flowering, the plants usually go into a dormant state and the frequency of watering can be reduced. Some species like *Cattleya warscewiczii* seem determined to make another growth even though they have just completed one and flowered. When this happens, the best thing to do is to continue regular watering until the new growth is mature. These post-flowering growths usually do not flower, but it is always desirable to produce a good-sized pseudobulb when you can. A little shriveling of the pseudo-bulbs is not serious while they are dormant since they will plump-up again as soon as the plants start to grow and you resume regular watering. Just be sure the pseudobulbs do not shrivel excessively.

Water Quality

Good quality water is essential for the successful cultivation of all orchids, including cattleyas. The water should be free of harmful contaminates and have a neutral or slightly acid pH. It should not be highly alkaline or excessively chlorinated. If your cattleyas are not growing well and there are no obvious cultural or pest problems, you should check the water to see if that is the problem. If you suspect the water, try collecting rain water and use it to water your plants for a while to see if they improve. Rain water was used by orchid growers on most private estates both in Europe and the United States during the 1800s and well into the 1900s. The rain that fell on the greenhouse was funneled into large rectangular concrete holding tanks that usually ran under the center bench.

Containers

Most cattleya plants in cultivation are grown in plastic or clay flower pots. This is a convenient and practical way to grow a number of individual plants in a relatively small area. Clay pots are better than plastic pots for growing cattleyas because they allow a better exchange of air with the plants' roots than plastic and allow the plants to dry out faster. Clay pots are also heavy enough to prevent the plants from tipping over when a new growth or flower spike leans too heavily over the edge of the pot.

The potted cattleya plants can be placed either on a typical 36- to 38-inch-high flat greenhouse bench or on a stepped bench. They can also be hung overhead from a horizontal pipe in the greenhouse using a metal hanger. Stepped benches have the advantage that it is easier to see the individual plants than on a flat bench and the flowers open better because they stand above the plants in front of them. Stepped benches are, however, more expensive to construct than flat benches. Regardless of which type of bench is used, it is desirable to put ¼-inch wire, like galvanized hardware cloth, about 2 inches high along the outer edge to prevent plants from being knocked off by people as they walk through the greenhouse.

Hanging baskets are sometimes used when a grower wants to develop a large exhibition plant and there is no room for the plant on the bench. The basket can be made from wood or metal. Metal baskets are normally lined with a porous material like a coconut husk pad that prevents the medium from being washed out when it is watered.

Two-inch high wire, like galvanized hardware cloth, along the front edge of the bench prevents plants from being knocked off the bench as people walk through the greenhouse.

When hanging pots or baskets overhead, place them over the aisle so they will not drip on plants below them when they are watered. Cattleyas are not usually grown on slabs of cork, tree fern, or bark because these dry out too quickly and must be watered several times a day to get the same results you get from growing the plants in pots.

Potting Mediums

Since orchid roots grow inside a pot under greenhouse cultivation and not in the open air on a tree trunk as they do in nature, the medium used in the pot to support the plant must provide good aeration or the roots will rot and die. Ordinary garden soil cannot be used to grow cattleyas because it lacks this aeration. Instead, a number of products have been developed to provide an open, air-filled medium that still provides enough water to the plant's roots so the plants do not have to be watered every day. Since the main requirement for producing healthy roots in cattleyas is good aeration, any material that provides this aeration can be used to grow them.

In the United States the most commonly used materials are ground fir bark, redwood bark, chipped and fibrous wood products like cypress mulch, chopped coconut husks, and sphagnum moss. The list of materials that have been used to grow cattleya plants successfully, however, is endless and includes tropical tree fern, osmunda, lava rock, washed pebbles, plastic peanuts, wine corks, rock wool, chunk peat, charcoal, redwood fiber, and mixtures of these and many more. A friend of ours even grew some cattleyas in the washed empty seed cases of our native Delaware sweet gum trees (*Liquidambar styraciflua*). He did this just to prove cattleyas will grow well in any neutral airfilled medium.

Fir Bark

Fir bark is the most commonly used medium to grow cattleyas in the United States today because it is inexpensive, widely available, easy to use, and good for stimulating root growth. Fir bark is a by-product of the lumber industry in the western United States and is sold in 2-cubic-foot plastic bags. It comes in three sizes: fine (approx. ¼-inch pieces), medium (½- to ¾-inch pieces), and large or coarse (¾- to 1-inch pieces). The fine fir bark is used to make seedling cattleya mixes for plants in 1½- to 3-inch pots, while the medium-size bark is used for flowering-size cattleya plants in pot sizes of 4 inches and above. The coarse-size bark is normally used for vandaceous orchids that have a bulky, more rigid root system than cattleyas.

Since fir bark holds very little water itself, a water-retention material is added to the bark to produce what are called "bark mixes." These mixes provide a good moisture balance in the medium while still retaining the aeration needed for the roots to grow well. Water-retention materials that are added to the bark include chunk peat moss, redwood and other wood fibers, synthetic products like perlite and vermiculite, charcoal, sphagnum, and mixtures of these. Commercially available proprietary orchid mixes and bark mixes can be found in many garden stores today or purchased from orchid plant growers.

If you decide to use a fir bark mix to grow your orchids, you should be aware of two problems. Fir bark that has not been heat-treated can harbor bush snails that love to eat orchid roots (see chapter ten for details). Fir bark can also carry a yellow fungus that over time can grow to block the flow of water through the medium. You know you have this yellow fungus if you see small yellow mushrooms coming up through the bark. These problems can be avoided by checking to see the bark is heat-treated to kill these pests. Sometimes this is noted on the label, but if it is not, you should call the manufacturer and ask about it.

Cypress Mulch

One of the most economical mediums we have found for cattleyas is the standard 100-percent cypress mulch sold in many garden stores. The mulch usually comes in 2-cubic-foot plastic bags and is not intended for use as a growing medium for cattleyas but as a mulch for flower beds and shrubs around the outside of the house. The mulch is made from the ground-up and chipped wood of cypress trees that grow in very wet environments like swamps and marshes in the southern United States, so the mulch is highly resistant to deterioration from rot and decay. It is therefore a lot more durable than fir bark in orchid pots.

Cypress mulch contains not only chipped and shredded pieces of cypress wood, but a lot of fiber as well so it has a reasonable water retention and good aeration. It also contains an occasional large 2- or 3-inch chunk of cypress wood that should be discarded. It is important to use the premium grade, 100-percent cypress mulch, however, since some so-called cypress mulch products contain mostly non-cypress wood which does not last long and can become moldy and interfere with the water and aeration properties of the mulch. The 100-percent cypress mulch can be used just as it comes from the bag without the addition of separate water-retention materials.

Coconut Husk Chips

Coconut husk chips are a relatively new medium for growing cattleyas and have only been available from suppliers of orchid products since the 1980s or so. Coconut husk chips are usually sold in 40-pound compressed bales in two sizes, ½ inch and 1-inch chips. Either size, or a mixture of both, can be used to grow cattleyas.

Coconut husk chips contain sea salt which must be washed out of the chips before they are used as a potting medium. Washing consists of soaking the chips overnight in water. The water is then poured off and the process repeated two more times to be sure all the salt is removed. Coconut husk chips have very good water-retention properties and good aeration and can last several years without deterioration. The root systems produced by cattleya plants in coconut husk chips compare well with the best fir bark mixes.

Osmunda

Osmunda was the most widely used potting medium for cattleyas during the heyday of the cattleya cut-flower industry in the United States. It is the root of the *Osmunda* fern that grew extensively in bogs in Florida at the time and was harvested annually from the previous year's growth, so it was a renewable product. It was sold to the large commercial growers in 6-cubic-foot compressed bales containing 12- to 18-inch chunks of chopped osmunda fiber. It is still available commercially but in only limited quantities and is now packaged in 6-cubic-foot non-compressed bales.

Osmunda is a very long lasting medium, and cattleya plants can stay in it for several years if the pot is large enough to accommodate the plant's forward growth. Osmunda wets very well even when completely dry and provides a good aeration and moisture balance and a modest amount of natural nutrient for the plants. It requires less-frequent watering than most fir bark mixes.

Osmunda is not an easy medium to work with, however, and its tough fibers must be chopped into pieces small enough to work into the pot and around the plants and it must be packed tightly to hold the plant fast in the pot. When a cattleya is potted correctly in osmunda, you can pick it up by the pseudobulbs and it will not come out of the pot. Newly repotted plants in osmunda must also be watered carefully until new roots are well established or the roots may rot. Because of these handling and potting problems, osmunda was replaced by fir bark mixes fairly quickly after fir bark appeared as a practical medium for growing cattleyas. Fir bark mixes were simply easier to use, and plants could be watered more safely immediately after repotting.

Sphagnum Moss

Sphagnum moss is both an ingredient in bark mixes and a product that can be used alone to grow cattleyas. When used in bark mixes, it adds additional water retention and a wicking effect that helps move moisture around the medium. When used alone, sphagnum is an excellent medium for seedling cattleyas up to 3-inch pot sizes, and it encourages the development of roots on weak or shriveled plants.

Most sphagnum moss sold today is dried and compressed and must be soaked in water to re-hydrate it. As a growing medium, it has the advantage that it dries out quickly in small pots so it stimulates root growth and has mild anti-fungal properties that help newly emerging roots grow better. Sphagnum should not be used alone in pot sizes larger than 4 inches, however, because it can stay wet too long in these large pots and will actually work against rooting. Sphagnum should also be packed loosely in the pot for best results and the plants repotted at least annually.

Several types of sphagnum are available, and the types most commonly used for orchids are New Zealand and Chilean sphagnums which have relatively thick fibers and are usually free of pests like snails and slugs although grass weeds sometimes sprout in Chilean sphagnum. Most native sphagnum harvested in the United States is much less expensive to buy than the imported New Zealand and Chilean types, but it has less dense fibers and often harbors snails, slugs, and their eggs. We feel if you want to use these domestic sphagnum products, you should boil them for two or three minutes to kill any pests before using them. Let them cool, of course, to room temperature before actually potting the plants.

Charcoal

Charcoal is not used by itself as a medium for cattleyas but is sometimes used as an ingredient in bark mixes. Charcoal is a sweetening agent, which means it absorbs many chemicals that can be toxic to plant roots. It also absorbs water and releases it as the medium dries out. Charcoal comes in several sizes: #1 size is 1 to 2 inches, #2 is $\frac{1}{2}$ to $\frac{3}{4}$ inch, #3 is $\frac{1}{4}$ to $\frac{1}{2}$ inch, and #4 is $\frac{1}{8}$ to $\frac{1}{4}$ inch. Sizes #2 and #3 are normally used for cattleya mixes. Because charcoal is considered a potential fire hazard, it has shipping restrictions when sold in large packages of 50 pounds. Many garden stores, however, sell charcoal in 5-pound plastic re-sealable packages which is usually enough for small hobbyists.

Proprietary Mixes

Some orchid amateurs and commercial growers like to put together their own special combination of ingredients to produce what they consider to be "the best" medium for cattleyas. Considering how easy it is to grow cattleyas in any aerated material, these special mixes are certainly not necessary for success with these plants. In our opinion, there is no "best medium" to use to grow cattleyas, and how you water these plants is much more important to your success than the medium in which they grow. You should use a medium that is in common use for cattleyas, easy to pot, readily available, and not too expensive. If you are a beginner, this usually points to one of the commercially available bark mixes that are sold by orchid suppliers and sometimes garden stores or nurseries. It is important whenever you use any potting medium that you dampen it with water first so you do not breathe the fine particles of dust that all mediums produce when they are dry.

Fertilizer

Because cattleyas do not grow in the soil in the jungle, fertilizer is not an essential ingredient for growing them successfully in a greenhouse. An old-fashioned medium like osmunda, which contains some natural nutrients, does not require any fertilizer to grow cattleyas well. Plants in bark mixes, cypress mulch, and other non-nutrient containing mediums, however, do benefit from some dilute fertilizer when they are actively grow-ing. Dilute fertilizer can help you produce larger and more robust pseudobulbs and better flowers than you would get otherwise.

A variety of fertilizer products is sold on the market from soluble chemical fertiliz-ers to natural products like fish emulsion and guano. Since it is easy to overfertilize catt-leyas, you should be sure the label specifically recommends a dosage for orchids. It will probably not give a specific recommendation for cattleyas so use only one-third of the orchid dosage. The fertilizer should contain nitrogen (N), phosphorous (P), and potas-sium (K) in equal percentages (10–10–10, or 20–20–20, for example). Slow-release nitrogen products like ureaforms should not be used because they will continue to feed the plants when they are dormant and should not have fertilizer. Fertilizer should be applied only when the cattleya plants are actively growing.

Growing Cattleyas Without a Greenhouse

Although we normally think of cattleyas as greenhouse plants, they can still be grown successfully without a greenhouse if you adapt your culture to the seasonal needs of the plants. Most *Cattleya* species are exposed to distinct wet and dry seasons in their native habitats. During the wet season, they receive all the moisture they need to grow and produce strong pseudobulbs. During the dry season, most species produce their flowers and go into a dormant or resting condition.

In late spring and summer in the United States the outside weather is normally warm and humid and is very much like the wet season in the jungle. The days are also longer and more like those found near the tropical equator. If you put your cattleyas outside on a bench or stand during these warm, humid months, they can grow there as well as they would in a greenhouse. Since the plants are outside in the open air and receiving the full spectrum of the sun's rays, they are actually exposed to more natural conditions than those provided by a greenhouse. Often the plants produce tougher growths that are more resistant to disease.

By the time autumn arrives with its cooler temperatures, shorter days, and less humid air, the new growths on the cattleya plants should be mature and you can bring the plants inside your house. Put them on a windowsill or plant stand where they can get some morning or afternoon sun and they should flower for you during fall and winter. The plants are essentially dormant after they have completed their new growths and they no longer require the warm, moist atmosphere they did when they were actively growing. The drier conditions inside the house are usually satisfactory for them during their resting season. When you have only a few cattleya plants, putting them outside in the late spring and summer requires a minimum of effort, but if you have a few hundred plants you should consider investing in a greenhouse unless you have many sunny win-dowsills and lots of free time.

When cattleyas are grown outside during late spring and summer, they should be potted in a bark mix that is loose and allows for very good drainage since the plants may be watered frequently by nature's rain. It is also good to put the plants on a slatted or wire-covered bench which gives them maximum air and drainage. The bench should be placed in a sunny location and shaded enough to keep the leaf color of the plants a light green not yellow-green or yellow.

Greenhouses have a unique assortment of pests, including a few like mites and white fly that are normally not a problem outside. Outside culture, however, has its own menagerie of perils, including caterpillars, grasshoppers, field mice, slugs, springtails, and occasionally squirrels, rats, and raccoons that can cause serious problems. Fortunately, cattleya leaves and pseudobulbs are tough when mature and are not attractive to most insects and small animals. New growths, however, are soft and succulent and this is where you should look for problems.

Some people like to hang a cattleya plant or two from a tree limb outside where they get a scattering of sunshine and lots of moving air in the summer which is also satisfactory. Never put cattleya plants on the ground itself because this can block drainage from the pot and be an invitation to ground-inhabiting pests like springtails and slugs to enjoy them for dinner.

Some of the best *Cattleya* species to grow outside during the summer are *C. labiata*, *C. percivaliana*, *C. trianaei*, *C. schroederae*, and *C. mossiae*. *Cattleya labiata* should have already formed small buds in the sheath by the time you bring it inside in the fall, and these will develop into flowers by late September or October. *Cattleya percivaliana* is particularly nice because it flowers for Christmas, and *C. trianaei* and *C. schroederae* will give you their lovely, pastel-colored flowers during the dreary months of January and February. *Cattleya mossiae* will flower as spring comes along and its wonderful bright, flowery fragrance will make your home smell delicious. If you decide to grow some *Cattleya* hybrids, select those with growths that mature by the end of the summer and are not still growing when you bring them inside.

Do not despair that you lack a greenhouse for you can still grow a variety of cattleyas successfully by piggybacking on nature's abundance in the summertime. Since your house is designed for the comfort of people and not plants, however, it is difficult to be successful with the *Cattleya* species that make their active growths during winter in the United States like *C. warneri* and *C. lueddemanniana* because you cannot provide them with the warm, moist air they need. You can only grow those cattleyas when the weather outside is warm, humid, and tropical.

Care of Cattleya Flowers

The main reason we grow cattleya plants is so we can enjoy the flowers, so a few comments are in order on how to make cattleya flowers last longer and develop to their fullest. It takes three days from the time a cattleya bud begins to open until it is completely expanded and has its full color. On the first day the sepals, petals, and lip separate and hang in a half-open position. On the second day these flower parts lengthen, enlarge, and open more fully. Most of the flower's color develops on the third day as the flower stabilizes its shape and size. Many hobbyists have been disappointed to find the beautiful white-petaled *Cattleya trianaei* they saw on the second day become a lavender-petaled flower on the third day.

If you plan to cut the flowers for an arrangement or a corsage, never do so before the afternoon of the third day or preferably the morning of the fourth day. Unlike many common florist flowers like gladiolus, lilies, and roses, cattleya flowers will not continue to open once they are cut, so you must wait until the flowers are fully open and hardened before you pick them. Also, never cut through the ovary of the flower because this will significantly shorten its life. Cut the flower off just below the end of the ovary where it is attached to the stem of the flower spike.

If you want to enjoy the flowers on the plant itself, be sure the buds have plenty of room to separate and grow after they have emerged from the sheath. They should be able to spread themselves to their fullest so they will give the best display. A petal that touches the foliage of another plant may remain only half open when it matures while the other petal on the flower is fully open. Also, be sure the buds are facing in the direction of the sun, and do not move the plant until the flowers are completely open, otherwise the flowers may not all face in the same direction. If you want the cattleya flowers to last as long as possible on the plant after they are open, keep them in a cool (55°–60°F) greenhouse that is not too humid.

When you flower cattleya seedlings for the first time, do not throw them out if you find they are not as good as you expected. The first flowering of a seedling is usually not as good as subsequent flowerings will be because the plant is too young to have the strength to produce the best flowers it can. Always let the plant bloom a second year before deciding if it is worth keeping or not.

Summary

Growing cattleyas is very much like growing any plant. It is more of an art than a science because no one can give you a foolproof recipe to guarantee perfect results every time. We have given you some general guidelines to follow, but in the end success depends on your own observations of how your plants respond to the medium in which you plant them, and to how you water them, shade them, and otherwise care for them. If they like what you do, they will reward you with strong growths and beautiful large flowers. If they do not like what you do, you may have to change things from time to time until they do. There is no substitute for personal involvement and you cannot leave the plants in the care of your babysitter. Growing cattleyas is fun and very rewarding, but it is a do-it-yourself sport.

NINE

Repotting and Dividing Cattleyas

CATTLEYAS normally grow in one direction across a pot and, when they reach the outer edge, it is time to repot them. If a plant is not repotted when it reaches the edge of the pot, the next pseudobulb will go over the pot and its roots will have no medium in which to grow.

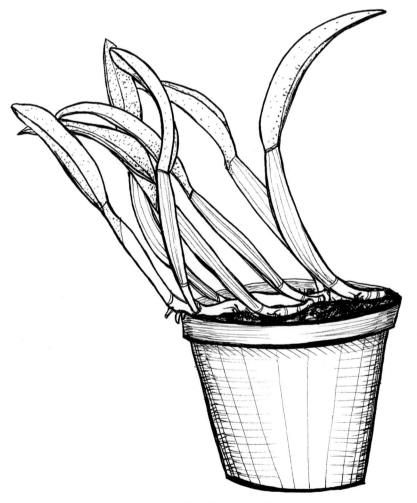

Front pseudobulb has grown to the edge of the pot and it is now time to repot the plant.

Potting On

The best way to handle a plant when it reaches the edge of the pot is to put it into the next larger size pot. This minimizes damage to the roots, and the plant will have virtually no reduction it its growth and vigor.

Before a plant is taken out of the pot, however, it should be watered until the whole medium is soaked. Let the plant drain, then sit for a few minutes so the moisture will have time to soften the outer layer of the roots that are adhering to the pot. If the plant is dry when you try to take it out of the pot, the roots will grip the sides of the pot so strongly that many of them will be torn and damaged, and the plant will take more time to recover. If the roots are growing all around the outside of the pot and cannot be loosened with water, you may have to cut some of them to get the plant out of the pot.

Once the roots have been loosened, you should be able to ease the plant out of the pot by gripping the sides of the pot with the fingers of both hands and applying a gentle upward pressure with your thumbs and index fingers at the base of the front pseudobulbs. The front of the plant should be facing away from you when you do this.

With the front of the pot facing away from you and using both hands, slowly ease the plant out of the pot by applying an upward pressure on the base of the front pseudobulbs with your thumbs and index fingers.

Assuming the roots and pseudobulbs look healthy, the plant should go into a pot that allows for one or two more years of growth. This means if the plant is now in a 5-inch pot it should go into a 6- or 7-inch pot. If it is in a 6-inch pot it should go into a 7- or 8-inch pot.

Dividing Plants

When a plant has become so large that it is no longer practical to repot it into a larger pot, the plant will have to be cut into two or more pieces so it will fit into smaller pots. Take the plant out of the pot and remove the four newest pseudobulbs by cutting the rhizome behind the fourth pseudobulb. Although fewer than four pseudobulbs can be used when you repot, a four-pseudobulb division has been found to produce the best plant for the next flowering.

The knife used to cut the rhizome should have been heat-sterilized to kill any virus particles that may be on it and cooled to room temperature before it is used. The knife should also be heat-sterilized between each plant that is cut to avoid the transfer of virus from one plant to another.

Put the four-pseudobulb plant into a new pot that will allow the plant two more years of growth. This will probably be a 5- or 6-inch pot depending on the size of the division. Be sure to put a slightly rounded piece of broken crock over the hole in the bottom of the

To divide a plant for repotting, cut through the rhizome of the fourth pseudobulb from the front of the plant and separate the plant into two parts—the front four bulbs will become the new plant and the remaining older bulbs will become the backpiece.

pot to prevent the new medium from blocking the hole and preventing water drainage.

Hold the four-pseudobulb division firmly with the rhizomes about ½ inch below the top rim of the pot and the oldest pseudobulb against the back of the pot, and fill the pot with whatever medium you are using. If you are using a bark mix, once the pot is filled with medium, put a pot clip on the edge of the pot so that the clip extends across the second or third rhizome to hold the plant firmly in place. Do not put the pot clip on the newest rhizome since this rhizome is softer than the others and the pot clip can damage it. The pot clip should fit tightly over the rim of the pot and it may have to be tapped on gently with a hammer to make it fit tightly.

It is important to keep the plant firmly pressed against the medium so the plant will not move or wiggle when it is watered or handled. If the plant moves, the new roots may break off and the plant will not be able to root well. When using a medium like osmunda, the osmunda should be pushed so tightly against the plant that you can literally pick the plant up by its pseudobulbs and the plant will not come out of the pot. A pot clip is not normally needed when you pot with osmunda unless the plant has virtually no root-ball to wedge it fast.

The final step in potting a plant is to tie up the pseudobulbs so they stand reasonably straight. This makes it easier to see the rhizomes and new growths when the plant is sitting among a group of plants on the greenhouse bench. When the plant flowers, it also helps to keep the flowers from blooming into the plants around them and the pot

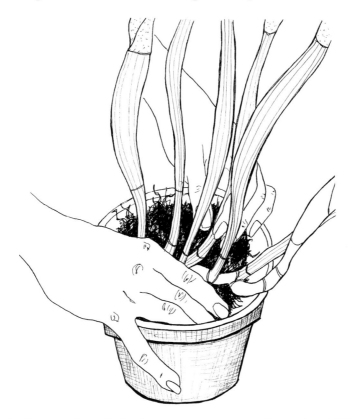

Put the plant in a larger pot that will allow for one or two more years of growth and fill the pot with additional medium.

from tipping over if the flower spike is too heavy and leans over the edge of the pot. A wood stake is usually placed toward the back of the plant against a rhizome that will prevent it from pulling forward when string is tied to the stake to pull the pseudobulbs upright. A metal stake that clips onto the edge of the pot can also be used.

Backbulbs

After the four front pseudobulbs are potted, you still have to do something with the backbulbs. The backbulbs are the older pseudobulbs behind the four front pseudobulbs and they can also produce a new plant. It usually requires two or more years for the backbulbs to grow into a plant that is strong enough to flower. The best way to make a new plant from the backbulbs is to cut through the rhizome of either the third or fourth pseudobulbs with a knife the season *before* you plan to repot the plant. This is extremely important and allows the backbulbs to use all their existing live roots to initiate a new growth. By the next season, when you want to repot the plant, the backbulbs should have made a new growth and begun sending out new roots. When you repot the plant now, you will have a four-pseudobulb division and an established backpiece that are two plants and can go into two separate pots.

If the backbulbs are only cut when the plant is repotted instead of the year before, the roots on the backbulbs will be damaged and this will reduce their ability to sprout from an old eye. Under these circumstances, unless the backbulbs are unusually strong and vigorous, it is best to put them into a plastic bag in a warm place (minimum 75°F) with a little moist sphagnum moss and tie the bag closed to encourage one of the eyes to begin to grow. The moisture-saturated atmosphere inside the plastic bag minimizes water-loss from the pseudobulbs and in a few weeks an old, dormant eye should break and start a new growth. Once the eye has broken and begins to grow and the growth is about ¼ inch long, it is important to remove the backbulbs from the plastic bag and put them in a pot with some sphagnum moss. If the plant is left in the plastic bag after it has begun to grow, the growth may rot from the effect of the stagnant, water-saturated atmosphere inside the bag.

If you have a large plant with several leads that needs repotting, the plant can either be cut into several four-pseudobulb divisions and put in separate, smaller pots, or a single large front section of the plant can be put back into a large pot. How you handle the plant depends on what you want to accomplish. The more leads there are in a pot, the more spectacular the plant will look when it flowers, so if you want the most flowers, keep the front part of the plant intact with as many leads on it as possible. If you want as many plants as possible, cutting it into four-pseudobulb divisions is the way to go.

The best time to repot a cattleya plant is when it just begins sending out a flush of new roots from the base of the newest pseudobulb. The sooner you repot it once the roots begin to appear, the less damage you will do to the emerging roots. Since not all cattleyas root at the same time during their growth cycle, a plant's desire to root is the most reliable guide for repotting. You should never repot a plant when it is in bud or in flower because it takes a lot of the plant's energy to produce the buds and hold the flowers and it needs all the roots it has to do this.

TEN

Pests, Diseases, and Environmental Problems

INSECTS, mollusks, and diseases can do serious damage to cattleyas. Some of these pests attack the leaves, pseudobulbs, or roots, while others primarily attack the flower. We have grouped the pests according to the part of the cattleya plant where they do their damage and where you are most likely to find them. We hope this makes it easier to recognize the problems and treat them.

Pests Attacking Cattleya Pseudobulbs and Leaves

Cattleyas are tough plants that have thick pseudobulbs and leathery leaves, so most insects avoid them because there are easier things to eat. A few insects, however, do feed on tough cattleya tissue, and others eat the new growths when they are young and succulent.

Scale Insects

White scale (*Diaspis boisduvalii*) is the most serious insect affecting cattleyas under greenhouse cultivation. It is one of the few insects that can actually kill a plant if left uncontrolled. It is also an insidious pest that can hide under dead sheathing, in the axils of leaves, and along the base of the rhizomes where it often goes undetected. Most amateur collections have some white scale on their cattleya plants, and it is still the most common insect found in the United States in these collections.

One of the telltale signs of white scale is a yellow area on the upper side of an otherwise green leaf (see left photo on page 224). Turn the leaf over to find the scales (see right photo on page 224). The size of the yellow area is an indication of the number of scales present. A single scale can produce a small yellow spot while a few dozen scales can produce a large yellow area.

It is always important to tear down and remove the dead sheathing on a cattleya pseudobulb because the sheathing can hide scale that can be actively feeding on the pseudobulb. The pseudobulb on page 225 (upper left) looks free of scale until the dead sheathing is pulled down (page 225, upper right). A favorite place for scale is at the base of a leaf where the leaf attaches to the pseudobulb. Because the scale can build up and become several layers thick here, spraying the top surface of the scale will not always kill all the scale. A toothbrush should be used to gently scrub the area to dislodge the insects.

White scale is a tiny insect with piercing mouth parts that enable it to suck the juices out of cattleya leaves, pseudobulbs, and rhizomes. In the adult stage, the female is protected by a round, white, tentlike armor while she feeds on the plant and hatches her young. When the larvae are old enough, they emerge from under the armor as crawlers that move around the leaf to find new places to settle down and feed. One of the reasons scale spreads so rapidly around a greenhouse is that the mobile crawler stage can be easily washed off the leaf of one plant and onto other plants when water is sprayed over the plants on a hot day. A whole group of crawlers can be washed several feet with a typical hose-type spray and, in the process, spread the scale to dozens of plants.

Scale is relatively easy to control when you have only two or three cattleya plants. A soft toothbrush and mild soap and water can handle the job well. When you have a dozen cattleya plants, a quart spray-bottle full of a 1- to 2-percent suspension of a highly refined horticultural oil in water is effective and convenient. When using horticultural oil, it is important to shake the emulsion constantly to be sure the oil is kept suspended in the water. If the oil is not well suspended, a higher amount of oil may be deposited on the plant and this may burn the foliage. It is also important to apply the oil on a cloudy day and only when the temperature is below 75°F. At higher temperatures oil can burn the plant as well as suffocate the scale.

If you have a whole greenhouse full of cattleya plants to treat for scale, you will need a 1- or 2-gallon sprayer for good control and you will have to wear a face mask, rubber gloves, and protective clothing for safety when you make an insecticide application. Commercial growers often use fogging machines that allow them to treat an entire greenhouse automatically without anyone being present when the insecticide is being applied. These foggers are expensive, however, and are usually only used by large greenhouse operations.

Yellow areas on upper surface of leaf may indicate live scales on the underside.

Underside of leaf showing scale insects

Healthy-looking pseudobulb

Same pseudobulb as in previous photo, showing scales hidden by sheathing

It is important whenever you use any pesticide that you follow the label directions exactly. If the product is sold in the United States, the label has been approved by the U.S. Environmental Protection Agency and carries not only recommended dosages, but also important precautions for using it safely.

White scale is not normally found on house plants or greenhouse plants other than orchids. Once the insects are eradicated from a cattleya collection, the only way to get them again is by adding new orchids to the collection that have scale on them. It is important to thoroughly examine any new orchid plants received from friends or even commercial growers to be certain they do not have scale hidden on them somewhere. When in doubt, treat the new plants for scale before putting them in with your other plants.

Although white scale is by far the most serious and difficult to eradicate of the scale insects

Scale crawlers have just emerged from under female scale.

that attack cattleyas in a greenhouse, a few other scales can occasionally find their way onto these plants. The most common of these are soft brown scale, *Coccus hesperidum*, and black scale, *Saissetia oleae*. These scales are larger than white scale and have a soft, raised waxy covering rather than the hard shell of an armored scale. They are generally easier to find than white scale and do not really seem to like cattleyas the way white scale does. Soft scales can usually be controlled with natural pyrethrum, synthetic pyrethrum products like permethrin, or horticultural oil. Unlike white scale, however, the soft scales can come into your home or greenhouse on other house plants.

Mealy Bugs

Mealy bugs, *Pseudococcus* spp., are oval-shaped sucking insects $\frac{1}{4}$ to $\frac{1}{3}$ inch long that have a cottony appearance. They are related to scale insects but generally attack softer tissue than the armored scales. Mealy bugs are common greenhouse pests found on many soft-stemmed foliage plants like coleus, fuchsia, croton, dracaena, and begonia and usually find their way onto orchids from these other plants. Female mealy bugs often bear live young and can lay several hundred eggs so they can create a serious problem in a short time. The nymphal stage of the insect can move around to some extent over the plant and it takes about a month for the completion of a generation under greenhouse conditions.

Mealy bugs should never be a problem in a cattleya collection if all new plants added to the collection are carefully inspected and treated for the insect. Once mealy bugs are found on a cattleya plant, however, it is important to control them immediately before they increase in number and spread around the greenhouse. Mealy bugs will usually attack softer-foliage orchids like *Phalaenopsis* before they bother cattleyas, and when they do attack cattleyas, they will usually feed on the soft, succulent cattleya flowers or flower buds. Natural pyrethrum, permethrin, and horticultural oil give good control of the active stages of mealy bug.

Grasshoppers, Crickets, and Caterpillars

When greenhouse ventilators are open during the warm summer months, a variety of outside leaf-feeding insects like grasshoppers, crickets, and caterpillars occasionally finds its way into the greenhouse. There they will eat any soft, succulent new growths and cause considerable damage to individual plants. Unlike white scale, these insects are not permanent residents of the greenhouse. They are strictly seasonal pests and usually damage only a plant or two. If they are found feeding on a plant, they can often be picked off by hand or killed with a knockdown aerosol spray. Putting screens over the ventilator openings can significantly reduce the chance of having these insects.

Cattleya Fly

Cattleya fly, *Isosoma orchidearum*, is a rare insect in orchid collections today, but it was a serious problem in the late 1800s and early 1900s when large numbers of cattleya plants were being imported into the United States from the jungles of South America. Cattleya fly deposits from 10 to 15 eggs inside the new growths of cattleyas when the growths are less than 1 inch long. The larvae of the fly eat their way through the developing pseudobulb and do considerable damage as they feed. A swelling at the base of the new pseudobulb is the first sign that eggs have been laid in the new growth.

For many years the only remedy for this pest was to cut off the new growth below the swelling and destroy it. When the insecticide DDT was first used in orchid green houses in the 1940s, cattleya fly was controlled so well it literally disappeared from these collections everywhere and the insect has not been a problem since. It is still possible to get cattleya fly, however, if you acquire cattleya plants that have come from the wild into the United States without having been inspected by the Animal and Plant Health Inspection Service of the U.S. Department of Agriculture.

Pests Attacking Cattleya Roots

Some of the most insidious and damaging pests of cattleyas are those that attack the roots of the plants. These pests either eat the whole root tip or leave small chewed areas on the roots which stop the roots from growing and allow pathogens to infect the roots and kill them. The pest is frequently hidden down in the medium where its damage goes unnoticed until the plant's pseudobulbs begin to shrivel excessively from the lost roots. When a plant is growing poorly, the blame is often put on poor culture like improper watering or the wrong medium or fertilizer when the real culprit is one or more root pests.

Millipedes

Millipedes, *Cambala annulata*, feed primarily on decaying organic matter, but they also feed on orchid roots and are one of the most insidious of all the pests of cattleyas. Adult millipedes are brown or brownish gray in color with long cylindrical wirelike bodies

Roots showing the nibbling-type feeding damage from millipedes

about an inch long and, because of their shape, are sometimes mistakenly called "wire worms." The bodies have 20 or more segments and each segment has a pair of tiny legs. Young millipedes are the same shape but much smaller in size than the adults.

If millipedes are present in a plant, they can often be seen curled up or moving around the bottom of the pot when you remove the plant for repotting. Millipedes can feed on orchid roots that are inside the pot where they are completely hidden, or they can be found nibbling on exposed roots on the surface of the pot. When they are on the surface of the pot, they do most of their feeding at night. If new roots appear to have died just as they are emerging from the base of a pseudobulb, millipedes are one possible cause and the plant should be taken out of the pot to see if millipedes are present. Millipedes are usually easy to find because they tend to congregate on the bottom of the pot.

Surface sprays with insecticides are usually not effective in controlling millipedes and you have to use a drench that gets to all parts of the medium, including the inside surface of the bottom of the pot. Millipedes are relatively easy to kill with most insecticides, including pyrethrum and permethrin.

Cockroaches

Cockroaches are one of the most serious pests that eat cattleya roots and are one of the most difficult to control. They can eat the exposed root tips of dozens of plants in just one evening and will eat the whole root tip rather than nibble holes in it as millipedes do. Cockroaches are very mobile, fast-moving insects that can cover a wide area of the bench in a short time and can even feed on orchid plants that are hanging from overhead pipes. They are nocturnal insects and do not come out to feed until the greenhouse is dark and quiet.

Cockroaches are one of the oldest known insects to attack orchids, and remedies for

Cockroaches damage roots by eating the growing tips.

their control have filled orchid literature since the early 1800s. The most common way to control cockroaches for many years was through the use of poison baits. The problem with baits, however, is that the bait is seldom as enticing to the roaches as the orchid roots and only a few foods like squeezed orange halves and beer are really guaranteed to attract the roaches more than the orchid roots. Domesticated cockroaches, like the German cockroach, *Blattela germanica*, and the American cockroach, *Periplaneta americana*, are very comfortable as permanent residents of homes and greenhouses and once they are established, it can take a concentrated and dedicated effort to eliminate them.

Before the discovery and widespread use of modern insecticides like insect growth regulators, the most common source for cockroaches was food stores that sent the roaches home with the customers in their grocery bags. Most food establishments now have professional pest control services that treat for cockroaches on a regular basis and food stores are seldom a source for these insects today. It is possible to acquire cockroaches, however, when you buy orchid plants in pots if the grower from whom you buy the plants has cockroaches.

Cockroaches lay dark brown egg-cases about $\frac{1}{2}$ inch long and $\frac{1}{8}$ inch wide that can be hidden in the pot. The egg-cases contain from 14 to 30 eggs depending on the species of cockroach. Tiny cockroaches emerge from these egg-cases in a few weeks and after passing through 7 to 13 or more molts, they become adults. The female adult cockroach can lay from 1 to 90 egg-cases over her lifetime which can produce a large population of very destructive root-eating insects in a greenhouse.

Unlike many root-damaging insects that can be seen when a cattleya plant is pulled out of the pot, cockroaches are seldom found in the pot unless an egg-case has recently hatched and the baby roaches are still scurrying around the bottom of the pot. Natural pyrethrum or permethrin is effective as a spray for controlling baby cockroaches but may require several applications to do the job. Adult cockroaches are difficult to kill with insecticides and they are very adept at avoiding sticky traps and poison baits so it is best to concentrate your control efforts on the more easily killed baby cockroaches.

Cockroaches usually feed on exposed root tips of cattleyas, so if the plant's pseudobulbs rest tightly against the medium in which they are potted and the roots go directly into the medium, they are difficult for the cockroach to eat and it will look elsewhere for a meal. To discourage cockroaches, you should always keep the area under the benches clean and free of debris.

Earwigs

Earwigs, *Dermaptera* spp., are another important insect that attack cattleya roots in a greenhouse. The damage they cause is similar to that of millipedes, and they often feed on roots that are inside the pot where the damage goes undetected. The first indication that earwigs are present in a pot is often a severe shriveling of the pseudobulbs that reflects the loss of roots eaten by the insect. When you see shriveled pseudobulbs, you should take the plant out of the pot and examine the root-ball and pot for live insects.

Earwigs are beetlelike insects with distinctive prominent pincers at the rear end of the body. They are $\frac{3}{4}$ to 1 inch long and have a blue-purple color. Earwigs have chewing mouth parts and are general feeders that attack many annual and perennial garden plants, and they often find their way into the greenhouse in the pots of these plants. Earwigs can be controlled with a drench of pyrethrum or permethrin, and just repotting the infested plants with a clean medium can often eliminate them. It is always desirable to keep grass and weeds away from the greenhouse walls to discourage these and other insects from entering the greenhouse.

Pillbugs

Pillbugs, *Armadillidium vulgare*, are strange little creatures that can roll themselves into a spherical shape when disturbed. They are not insects but are closely related to crayfish. They are usually not a problem in cattleyas but can find their way into the potting medium and eat the roots of cattleyas if the plants are kept too wet. These pests must have a moist environment, and most bark mixes dry out too fast for them to survive. They are common in many greenhouses on the floor and in many common pot plants. They are easy to kill with most insecticide drenches, but should never really be a problem if you allow your cattleyas to dry out thoroughly between waterings.

Bush Snails

Bush snails are about ⅛ inch long and often found in fir bark that has not been heat-sterilized. The root-tips of cattleyas are a favorite food of bush snails, and the snails can do considerable damage when they occur in large numbers. The best control for bush snails is to use only heat-sterilized fir bark to grow your cattleyas. If bush snails have already appeared in your collection, however, changing the medium will not eliminate them because once they are established, bush snails can live in most aerated mediums.

Bush snails will feed on cattleya roots both during the day and at night and can be found now and then on young, tender cattleya growths although they do little damage to these growths. Their main damage is to the roots. Most insecticides will not control bush snails and, if snails are found on a plant, the only way to get rid of them is often to take the plant out of the pot and wash off all the medium and repot the plant in a sterilized bark mix. Be sure the old medium is disposed of outside the greenhouse since it can contain both the bush snails and their eggs.

Pests Affecting Cattleya Flowers

The most frustrating pests of cattleyas are those that feed on the flowers. After you have successfully grown strong, healthy pseudobulbs and stimulated the plant to produce a number of large, beautiful flowers, the last thing you want to see is the flowers ruined by some hungry insect or slimy mollusk.

Slugs

The most damaging pests that feed on cattleya flowers are the various species of garden slugs. Slugs are similar to snails, but they have no shell to protect their bodies as snails do. Slugs are common in damp or wet areas outside the greenhouse and can find their way into the greenhouse by crawling up the outside walls and through open ventilators. They can also be introduced into the greenhouse in the pots of garden plants that have

Cattleya flowers partially eaten by slugs

been grown outside during the warm summer months and brought into the greenhouse in the fall.

Slugs vary in size from ½ to 4 inches, and they leave a telltale sticky, viscid secretion behind them as they move across the greenhouse bench or cattleya plants. The sticky trail makes it easy to identify the pest that caused the damage, and by following the trail, you can sometimes find the culprit, pick it up, and dispose of it. Slugs can ravage cattleya flowers and buds sometimes eating them to the point where they are barely recognizable. They eat holes though buds and rag flower petals, sepals, and lips, while leaving their sticky trademark secretions. Colorless slug eggs are laid in sticky clumps in damp places around the greenhouse floor where they hatch in about a month and give rise to tiny replicas of the adult.

Most insecticides have no effect on slugs and the standard treatment for slug control today is a pelleted product which contains iron phosphate as the active ingredient. The pellets are scattered over the floor of the greenhouse and around plants and usually eliminate this pest with one or two applications three months apart.

Aphids and Ants

Aphids are small sucking insects that attack many garden plants and fruit trees during the outdoor growing season. Many of them, like the green peach aphid, *Myzus persicae*, are pale green in color and are difficult to see on green cattleya flower buds. Aphids are particularly abundant in the cool spring season when females can produce living young without mating with a male. These young aphids become adults within a week and can begin producing their own young almost immediately, so aphids can become very numerous in a short time if not controlled.

Aphids can be introduced into a greenhouse when winged sexual forms fly through open ventilators in late summer or early autumn, and they can be brought in by ants. Ants feed on the sweet exudate of the aphids and will aggressively protect the aphids from their predators. Tough cattleya foliage is not attractive to aphids and they only feed on succulent buds and flowers.

Aphids are easily controlled with pyrethrum or permethrin. If there are only a few aphids on a flower bud or two, they can usually be wiped off with a soapy cloth. Aphids are dangerous insects to have in a greenhouse because they can transmit viruses from one plant to another. For this reason, it is always wise to eliminate aphids as soon as you see them. It is also good to stop ants from becoming established in the greenhouse since they are often the main source for the introduction of aphids.

One of the most effective predators of aphids is the lady beetle, *Hippodamia convergens*, which can eat dozens of aphids in a day. These lady beetles are sometimes sold in containers of 100 or more beetles which can be released into the greenhouse to control aphids. The problem with this approach is that it takes time to order and receive these insects, and the aphids are multiplying vigorously while you do this. Once the aphids are gone, the lady beetles will also leave to look for more food and you will be left with no lady beetles when aphids re-appear in the greenhouse.

Thrips

Thrips are an increasingly common pest of cattleya flowers in the United States because so many young orchid plants are grown in tropical and subtropical areas today where the pest is found naturally. The adults look like tiny oval black specks that move quickly around the flowers, and their feeding creates a silvery effect that is most noticeable along the edges of the petals. Thrips cannot be effectively controlled on the flowers without damaging the flowers further, so it is best to remove the flowers and spray the whole plant to stop them from spreading to other plants. We have found that pyrethrum will control both the adult and larval stages of this pest, but it may require several applications for complete control.

Diseases of Cattleyas

Most fungus and bacterial diseases of cattleyas are the result of poor cultural practices and can be prevented by using good culture. Fungi are dependent on moisture and temperature to grow and infect plants, and most fungi are active when temperatures are in the 50°F range. The spores of many pathogenic fungi are floating in the air in the greenhouse all the time, but when conditions are dry they remain dormant and do not bother anything. The spores begin to grow when moisture is added to their environment particularly as temperatures begin to fall. Fungus infections, such as black rot on foliage or spotting on flowers, can become a problem when there is water on the plants at night or the air is saturated with moisture and the temperature drops below 65°F. Correcting the environmental conditions is far more effective in controlling these diseases than applying fungicides and bactericides.

Black Rot

Black rot of cattleyas can develop whenever there is water on the leaves or young growths of cattleya plants at night. To avoid black rot, simply do not water or spray cattleya plants in the late afternoon or evening. Water them only in the morning on a sunny day. If there is no water on the plants at night, there will be no black rot. If you have somehow allowed water to collect in the crown of a pseudobulb or the young leaf of a new growth and it remained wet all night and you developed black rot, cut the rotted leaf off at least 1 inch below the last point of black tissue. Dust the cut with sulfur to dry it out and put the plant in a dry place for about a week. Be careful not to get water on the leaf for a few weeks after you return the plant to the greenhouse bench since the fungus is probably still there in an infective form.

Spotting on Flowers

Small dark brown or black spots on cattleya flowers can occur when the atmosphere in the

Black rot beginning on young, developing cattleya leaf

Spotting on cattleya flower

greenhouse is extremely humid and ventilation is poor. To prevent further spotting of the flowers you should avoid spraying and watering and should increase the ventilation and air movement in the greenhouse. Unfortunately, once the cattleya flowers are spotted nothing can be done to remove the spots since they are now an integral part of the flower itself. Spotting of cattleya flowers can occur at any time of the year when conditions are excessively wet and humid.

Pseudobulb rot

One of the most serious diseases of cattleyas is pseudobulb rot. The condition is found most often in *Cattleya dowiana*, although it can occur in any cattleya plant under the right conditions. While most rots of cattleyas start on the newest and youngest pseudobulb, pseudobulb rot usually starts on the oldest pseudobulb, and it first appears as a browning at the base of the pseudobulb. The browning progresses up the old pseudobulb and along the inside of the rhizomes and into the forward pseudobulbs and eventually kills the plant. Pseudobulb rot develops when the medium in which the cattleya is growing becomes too wet when the greenhouse is cold during the winter months.

Plant killed by pseudobulb rot

The only way to prevent pseudobulb rot is to keep plants like *Cattleya dowiana* as dry as possible when the temperature drops below 65°F. Once symptoms appear in the old pseudobulbs, it is usually too late to save the plant. Standard 3-percent hydrogen peroxide, poured straight from the bottle over the rhizomes when symptoms first appear, will sometimes stop the progress of the disease but not always. Cutting off the front two or three pseudobulbs usually does not save these pseudobulbs either because their rhizomes are usually already infected even though they show no symptoms.

Pseudobulb rot killed literally thousands of *Cattleya dowiana* plants during the 1800s and 1900s. Almost all imported plants at the time were dead within five years after importation due to the disease.

Virus Diseases

Virus diseases are common problems in cattleya collections because many of the fine, old varieties of cattleyas acquired these viruses before viruses were recognized as contagious diseases. These viruses do not usually kill cattleya plants, but they can severely reduce plant vigor and cause undesirable leaf and flower symptoms.

Cymbidium Mosaic Virus

The most common virus of cattleyas is cymbidium mosaic virus (CyMV) which, as its name implies, was originally transmitted to cattleyas from infected *Cymbidium* plants. The most common symptoms of CyMV appear in the flowers, which seem to age prematurely and show translucent and sometimes brown flecks in the petals. Severe cases show a necrosis or browning along the center vein of the petals (see photo below). The

Cattleya flower showing browning on sepals and petals from CyMV

In very severe cases, CyMV symptoms appear as vertical light and dark areas in the leaves and the plants are noticeably stunted.

flowers appear normal when they first open and symptoms do not begin to appear in the petals for a week or ten days.

CyMV can also produce irregular black markings on a plant's leaves, and this shows up primarily on the older cattleya leaves where the number of virus particles is greatest (see photo below). Bars of irregular shades of green can also appear in the new growths of cattleya plants that are severely infected with the virus. Such plants appear stunted and have such poor vigor that they are only able to flower every three or four years (see photo to left).

Some cattleya plants are fairly resistant to CyMV and show no symptoms on their leaves and only faint flecking in the petals of the flowers after three or four weeks. These plants, however, are carriers of the virus and can act as a source for transmission to other cattleya plants. CyMV is not transmitted through cattleya seeds, but can be transmitted by green-pod planting or meristemming. Infected meristemmed seed-

Symptoms of CyMV will often appear on older cattleya leaves as irregular black spotting.

lings normally do not show symptoms of the virus until the plants are mature and begin to flower.

There is no practical way to cure cattleya plants of CyMV at the present time, and a grower is faced with either throwing a plant out or isolating it to avoid possible transmission to the other plants. The most common way to transmit CyMV and most other cattleya viruses is through the mechanical cutting of the rhizome during repotting when small amounts of plant sap adhere to the cutting knife. Cutting knives and shears should be heat-sterilized between plants that are repotted or flowers that are cut to kill any virus that is in the sap. Throw-away single-edge razor blades can also be used.

Many growers use inexpensive latex or vinyl gloves which they throw away before they pot the next plant to avoid transmitting the virus on their hands. They also pot the plants on newspapers to keep the plant's sap off the potting bench and throw away the newspaper after each plant is repotted. Old clay pots should be heat-sterilized before they are re-used. We cook our pots in a 375°F oven for one hour. Plastic pots cannot be heat-sterilized and should be thrown away.

Laboratory tests are available if you want to confirm that a plant has hidden CyMV. Companies that supply these usually advertise in the American Orchid Society's magazine, *Orchids*.

Color-Break Virus

The most destructive virus that damages cattleyas is color-break virus which causes an irregular color splashing in the flowers and makes them worthless. Plants with color-

Cattleya flower infected with color-break virus (ORSV) showing typical irregular pigmentation of color in petals with characteristic circular lesions

break virus often do not show symptoms on the vegetative parts of the plant and you are not aware the plant has the virus until it flowers. Color-break is caused by tobacco mosaic virus (TMV-O), also known as odontoglossum ringspot virus (ORSV). Fortunately, this virus is not as common in orchid collections today as it once was. The intensity of color-breaking in the flowers is related to the number of virus particles in the plant tissue. Growers normally throw out plants with color-break virus as soon as they see the symptoms because of the severity of the flower damage and its ease of transmission.

For more information on virus diseases of orchids, see the American Orchid Society's *Guide to Orchid Pests and Diseases*, which is available from the American Orchid Society, 16700 AOS Lane, Delray Beach, Florida 33446-4351.

Environmental Problems

Some of the most difficult problems to diagnose when growing cattleyas are caused by environmental conditions. These conditions may or may not be under the control of the grower and the damage cannot always be avoided. Flowers and flower stems, where tissues are soft and often rapidly expanding, are most susceptible to a poor environment and the injury usually makes them worthless. Since flowers are particularly sensitive to environmental changes, cattleya plants should not be moved from one place to another when the buds are ready to open or have begun to open.

Watery Flowers

If a cattleya plant is watered heavily on a very humid day when the flowers are opening, the plant can occasionally pull too much water into the flowers and cause an accumu-

Cattleya trianaei flower showing water accumulation in petal

lation of water in the petals or lip. These watery flowers look bad and are relatively short lived. If the plant can be dried out by putting it in a dry place out of the sun for a day or two, the condition will sometimes correct itself but not always. The worst thing to do is put the plant in the sun because this will usually pull more water into the flower. When flowers are open or the buds have begun to crack, the plant should be watered only lightly or just sprayed to avoid this problem.

Drooping Flower Stems

Cattleya flower stems normally stand erect. When a stem bends or droops, the plant has probably been overwatered and subjected to too much heat particularly at night. Too much water and heat can cause the flower stem to grow too fast and produce a soft stem that cannot support the weight of the flower buds, and the whole stem will bend over. While the stem does not usually break off, the flowers open at odd angles, ruining their presentation.

Sepal Wilt

Sepal wilt is a condition where the sepals become prematurely thin and dried. The condition usually appears as the flower is opening and is caused by the accumulation of gases like ethylene around the flower. Sepal wilt is common in areas that have a high amount of auto traffic, and it can be reduced by installing fans to keep the air in the greenhouse moving fast enough to prevent the accumulation of gases around the flowers. The fans should operate 24 hours a day to be effective. Very low humidity can also occasionally cause sepal wilt.

Back sepals of cattleya flowers showing dried appearance of sepal wilt

Random mutation in cattleya flower causing no petals

Flower Abnormalities

Some *Cattleya* hybrids are pre-disposed to producing abnormal flowers. Many of these hybrids are crosses between full-lip *Cattleya* species and cut-lip species where a certain amount of genetic incompatibility exists in the formation of the lips and petals. Several cattleyas also have a tendency to produce elongated petals when the buds are forming under high-temperature conditions. Some varieties of *C. gaskelliana* have this trait as does an occasional selfing of *C.* Bow Bells. These types of flower abnormalities are inherent in the plant and will occur again and again for the life of the plant.

Another type of flower abnormality is the random mutation which usually occurs only once in a plant's lifetime. The random mutation is caused by damage to the flower buds in their early stages of development. We made a study of random mutations some years ago and found that about one percent of all the flowers produced in any given year are randomly mutated in various ways. These randomly mutated flowers appear in everyone's cattleya collection and do not appear to be related to any specific cultural practice. They occur equally on the best-grown and most poorly grown plants. Nature is a great experimenter and these mutations can be looked at as examples of some of her unsuccessful efforts to improve the flowers.

Random mutation in cattleya flower causing no lip

Conversion Tables

INCHES	CENTIMETERS		FEET	METERS		FEET	METERS
$1/4$ in.	0.6 cm		1 ft.	0.3 m		100 ft.	30 m
$1/3$ in.	0.8 cm		2 ft.	0.6 m		200 ft.	60 m
$1/2$ in.	1 cm		3 ft.	0.9 m		300 ft.	90 m
$3/4$ in.	2 cm		4 ft.	1.2 m		400 ft.	120 m
1 in.	2.5 cm		5 ft.	1.5 m		500 ft.	150 m
2 in.	5 cm		6 ft.	1.8 m		600 ft.	180 m
3 in.	8 cm		7 ft.	2.1 m		700 ft.	210 m
4 in.	10 cm		8 ft.	2.4 m		800 ft.	240 m
5 in.	13 cm		9 ft.	2.7 m		900 ft.	270 m
6 in.	15 cm		10 ft.	3 m		1000 ft.	300m
7 in.	18 cm		20 ft.	6 m		2000 ft.	610 m
8 in.	20 cm		30 ft.	9 m		3000 ft.	910 m
9 in.	23 cm		40 ft.	12 m		4000 ft.	1200 m
10 in.	25 cm		50 ft.	15 m		5000 ft.	1500 m
20 in.	50 cm		60 ft.	18 m		6000 ft.	1800 m
30 in.	76 cm		70 ft.	21 m		7000 ft.	2100 m
40 in.	100 cm		80 ft.	24 m		8000 ft.	2400 m
			90 ft.	27 m			

POUNDS	KILOGRAMS		FAHRENHEIT	CELSIUS		FAHRENHEIT	CELSIUS
1 lb.	0.45 kg		45°F	7°C		65°F	18°C
5 lbs.	2.25 kg		50°F	10°C		70°F	21°C
10 lbs.	4.5 kg		55°F	13°C		75°F	24°C
20 lbs.	9 kg		58°F	14°C		80°F	27°C
30 lbs.	14 kg		60°F	16°C		85°F	29°C
40 lbs.	18 kg		63°F	17.2°C		90°F	32°C
50 lbs.	23 kg		64°F	17.8°C		375°F	190°C

600 miles = 960 kilometers
1 square foot = 0.09 square meter
1 acre = 0.4 hectare
1 cubic foot = 0.03 cubic meter
$1/4$ teaspoon = 5 milliliters
1 U.S. quart liquid = 0.9 liter
1 U.S. gallon = 3.8 liters

Bibliography

American Orchid Society. 1932–2002. *Bulletin*. Quarterly/Monthly of the American Orchid Society; re-named *Orchids* 2003.

American Orchid Society. 2003–present. *Orchids*. Monthly. American Orchid Society.

Arditti, Joseph. 1992. *Fundamentals of Orchid Biology*. New York: John Wiley.

Aulisi, C., and E. Foldats. 1989. *Monograph of the Venezuelan Cattleyas*. Venezuela: Carlo Aulisi.

Baker, C., and M. Baker. 2000. *Orchid Species Culture–Cattleya*. Portland: C. Baker and M. Baker.

Bentham, G., and J. D. Hooker. 1883. *Genera Plantarum*. London: Reeve and Company.

Blunt, W. 1955. *The Art of Botanical Illustration*. 3d edition. London: Collins.

Boyle, F. 1901. *The Woodlands Orchids*. New York: Macmillan.

Curtis, W., et al. 1827–1844. Curtis's *Botanical Magazine*. London: Edward Couchman.

Du Buysson, F. 1878. *L'Orchidophile*. Paris: Auguste Goin.

Dunsterville, G., and L. Garay. 1959. *Venezuelan Orchids Illustrated*, vols. 1–6. André Deutsch.

Duval, L. 1907. *Traité de Culture Pratique des Cattleya*. Paris: Octave Doin.

Edwards, S. 1815–1842. Edwards's *Botanical Register*. London: James Ridgway.

Gardeners' Chronicle, The. 1841–1901. Weekly publication. London.

Hackney, C. 2004. *American Cattleyas*. Wilmington, North Carolina: Hackney.

Kaiser, Roman. 1993. *The Scent of Orchids*. Basel: Editiones Roche.

Knudson, L. 1922. "Nonsymbiotic Germination of Orchid Seed." *Botanical Gazette* 73: 1–25.

Knudson, L. 1924. "Further Observations on Nonsymbiotic Germination of Orchid Seed." *Botanical Gazette* 77: 212–219.

Knudson, L. 1930. "Flower Production by Orchid Grown Non-symbiotically." *Botanical Gazette* 89: 192–199.

Lindley, J. 1821. *Collectanea Botanica*. London: Taylor.

Lindley, J. 1830. *Genera and Species of Orchidaceous Plants*. London: Ridgways.

Linden, J. 1883. *L'Illustration Horticole*. Belgium: Linden.

Linden, J. 1885–1906. *Lindenia: Iconographie des Orchidées*. Ghent, Belgium: Linden.

Macfarlane, A., and G. Martin. 2002. *Glass: A World History*. Chicago: University of Chicago Press.

Menezes, L. C. 1994. *Cattleya Warneri*. Turriers, France: Naturalia Publications.

Menezes, L. C. 1995. *Laelia purpurata*. Rio de Janeiro: Expressão e Cultura.

Menezes, L. C. 2002. *Cattleya labiata autumnalis*. Brasilia: Edições.

Miranda, F. 1996. *Orchids from the Brazilian Amazon*. Rio de Janeiro: Expressão e Cultura.

Orchid Digest Corporation. 1937–present. *Orchid Digest*. Bimonthly/quarterly. Orchid Digest Corporation.

Ospina H. M. 1958. *Ochideas Colombianas*. Bogota: La Liberia Voluntad.

Ospina H. M. 1996. *Orchids and Ecology in Colombia*. Bogota: Orchideas Eldorado.

Paxton, J. 1834–1849. *Paxton's Magazine of Botany*. London: Orr and Smith.

Paxton, J. 1850. *Paxton's Flower Garden*. London: Cassell and Company.

Persson, R. 1969. *Flat Glass Technology*. London: Plenum Press.

Rolfe, R. A. 1893–1920. *The Orchid Review*. London: West Newman.

Reinikka, M. A. 1995. *A History of the Orchid*. Portland: Timber Press.

Rogerson, W. P. 2004. "*Cattleya* Species and Their Culture." *Orchid Digest* 68 (4): 203.

Ronaele Manor Collection of Orchids, The. 1931. Elkins Park, Pennsylvania: Dixon.

Sander, C. F., F. K. Sander, and L. L. Sander. 1927. *Sanders' Orchid Guide*. Rev. ed. St. Albans, England: F. Sander and Company.

Sander, D., and W. J. Wreford. 1946–1960. *David Sander's One Table List of Orchid Hybrids*. David Sander's Orchids.

Sander, F. 1888–1894. *Reichenbachia: Orchids Illustrated and Described*. 4 vols. St. Albans, England: F. Sander and Company.

Sander's Complete List of Orchid Hybrids to 1 January 1946. St. Albans, England: Sanders.

Sander's List of Orchid Hybrids. 1961–2004. London: Royal Horticultural Society.

Swainson, W. 1819. Sketch of Journey through Brazil 1817 and 1818. *Edinburgh Philosophical Journal* 1: 369–373.

Swinson, A. 1970. *Frederick Sander: the Orchid King*. London: Hodder and Stouchton.

Stearn, W. T. 1992. *Botanical Latin*. 4th ed. Devon: David and Charles; Portland, Oregon: Timber Press.

Stearn, W. T. 1999. *John Lindley*. Suffolk: Antique Collectors' Club.

Toulemonde, T. 2004. *The Colombian Cattleya*. Colombia: Toulemonde.

Van den Berg, C., W. E. Higgins, R. L. Dressler, W. M. Whitten, M. A. Soto Arénas, A. Culham, and M. W. Chase. 2000. "A Phylogenic Analysis of Laeliinae." *Lindleyana* 15 (2): 96–114.

Van Houtte, L. 1869–1870. *Flore des Serres et des Jardins de l'Europe*. Gand, Belgium.

Veitch, J. 1887. A *Manual of Orchidaceous Plants*. Vol. 1, *Epidendreae*. Chelsea: Veitch.

Veitch, J. 1906. *Hortus Veitchii*. London: Veitch.

Warner, R. 1865. *Select Orchidaceous Plants*. London: Crescent, Cripplegate.

Warner, R., and B. S. Williams. 1882–1897. *The Orchid Album*, 11 vols. London: Williams.

Watson, W. 1890. *Orchids: Their Culture and Management*. London: L. Upcott Gill.

White, E. A. 1939. *American Orchid Culture*. 2d edition. New York: A. T. De La Mar.

Williams, B. S. 1852. *The Orchid-Grower's Manual*. London.

Williams, B. S. 1862. *The Orchid-Grower's Manual*. 2d edition. London.

Williams, B. S. 1868. *The Orchid-Grower's Manual*. 3d edition. London.

Williams, B. S. 1871. *The Orchid-Grower's Manual*. 4th edition. London.

Williams, B. S. 1877. *The Orchid-Grower's Manual.* 5th edition. London.

Williams, B. S. 1885. *The Orchid-Grower's Manual.* 6th edition. London.

Williams, B. S., and H. Williams. 1894. *The Orchid-Grower's Manual.* 7th edition. London.

Withner, C. L. 1988. *The Cattleyas and Their Relatives.* Vol. 1, *The Cattleyas.* Portland, Oregon: Timber Press.

Withner, C. L. 1990. *The Cattleyas and Their Relatives.* Vol. 2, *The Laelias.* Portland, Oregon: Timber Press.

World Orchid Conference. 1974. *Proceedings of the 7th World Orchid Conference.* Colombia: Medellin.

Index